Six Sigma Statistics using Minitab® 17

Green Belt Edition

By Rehman M. Khan

Chartered Chemical Engineer

& Six Sigma Master Black Belt

Portions of information contained in this publication/book are printed with permission of Minitab Inc. All such material remains the exclusive property and copyright of Minitab Inc. All rights reserved.

MINITAB® and all other trademarks and logos for the Company's products and services are the exclusive property of Minitab Inc. All other marks referenced remain the property of their respective owners. See minitab.com for more information.

ISBN-10: 1539155056

ISBN-13: 978-1539155058

DEDICATION

For Mum & Dad, Mahwish, Iqra, Humzah and Raeesa.

CONTENTS

Acknowledgments

Detailed Contents

ACKNOWLEDGMENTS

I would like to thank God for giving me the ability and circumstance to put pen to paper for the second time and complete this book.

I would like to thank my family for being patient with me while I completed this work over three years. These were three years where we also moved house and I started work at FMC Chemicals Ltd in Bromborough, Wirral.

FMC has been a great place to work and I feel proud to work at a Chemical Manufacturing site in the UK with such a fantastic team. Earlier this year we achieved something truly great for a site of 55 people. We won the Chemical Industry Association 2016 awards for Manufacturing and Resource Efficiency and also the Environmental Management Award.

I would like to thank Sigma Pro for helping me achieve a greater understanding of Six Sigma and becoming a Master Black Belt.

Finally, I would like to thank the great people at Minitab for supporting me.

.

1 INTRODUCTION

1.1 Introduction
1.2 What to expect
1.3 How the book should be used
1.4 Who the book is aimed at

1.1 Introduction

'The capacity to learn is a gift; the ability to learn is a skill; the willingness to learn is a choice.' Welcome and thank you for buying this book. You have made the choice and now it is up to me to teach you how to use Minitab for Six Sigma Statistics.

I am assuming you have already done your Green Belt training and you have your course notes. What you need is support in understanding how to use Minitab for those common topics that all Green Belts should cover. This book is very much focussed on Minitab 17. Some of the more fun topics covered using the Assistant like Multiple Regression and Sequential Design of Experiment do not appear in Minitab 16. If you have the option or the cash you might want to upgrade.

I wrote my first book, Problem Solving and Data Analysis using Minitab, after deciding that there was not enough support for Six Sigma Practitioners following the initial training, especially on Minitab. I felt the soft tools could be understood following the initial training but as most people had not covered statistical tools before they needed more support. This book follows on in the same fashion but focuses on the needs of Green Belts.

It is my intention to have two versions of this book a Green Belt edition, the one you are holding, and a Black belt edition, the one you will buy after learning from this one.

1.2 What to expect

Confucius said "I hear and I forget. I see and I remember. I do and I understand". I still love this Confucius quote as it describes what I want to achieve with the book. This book is a teaching companion not a reference book or a text book.

The aim of this book is to teach the reader how to use Minitab to perform Six Sigma statistics at the Green Belt level. The non-statistical tools of Six Sigma are not covered and indeed there is not much coverage of completing DMAIC projects. However, if you work through this book it should improve your ability to use Minitab and make decisions based on your analysis, which is the most challenging element of Six Sigma when you start.

The order of the chapters is selected deliberately to build the understanding of the reader so that by the end of the book the reader is using fairly complex Six Sigma tools such as Multiple Regression. They are not in the order you would use the tools in DMAIC. This is what we will be covering

Chapter 2, Minitab Boot Camp- we learn the basics like opening files and navigation between the different windows.

Chapter 3, Data Manipulation- we learn how to handle data by using techniques that allow us to extract and concentrate relevant information

Chapter 4, Generating Graphs- we learn how to produce a number of graphs and build on what we learned in Boot Camp.

Chapter 5, Core Statistics- we review the core statistics that you should understand.

Chapter 6, An overview of Hypothesis Testing- A lot of the statistical decision making within Minitab is done using Hypothesis Tests. Therefore, it is very useful to understand what is happening at a basic level. Having a good understanding of Hypothesis Testing is the key for furthering your understanding of Six Sigma statistics.

Chapter 7, Hypothesis Testing- we learn how to conduct the simple statistical tests that are collectively known as Hypothesis Tests.

Chapter 8, ANOVA- we build on the simple Hypothesis Testing that we learnt in the previous chapter. Chapter 7 was about testing either one sample against a target or two samples against each other. Chapter 8 is about testing more than two samples against each other.

Chapter 9, Control Charts- we learn how to assess whether our process is stable or whether there are uncontrolled forces disrupting our key variables. Producing control charts at the start and end of a project is a good way of demonstrating improvement when there are stability issues.

Chapter 10, Process Capability. These are a set of tools used to assess how your process performs against the customer requirements, which are usually set in specifications. Conducting capability studies at the start and end of a project is a good way of demonstrating improvement against a specification limit.

Chapter 11, Measurement System Analysis (MSA)- This is a fundamental tool that is used early on in a project to understand whether we can measure our key parameters. If we are weak on this step we may conduct a lot of abortive work just because we assumed we could measure with accuracy and precision when we could not.

Chapter 12- Regression Tools are a set of statistical tools used to mathematically assess the link between input variables with output variables. You will get to see the new magical Multiple Regression routine within the Assistant. Minitab have done a fantastic job to make it easy and accessible . I really believe that Green Belts will benefit from this new routine whereas in the past it might have been left to the Black Belts.

Chapter 13 Design of Experiment is very much like Regression but you spend more time on the initial design of the study. The payback is an optimised number of experimental runs to make a conclusion. Again Minitab have done an absolutely fantastic job on the new routine in the Assistant. When I did my Green Belt training we were not even taught DOE as it was thought to be beyond Green Belts, However, the sequential DOE routine that Minitab have delivered here is a marvel and should be used by Green Belts.

We cover a lot of the basics but as you can imagine we don't cover some material that is intended to be in the Black Belt Edition. And although I am years from finishing the Black Belt Edition here are some of the topics that I am thinking about including.

Non Parametric Testing
GR&R Expanded
Understanding Distributions
Advanced Regression
Advanced Process Capability
Advanced DOE.

When I started this book it was 2014 and I was using the launch version of Minitab 16. I finished the first draft of the book in July 2016 and the version has changed to 17.3.1. With the last couple of updates the look of Minitab and some of my screenshots has changed so you might notice minor differences between my screenshots and the ones you get from Minitab. On Occasion, I edit the screens within Minitab before I capture the shot to clarify the message. This will also result in minor changes to the screen shots that you will see in your version of Minitab.

1.3 How the book should be used

As stated in the previous section the aim of this book is to teach how to use Minitab. Most chapters will start with a simple explanation of the statistical tool being taught and will then go into an example. At the end of the chapter there will usually be a number of exercises for the reader to try. A detailed solution for each of the exercises is available from the website so the reader can check that the topic has been understood.
All of the data for the examples and exercises can be downloaded at www.rmksixsigma.com.
I would strongly advise that you download all the data files and put them on your desktop for easy access. Then work through each chapter in turn, first going through the worked example. When you can go through the worked example without looking at the book then try the associated exercise. Finally, review the answer to the exercise to ensure you got the same result as on the website.

1.4 Who this book is aimed at

Six Sigma uses a system of coloured belts to describe the individuals level of proficiency as seen in martial arts. Many years ago I used to do Tae Kwon Do (TKD) where the increasing level of the belts are described as a plant taking root and gaining strength.
I have given the TKD belt descriptions below and inserted Six Sigma where appropriate.
Yellow represents the earth where the seed of Six Sigma is planted as the foundation of Six Sigma is being laid.
Green represents the plant growing as the skills of Six Sigma develop.
Black : The opposite of white, therefore signifying a maturity and proficiency in Six Sigma. It also indicates the holder's imperviousness to darkness and fear.
The analogy works well for Yellow and Green belt and although a Six Sigma Black Belt won't make you 'impervious to darkness and fear' you should be a much more experienced and knowledgeable practitioner. The point is that at Green Belt you are still within the development process. In order to help you develop this book focuses on methods within Minitab that make the statistical tools easier to use. Minitab uses two systems of conducting tests within the program. One is the classic method which relies on graphical outputs and session window outputs to convey test results. However, interpretation is totally up to the user. The classic method tends to be preferred by experienced users who prefer the flexibility and greater number of options.

The other method, which Minitab is continuing to develop, is the Assistant. This appeared in Minitab 16. The tools within the assistant are easier to use for beginners as they provide graphical advice on the test procedures and also help with interpretation. I remember one person on the Minitab course I was delivering saying 'Why would anyone not use the Assistant?'. For these reasons the Green Belt edition will focus on the Assistant and the Black Belt edition will focus on the Classic Menu's.

Finally, As you are my customers I really want to understand your thoughts and customer needs. Therefore, one of the download files is a feedback form for this book. I would very much appreciated it if you could complete this once you have finished working through the book. and email the form back to me at admin@rmksixsigma.com. All email addresses will remain private and won't be used for email distribution lists or distributed to third parties.

2 MINITAB BOOT CAMP

2.1 The Initial layout
2.2 Opening a File
2.3 Moving Between the 3 Main Windows
2.4 Column Formats
2.5 The Show Info Icon
2.6 Sending Minitab Outputs to Microsoft Office Products

2.1 The Initial layout

Start your copy of Minitab 17 by double clicking on your Minitab Icon or running the program from the Start menu. The first screen that you will see will look like the one shown on the left. Like most windows based productivity programs Minitab has a number of drop-down menu's. It also has a number of buttons for quick access to important commands or tools. Below that we see the Session Window. This is where Minitab gives us the textual results of statistical test procedures when using the Classic Menu's.

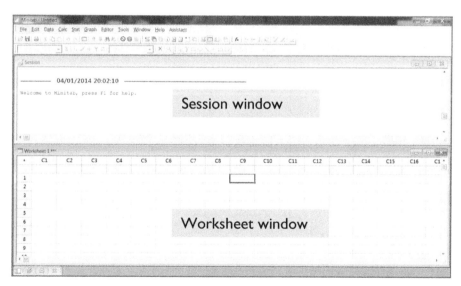

Underneath the Session Window we have the Worksheet Window. This is where we enter the data that we want Minitab to analyse. Later in the book you will see how we can manipulate data within Worksheets.

In my last Minitab book I asked the trainee to enter commands both in the text frames and graphically. However, I now feel there will be more benefit in terms of saving space if I just give you the command I want you to complete in the text frame.

For example,

1. Click *Stat<<BasicStatistics<< Graphical Summary.*

If the trainee wants to work along with the example I want them to left click on the Stat Menu and then select the next two sub-commands and then left click again on 'Graphical Summary'. Please do this now.
If you did it correctly the Graphical Summary menu box will open. Just press cancel for now or I should say

2. Click on the *Cancel* button.

2.2 Opening a File

Download the support files for this chapter. First we are going to open the Minitab project file called 02 Minitab Boot Camp.MPJ. Where the MPJ file extension refers to a Minitab project file. You can also have the following Minitab file extensions.
MGF for Minitab Graph
MTW for Minitab Worksheet

If you want you can simply navigate to the required folder and double click on any of the Minitab file types and Minitab will be launched with your chosen file. The other way is to do the following

1. Launch Minitab and click *File<<Open.*
2. Navigate to where you have stored 02 Minitab Boot Camp.MPJ and select the file. The type of each file can be seen within the menu window. Note, we have a filter on the bottom left of the menu. This can be used to restrict the type of items seen within the menu.
3. Click the *Open* button.
Minitab will open the project for you.

Minitab only lets you have one project open at a time. If you try and use the **File<<Open** with another project file Minitab will close the active project first and then open the new project. However, you can open additional worksheets and graphs. They will be added to the current project as additional worksheets or graphs.

4. Try this now by using **File<<Open** then open the worksheet called Testworksheet.MTW. Click OK on the pop-up box that opens.

We don't need this right now so close testworksheet.MTW.

Another useful way of bringing information into Minitab is simply to copy it from the host program and then paste it into a blank Minitab Worksheet. This is the method we will use for the remainder of the book. The host program for the data files for the examples and exercises that I use is Microsoft Excel.

If you have a project already open within a Minitab program and then double click on a Minitab project file from the windows environment a second instance of a Minitab program will be opened.

↓	C1	C2	C3
	Type1	Type2	Result
1	6.86934	18.6242	*
2	0.97162	18.2804	12.9716
3	3.49401	19.7060	15.4940

2.3 Moving Between the 3 Main Windows

Minitab has 3 main work areas for taking inputs and giving you outputs. These are the Session Window, the Worksheet Window and the Graph Window. We need to know how to move around these windows.

When you opened the Minitab Boot Camp project you should have been faced with this view. This is the Worksheet Window and the Project Manager.

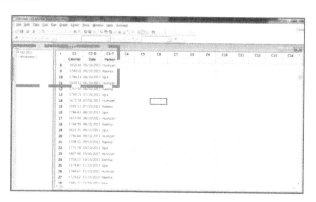

The next screenshot shows the view when we zoom in to the area indicated by the dashed rectangle.

The current worksheet is called Oct 2013, we can see some of the data within the

↓	C1	C2-D	C3-T
	Calories	Date	Person
8	1650.41	05/10/2013	Humzah
9	1740.92	05/10/2013	Raeesa

worksheet. The Project Manager on the left of the worksheet tells us that this project contains two worksheets, the other is called Worksheet 2.

To have a look at the contents of the other worksheet do the following.

5.   Double click on "Worksheet 2" within the Project Manager Window.
6.   Have a look at the data within Worksheet 2 and then return to the first worksheet by double clicking on "Oct 2013" within the Project Manager.

You may have noticed that Worksheet 2 contains data that relates to November 2013. It would be a good idea to rename the worksheet to follow the same nomenclature as the first worksheet.
7.   Right click on "Worksheet 2" and select 'Rename' from the drop down list.
8.   Change the name to Nov 2013 and then press enter. It should look like the screenshot shown.

Let's just check, we should be on the worksheet window and the Project Manager should be open. We are now going to learn how to move about the main windows within Minitab.

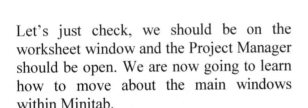

9.   Look at the graphic above.

10. If we wanted to look at statistical test results we would go to the Session Window. Click on the Session Window Icon now.

11. Scroll up the screen. You will see the results of a number of tests that I did earlier and saved in the file.

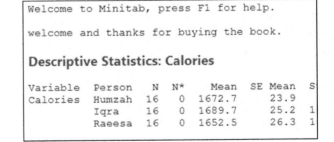

12. Now click on the Graph Window icon. You will see that one of the graphs is displayed.

Graph

13. Look at the Project Manager and you will see that there are 3 additional graphs.

14. Double click on each of the other graph titles to display that particular graph in the window.

15. Please return to the worksheet window.

2.4 Column Formats

16. Go to worksheet Oct 2013 and look at the top section of the columns.

Minitab uses the 1st Row to denote the column number, C1, C2, C3 etc, and the data type used within the column. Minitab only allows one type of data within each column.

In Worksheet Oct 2013 there are 3 columns and each has one of the 3 different column data types used by Minitab.

T indicates the **Text** data type within the column.
D indicates a **Date/Time** data type within the column.
No letter after the column number indicates a numeric data type.

Go to worksheet Nov 2013 and look at the top of the worksheet at the data formats used within the columns.

We can see that there has been an error of some sort and that C1 is not formatted as numeric data but text data. This needs to be corrected or Minitab won't let us carry out any of the tests used on numeric data.

Oct 2013

C1	C2-D	C3-T
Calories	Date	Person
1750.62	04/10/2013	Iqra
1532.81	04/10/2013	Humzah
1535.23	04/10/2013	Raeesa

Nov 2013

C1-T	C2-D	C3-T
Calories	Date	Person
R1669.52	03/11/2013	Iqra
1631.48	03/11/2013	Humzah
1687.58	03/11/2013	Raeesa

17. Place the cursor in Row01,C1. Then double click within the cell. You can now edit the contents using the cursor. Remove the 'R' from in front of '1669.52'.

We can see that removing the 'R' does not change the formatting of the column. We must change the formatting manually, even though all the data in the column is now actually numeric.

18. To change the column format click **Data<<Change Data Type.**
19. Select Calories as the column to be modified.
20. Then click OK and the format will be corrected.

If you are copying and pasting data from any spread-sheeting program into Minitab make sure it is correctly formatted, with the data in columns and without mixing data types, before you copy it to Minitab.

A useful function to know in Microsoft Excel is the Transpose function as it can be used to turn your data by 90 degrees in Excel. If you have never used it before use the Help menu in Excel to find out how to use it.

2.5 The Show Info Icon

A useful way of looking at features of your data is use the Show Info tool, which gives a summary of the data within the active worksheet.

21. Click on the Show Info Icon.

You will see that the project manager gives us a summary of our data. This includes the number of rows of data within each column, whether any cells contain missing data and the format of each column.

Nov 2013

C1-T	C2-D	C3-T
Calories	Date	Person
1669.52	03/11/2013	Iqra
1631.48	03/11/2013	Humzah
1687.58	03/11/2013	Raeesa

Variables:

Calories

Choose type: Automatic numeric ▼

C1	C2-D	C3-T
Calories	Date	Person
1669.52	03/11/2013	Iqra
1631.48	03/11/2013	Humzah
1687.58	03/11/2013	Raeesa

Project Manager

Name	Id	Count	Missing	Type
Calories	C1	48	0	T
Date	C2	48	0	D
Person	C3	48	0	T

2.6 Sending Minitab Outputs to Microsoft Office Products

Most people use Microsoft Office products for report writing so this section reviews how to transfer Minitab outputs to Word, Excel and Powerpoint.

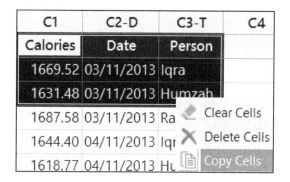

22. In order to transfer data from the Worksheet window highlight the area you wish to transfer and then right click and then click on 'Copy Cells'. The selection can then be pasted into Office. Depending on which program has received the data it will be in cells or text boxes and can be edited.

23. Outputs in the Session window are separated by their titles. In order to transfer a section from the Session window right click anywhere in that section then click on 'Send Section to ....'. The section will appear as a text box and can be edited. If you want to send more than one section highlight the area you want transferred and then right click.

24. Transferring a graph is probably the easiest. Select the graph you want to transfer and then right click and then select 'Send Section to ....'. Graphs will be treated as pictures in Word and Powerpoint and cannot be edited but you can place items on top, such as text boxes. As Assistant Reports are treated as graphs they can be sent to Word and Powerpoint using the same method.

3 DATA MANIPULATION

3.1 Introduction to Data Manipulation
3.2 Split a Worksheet
3.3 Using Code
3.4 Subsetting the Worksheet
3.5 Extract numeric data from a cell with Date/Time format
3.6 Using the calculator
3.7 Assigning a Function
3.8 Setting the Decimal Places & Rounding Values
3.9 Deleting data
3.10 Conditional Formatting

3.1 Introduction to Data Manipulation

The aim of this chapter is to teach you how to manipulate data within the worksheet window. It is very useful to have these skills so that you can reduce a large worksheet into a much smaller and focused one. This helps to focus the mind and reduce errors. So these skills will come in useful early on in a project when you are required to sanitise your data before applying your analysis skills.

We will only be working with data in the worksheet window and we will be using a single example throughout the chapter.

This can be found in the file 03 Data Manipulation.xlsx. When you are ready copy the data from that file into a new worksheet within Minitab. Have a look at the data in the worksheet window. Get a feel for the type of data in each column and the type and magnitude of the data elements

↓	C1-T	C2	C3	C4	C5	C6-D
	Factory	A Conc	A Feeder2	B Conc	Product Code	Reaction Time
1	UK	54.6	2.02375	75.7652	903	12:03:01 AM
2	Nigeria	63.5	2.92875	80.9307	106	12:00:48 AM
3	Spain	74.0	0.57250	88.7614	605	12:00:45 AM
4	Dubai	86.3	1.94000	89.3517	903	12:04:39 AM
5	Nigeria	87.9	1.80375	75.9439	605	12:04:46 AM
6	UK	65.8	3.81250	86.4065	903	12:03:43 AM

In this example you have been asked by a company to analyse how reaction time of a product varies with the concentration of two additives called A & B. The company are only interested in data from their UK site and their Low Fat product. As you can see from the screen-shot they have supplied data from a number of sites and for all the product range. Additionally, the product range is listed in terms of the company's own internal codes. Also, they have two feeders for ingredient A and they both carry out the same function.

We are going to learn how to use a number of functions within Minitab to focus our data on what we feel are the relevant parameters. We are also going to make the data easier to interpret. By that I mean we will change the format of the Reaction Time column into a numeric column and we will only display a single figure which will be in units of seconds only. Although Minitab will allow us to use the Date/Time format as shown within calculations I would much rather see this converted to number of seconds only

3.2 Splitting a Worksheet

The first thing we are going to do is to isolate the UK data into a separate worksheet.

1.   Click *Data<<Split Worksheet.*
2.   Select Factory as the variable to be used to split the worksheet.
3.   Click OK. This action will leave our original worksheet intact and form four new worksheets. These will be split by the four factory locations that were listed in the 'Factory' column.

4.   Click on the Worksheet window icon. This will tidy-up all those worksheets.

5.   Ensure that the worksheet relating to the UK data is active by double clicking on it within the Project Manager.

We now have 5 worksheets. The original and one each for each of the different countries, although we are only interested in the one for the UK.

3.3 Using Code

We are now going to change the data within the Product Code column to make it more user friendly. Presently, it contains four numbers which represent the products that the company makes. These are

    106→Herbal
    109→Organic
    605→Sugar Free
    903→Low Fat

We will make this conversion on the worksheet.

6.   Click *Data<<Recode<<To Text.*
7.   Under Recode values in the following columns select the Product Code column.
8.   Under Method select in 'Recode individual values' from the drop down list.
9.   Enter the text as shown against each of the product codes.

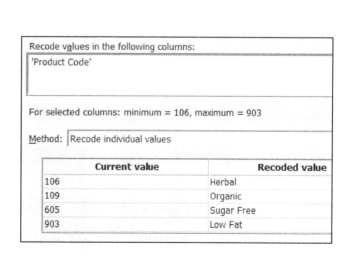

10. Minitab is then asking us where we want to put our converted data. We are going to tell it to put the data into a specified column. We tell it to put the converted data into a new column called 'Product'. As the column does not exist Minitab will create it. Complete this section as shown.

Storage location for the recoded columns:
In specified columns of the current worksheet

Columns:

Product

C7-T
Product
Low Fat
Low Fat
Low Fat
Herbal

11. Click OK. Minitab creates the data column in C7.

3.4 Subsetting the Worksheet

We used the 'Split Worksheet' command to produce worksheets specifically for each country. We then started working on the UK worksheet. We will now use the 'Subset Worksheet' command to draw out data only for the Low Fat product. 'Subset Worksheet' only produces a single worksheet unlike 'Split Worksheet'.

12. Click *Data<<Subset Worksheet.*

13. Leave the default selection in the first two drop down lists. This sets the selection so we include rows that match a certain condition.

14. Next we need to specify the column that will be used to split the worksheet. Under Column enter Product.

15. Now we need to specify that whenever the value in the Product column is equal to Low Fat put that row into the new worksheet. Under Condition select 'Equals set of values' from the drop-down list. Then select 'Low Fat'.

16. At the bottom of the menu we have the option of specifying a new worksheet name but we are going to leave that blank.

17. Click OK to generate the new worksheet.

18. Delete columns 1,5 & 7, **Factory, Product & Product Code,** by clicking in the cell where the column headers (C1 etc) are to select the column and then right click

How do you want to create a subset?

Use rows that match a condition

Do you want to include or exclude rows?

Include rows that match the condition

Column: | Product |

Condition: | Equals set of values |

Values:

- ☐ (Select All)
- ☐ Herbal
- ☑ Low Fat
- ☐ Organic
- ☐ Sugar Free

and select **Delete Cells**. This will leave 4 columns in the worksheet.

↓	C1	C2	C3	C4-D
	A Conc	A Feeder2	B Conc	Reaction Time
1	54.6	2.02375	75.7652	12:03:01 AM
2	65.8	3.81250	86.4065	12:03:43 AM
3	64.1	1.09000	83.5307	12:04:35 AM
4	60.3	4.08250	78.4096	12:02:54 AM

3.5 Extract numeric data from a cell with Date/Time format

19. Rename the active worksheet UK Low Fat.

20. The remainder of the worksheets can now be deleted.

UK Low Fat

Reaction Time is our response, it should be in C4. The formatting is not very appealing. It would be better if it were displayed in minutes and seconds as per the original Excel file or just in seconds. We are going to change the format so the response is the total number of seconds.

C4-D
Reaction Time
12:03:01 AM
12:03:43 AM
12:04:35 AM

Original Excel File

Reaction Time
0:03:01
0:00:48
0:00:45

21. Click on **Data<<Date/Time<<Extract to Numeric.**

22. Select Reaction Time as the target column and enter **Mins** as the name of the column that we will store the number of minutes in.

Extract from date/time column: 'Reaction Time'

Store numeric column in: Mins

23. In the selection box at the bottom of the menu specify 'Minute' as the data to be extracted.

24. Click OK.

Minitab will create a column with the minute data from our Reaction Time column.

We will now extract the number of seconds from our response data.

Specify at least one component to extract from date/time

- ☐ Year
  - ◉ Four Digit
  - ○ Two Digit
- ☐ Quarter
- ☐ Month
- ☐ Week
- ☐ Day of month
- ☐ Day of week
- ☐ Hour
- ☑ Minute
- ☐ Second
- ☐ Tenths
- ☐ Hundredths
- ☐ Thousandths

25. Click on the Edit Last Dialog Box icon or press Ctrl+E.

26. Enter **secs** as the name of the column that we will store the number of seconds in.

27. In the selection box at the bottom of the menu specify Second as the data to be extracted.

28. Click OK.

Minitab will create a column with the second data from our Reaction Time column.

Store numeric column in: secs

- ☐ Hour
- ☐ Minute
- ☑ Second
- ☐ Tenths
- ☐ Hundredths
- ☐ Thousandths

With a bit of mathematics we can convert our two new columns into a single column that contains only the total number of seconds.

Reaction Time	Mins	secs
12:03:01 AM	3	1
12:03:43 AM	3	43
12:04:35 AM	4	35

3.6 Using the Calculator

29. Click *Calc<<Calculator.*
In Excel a mathematical operation would be initiated in the worksheet by putting ' = ' in front of the instruction. In Minitab, we use the calculator, the difference is that Minitab works with columns of data but it conducts the operations across the rows of data.

1 We tell Minitab to store the results here.

2 We enter the mathematical expression here. Expressions can also use logic functions.

3 We have the option of using the buttons in this area to enter the expression.

4 This is a function selector that can be used to quickly select functions. If a function is selected the required formatting is shown underneath the selector.

5 This is an optional tick box for assigning the expression as a formula. We will learn more about this in the next section.

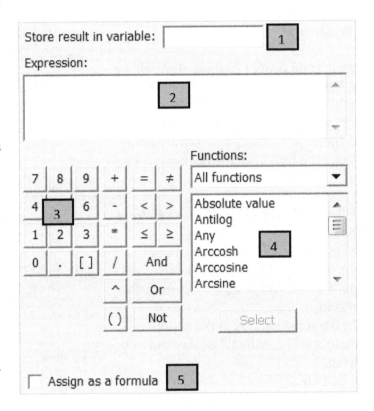

30. Enter **Time** as the name of a new column that will be used to store the results.
31. Enter the following under Expression **Mins*60+secs** . This will give us the total number of seconds. Remember, when you come across a column name you don't have to type it all in. You can just double click on the column name in the column select menu. Click OK.
Minitab will produce the new column called Time and it will contain the reaction time in terms of seconds.
32. Delete the columns that we don't need anymore; Reaction Time, Mins and secs. These should be C4, C5 & C6.

At the start of this example we said that the company uses 2 feeders for component A. We are going to simplify the worksheet by adding the two columns together. This is really an excuse to demonstrate how to Assign a Function. In the real world we might want to handle the two feeders independently.

3.7 Assigning a Function

The menu for Assigning a Function looks very similar to that for the Calculator. The only difference is that the Assign Function menu does not ask you for a storage location. The storage location for the results of the expression is set by placing the active cursor before you assign a function.

33. Move the active cursor to any cell within C5.
34. Click on the Assign Function button.
35. Enter the expression **A Conc + A Feeder2** .
36. Click OK.
37. Rename C5 as **Total A**.

Notice the green tick within the title cell of C5. This signifies that Assign Function has been used to generate this column of data and also that it will be updated if any values in the parent columns change. When the Calculator is used there is no automatic update of the calculated column as there is with Assign Function.

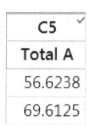

If you hover over the green arrow with your mouse pointer Minitab will show you the formula that has been used to generate that particular column.

If you try and delete one of the parent columns the warning shown will be displayed. Don't do this now but if you do delete one of the parent columns the values in the **Total A** column will no longer update.

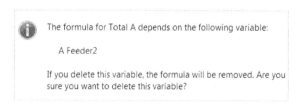

3.8 Setting the Decimal Places & Rounding Values

Let's say that I did not want to display the value in C5 to 4 decimal places (dp). I could format the column to only display 2 dp.

38. Place the active cursor on any cell within C5.

39. Click *Editor<<Format Column* or right click on the column and select *Format Column*.

40. Under Choose type change the selection to **Fixed decimal.** Then change the number or Decimal places to **2**.

41. Click OK.

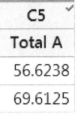

C5	
Total A	
56.6238	
69.6125	

Choose type:

Automatic numeric
Fixed decimal
Exponential
Currency
Percentage
Date
Time
Elapsed time
Text

Preview

1234.12

Decimal places: 2

The values to 4dp still exist but now C5 is only displayed to 2 dp. We also have the option to round the number and this will mean that the number to 4 dp will no longer exist.

42. Change the display back to 4 dp for C5 by using the Format Column command again

Total A
56.62
69.61
65.19

We can also use a function command to round the number of decimal places. Rounding is different to changing the display as it will change the value that is stored in the cell, whereas, in the last section we only changed the display.

43. Move the active cursor to any cell within C5.

44. Click on the Assign Function button. The existing expression is **A Conc + A Feeder2** .

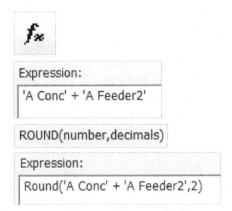

Expression:

'A Conc' + 'A Feeder2'

ROUND(number,decimals)

Expression:

Round('A Conc' + 'A Feeder2',2)

45. Select Round from the function selector. The basic form is shown here. Our expression will replace 'number' within the basic form. Change the expression as shown.

46. Click OK.

47. Take a look at C5. It has been rounded to 2 dp.

Total A
56.62
69.61
65.19

3.9 Deleting Data

48. Click on the **Show Info** icon. This will display information on the columns within the active worksheet window. The information will be displayed in a separate project manager window. We can see the headings for each of our columns and the number of rows of data that they contain. We see that within the **Time** column there are 5 missing data elements. 'Type' indicates the column format. We spoke about the three data types used in Minitab in the last chapter.

Name	Id	Count	Missing	Type
A Conc	C1	56	0	N
A Feeder2	C2	56	0	N
B Conc	C3	56	0	N
Time	C4	56	5	N
Total A	C5	56	0	N

78.41	174	64.38
75.48	*	52.69
81.01	600	76.29

49. Look at row 5 in the Time column. As a default Minitab uses the '*' to denote a cell with no data.

50. We will delete the empty cell by moving the active cursor onto the cell and then right clicking and selecting **Delete Cells**.

Deleting a single cell can cause big problems as demonstrated here. The missing cell is deleted but then all the cells below it are moved up one space. This means that the data within the row is not all related to one instance in time or one event as it was before the deletion.

78.41	174	64.38
75.48	600	52.69
81.01	127	76.29

51. Click on the **Undo** icon. If we want to delete the cell we must delete the complete row in order to stop the misalignment of data.

52. Left click on the row number for row 5. This highlights the complete row.

53. Right click in the same position. Then select **Delete Cells.** Notice that this action deletes the complete row.

54. Initially, there were 5 missing cells in the **Time** column so that means there are 4 left to delete. Let's pretend that the data set is really long, thousands of rows, and we want an easy way to locate the row numbers of missing data cells. We need a better method of deletion for this scenario.

55. Place the active cursor in C4 Row1.

56. Click *Editor<<Find and Replace<<Find*
57. Type in the asterix symbol in the **Find What** menu box.

58. Then click on the **Find Next** button on the same menu. Minitab will move the active cursor to the next occurrence of ' * '. Make a note of the row number.

59. Keep clicking on the **Find Next** button until you get to the bottom of the column. Row 19, 39, 41 and 54 should contain the missing data. Close the Find pop-up box.
60. In order to delete the data from these rows in one step click *Data<<Delete Rows.*

61. Enter the 4 rows of data into the menu with a space between each number. Then select all the columns in the next menu box. Then click OK.

The missing data and the rows associated with that data should have been deleted.

3.10 Conditional Formatting

Conditional Formatting was introduced in the 17.2 update. It is a very useful tool with lots of sub-options. I will give you a brief introduction but you should have a play and explore session yourself.

62. Click *Data<<Conditional Formatting<<High/Low<< Highest Percentage*
63. Select Time as the column that we will format.
64. Leave the Percent selection as 10. This means that the highest 10% of the Time data will be formatted. As there are 51 rows of data that means 5 cells will be formatted.

65. Under Style choose 'Red' as the formatting style.
66. Click OK and check the worksheet. Cells in row 5, 12, 20, 40 & 43 of the Time column should be highlighted.

67. Repeat the steps shown above to format the lowest 10 percent with a yellow background.

68. Click *Data<<Conditional Formatting<<Manage Rules*

This menu allows us to manage the rules that we created for conditional formatting and to some extent it allows editing. There is a drop-down menu at the top to select the appropriate column if you have formatted more than one column. Below that are the rules that you created. They are order specific. You can delete rules and change their order.
At the bottom of the menu there is a Format button. This allows you to edit the formatting and gives you more options than in the original menu.

4 GENERATING GRAPHS

4.1 INTRODUCTION TO GENERATING GRAPHS

A graph allows our minds to draw out patterns from thousands of data points. The starting point for all analysis should be to have a look at the data in a way our minds can understand.

This chapter starts you off on how to create, manipulate and analyse data using graphs.

This subject could easily produce a book in itself but I want to keep it reasonably brief so we can get down to the hard core statistics. To keep things brief we will only be covering the more useful graphs for Green Belts. I will completely miss out some of the ones like Stem & Leaf because I have never found them useful. We will cover a number of graphs within the chapter but we will also be learning more about graphical analysis as we work through the statistical modules. For example, Multi-Vari-Plot, Main Effects Plot and Interactions Plot will be covered in the ANOVA module. Also as the book focuses on the Assistant many graphs will be shown within the reports generated by the Assistant so they won't be covered in this chapter.

We will be covering the Boxplot, Dotplot, Individual value Plot, Bar Chart and Time Series Chart. Then we will show you how to manipulate these graphs and that will be applicable to all other graphs which are generated without the Assistant.

4.2 BOXPLOTS AND THE MENU SYSTEM

1.   The data that we are going to be using in this module is in the Excel file 04 Generating Graphs.xlsx. Open this file and transfer the data from Sheet 1 into a worksheet within a new Minitab Project.

We are working with a similar data set as the one used in Chapter 4, where we investigated product data for a company. Our numerical response data is called reaction time. We then have two columns of numerical data for the Concentration of A and B. There are two columns of categorical variables also. These are the Product Code and the Factory.

2.   To produce the first Boxplot click *Graph<<Boxplot.*
The first choice that we need to make is whether we want to display one variable or more than one variable. As we only want to display one variable without breaking it down into groups we select the One Y, Simple option on the top left of the four boxes, this is the default selection any way.

3.   For this example select A Conc as the variable to be plotted. Then click OK.

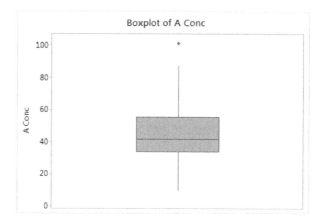

A simple boxplot is produced which shows the distribution of A Conc data. The top of the box on the boxplot is at the 75th percentile and the bottom of the box is at the 25th percentile. The horizontal line in the box represents the median. The asterisk at the top represents an outlier.

4.   Click on the show graphs folder icon. Take a look at the top left corner of the Boxplot, within the menu bar. There is a green tick with a double arrow circle below it. This is the graphical system that Minitab uses to tell us if the graph is currently up to date with the data within the worksheet. Let's see how this works with a fabricated example.
We will investigate the outlier within the data. Hover the mouse over the outlier on the graph. Minitab tells us that the data for the outlier is within Row 11. We will now pretend that the data was incorrectly recorded and the value for **A Conc** in Row 11 should be 61.3 and not 101.3.

5.   Correct the value for **A Conc** in row 11.

6.   Go back to the existing Boxplot and look at the graphic in the top left corner. The Yellow triangle with the exclamation mark denotes that the Boxplot no longer reflects the data from which it was produced.

Outlier symbol, Row 11: A Conc = 101.3

10	UK	44.4
11	Nigeria	61.3
12	Spain	38.7

7.   We have the option to update the Boxplot. Right Click on the actual display area of the Boxplot and then select '**Update Graph Now'** . If we had selected automatic updates then Minitab would always keep the graph up to date with the data.
Some graphs do not have an update facility and have to be redrawn through the menus. These types of graphs do not have the double arrow circle in the top left corner.

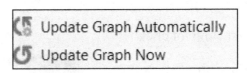

We are going to produce a 1Y simple boxplot with groups.

8.   Click *Graph<<Boxplot.*
9.   Click on the selector for **1Y with Groups**. Click OK.
10.   Again the 1Y that we are going to investigate is A Conc. Select 'A Conc' as the Graph Variable. If we want to split the groupings further we can add more than one categorical variable. Select 'Factory' as the Categorical Variable

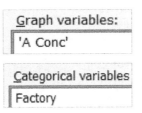

11. Click OK to produce the Boxplot.

Using this Boxplot we can compare the 'A Conc' variable across the different sites. We need to remember that there is a product range made by each site and this may change any conclusions we make regarding the variable we are investigating.

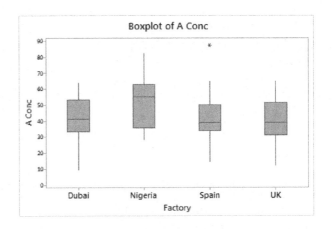

As a mini exercise produce a Boxplot using the Multiple Y's with Groups options as shown.

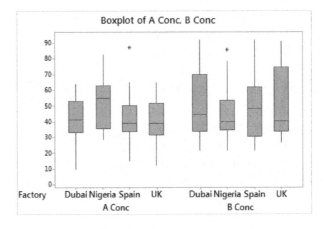

4.3 Editing Graphs

We are now going to learn how to edit the graph and change its physical appearance. The appearance of the graph can be changed considerably by editing it. Every area of the graph can be changed and the appearance modified. Once the graph has been selected by clicking on it, editing menus can be opened by further double clicking on the region you wish to modify.

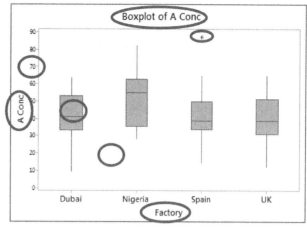

12. Open the editing menu's for the features I have circled and have a quick look at each menu in turn.

Below the graph I have shown the editing menu for the Y-Scale. You can see the number of tabs that are available for the different characteristics of the Y-scale that can be amended.

The tabs and the menu options are self-explanatory so I won't try and go through all the options within the book. I would suggest that you go through the menu's yourself and make some changes and observe their effects on the graph.

4.4 Duplicating Graphs

Here's one I made earlier. I have made quite a few changes to the graph. If I wanted to keep my formatting consistent over a number of graphs I would have to remember what changes I made and then make them each time. Thankfully there is an easier way of producing more graphs with the same formatting.

In this case I have the 1Y with Groups plot, my Y variable is 'A Conc' and my categorical variable is Factory. I want to keep the formatting but I want to produce another graph where 'Product Type' is the Categorical variable.

13. Ensure the parent graph is selected.
14. Click Editor<<Make Similar Graph.

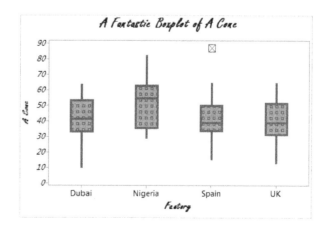

15. In the menu that opens change the Categorical Grouping from Factory to Product Type.

16. Click OK to produce the new graph.

We have made our new graph and retained the formatting that would otherwise have taken a fair amount of time to put into place.

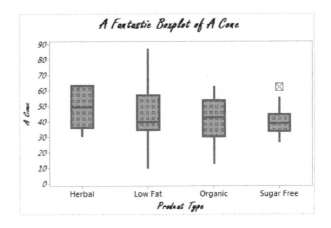

4.5 The Individual Value Plot

When I am conducting graphical analysis, which involves looking for trends within groups, I will start off with boxplots and then change to Individual value plots when I have seen a trend and want to see the real data in the trend.

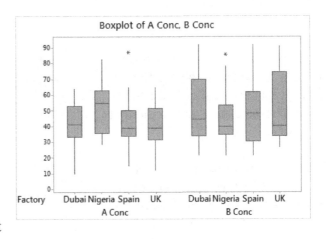

Have a look at the two charts shown here. The underlying data and the groupings are exactly the same. Even with the same data both charts look very different. This is a good reason not to rely on one type of chart when you are conducting graphical analysis.

To produce this Individual Value Plot
17. Click *Graph<<Individual Value Plot*

18. Click on the selector for **Multiple Y's, with Groups**. Click OK.

19. Select 'A Conc' and 'B Conc' as the graph variables.

20. Select Factory as the Categorical variable for Grouping.

21. Click OK to produce the plot.

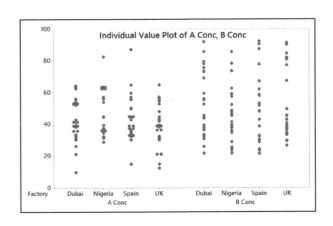

4.6 The Dot Plot

The Dotplot is an interesting graph as it comes with additional optional presentations using Stacking. Stack groups is another option for displaying the data points similar to a cumulative frequency plot.

To produce this Individual Value Plot

22. Click **Graph<<Dotplot**

23. Click on the selector for **Multiple Y's, Stack Groups**. Click OK.

24. Select 'A Conc' and 'B Conc' as the graph variables.

25. Select Product Type as the Categorical variable for Grouping.

26. Click OK to produce the plot.

4.7 The Bar Chart

Even though Excel is very good at producing Bar Charts it is worth knowing how to form them in Minitab as well. Especially, when you want to bring statistical calculations into the mix.
To produce a simple Bar Chart
27. Click **Graph<<Bar chart**

The Bar Chart options menu opens and the first thing we need to decide is what the Bars represent. This menu is for the numerical side of the chart and relates to the Y-axis. The next thing that we decide is what the X-axis will look like and this relates to the categorical variables that we use. The options for the X-axis are Simple, Cluster and Stack.
There are 3 main options for the Y-axis and 3 options for the X-axis; that makes 9 combinations altogether. (I'm not counting the Multiple Y versions of the Bar Chart). The examples shown in this section will cover only 3 combinations but use all the options for each category.

28. From the Bar represents drop-down menu select 'Counts of unique values'.

29. Select Simple then Click OK. The sub-menu opens for this type of Bar Chart.

30. Select Factory as the Categorical Variable.

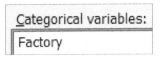

31. Click OK to produce the Chart.

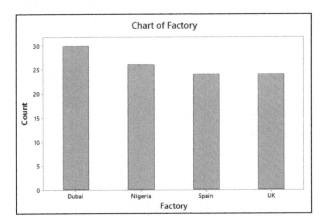

The Bar Chart gives a count of the number of times each factory appears in the data. Hence the name 'Counts of unique values'.

Functions of a variable is much more interesting. It offers to carry out stats functions through menu selections for a limited number of functions.

32. Click *Graph<<Bar chart*

33. From the Bar represents drop-down menu select 'A function of a variable'.

34. Select Cluster under the One Y heading then Click OK. The sub-menu opens for this type of Bar Chart.

35. Select 'StDev' from the function drop down menu. There are 9 other available functions.

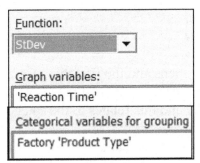

36. Select Reaction Time as the Graph variable.

37. Select Factory and Product Type as the Categorical Variables for grouping.

38. Click OK to produce the Chart.

The Bar Chart gives a us the values of StDev for Reaction Time with the data broken down by factory and then product.

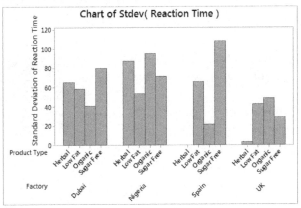

The final option is 'Values from a table'. This is simply the sum, or total, of the data of the selected categorical variables. It produces the same graph as using the Sum function when using the 'Functions of a variable' option from the drop-down list.

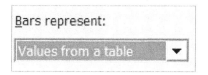

39. Click **Graph<<Bar chart**
40. From the Bar represents drop-down menu select 'Values from a table'.

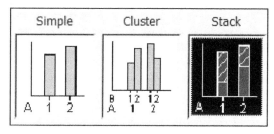

41. Select Stack under the One Y heading then Click OK. The sub-menu opens for this type of Bar Chart.

42. Select Reaction Time as the Graph variable.
43. Select Factory and Product Type as the Categorical Variables for grouping.
44. Click OK to produce the Chart.

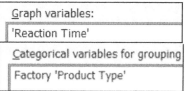

The Y-axis for the produced chart is the sum of Reaction Time within each of the categories.

Notice that for every other graph that we produced, as a default, Minitab ordered the Categorical variables in alphabetical order but it did not do this on this occasion.

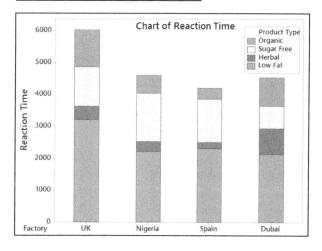

4.8 Changing the order on a Categorical Axis

Learning how to change the order on a categorical axis is something that not many people know how to do. Once you learn it you will be able to impress your colleagues with your understanding of Minitab. I must admit that I don't know why the last Bar Chart has not selected alphabetical order for the X-axis but has defaulted to order of appearance in the spreadsheet. Let's correct that now. This only works on graphs produced using the Classic Menus and not on graphs produced using the Assistant.

45. Place the active cursor in the column that you wish to correct.

46. Click *Editor<<Column Properties<<Value Order*
47. Using the radio buttons at the top of the menu select 'User-specified order'.
48. The box for Define an order should pre-populate with the alphabetical list but if it does not type it in.
49. Click OK.

The graph produced will have the X-axis categorical variables in alphabetical order. Did you notice that there is a radio button for 'Alphabetical order' but I opted not to use that. It does not work for this graph on my copy of Minitab.

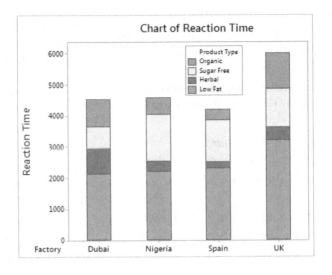

4.9 The Time Series Plot

Time series plots are very valuable for looking for patterns in time ordered data. Your goal might be to look for complete randomness in the data and no trends, you might want to look for cyclic trends or simply increasing or decreasing trends.

For this example we are going to use the data on worksheet 'Sheet2'. This has 3 columns of data. The first column is time in 10 minute intervals and the second and third are the feed rate of two components called C and D.

50. Please load the data from 'Sheet2' into a new Minitab project worksheet.

51. Click *Graph<<Time Series Plot*

52. For the grouping options select Multiple. Click OK.

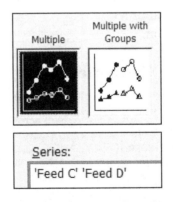

53. For the Series select Feed C and Feed D.
54. Click on the *Time/Scale* button.

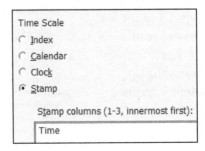

55. Click on the radio button for 'Stamp' and select the Time column as the Stamp Column. This will replace the X-axis with the data stored in the time column.

56. Click OK and OK again to produce the chart.

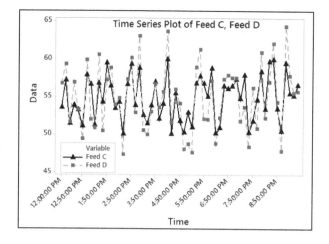

A quick examination of the chart indicates that Feed D is following Feed C.
Adding the Time Stamp is only available on graphs produced via the classic menus.

4.10 The Scatter Plot

The scatter plot is usually covered in the Regression Module but as we use the Assistant predominantly in that section it won't be covered in the Regression chapter.
Following on from the Time Series Plot we just produced and found that Feed D was following Feed C we can create a Scatter Plot and check the variables against each other.

57. Click **Graph<<Scatter Plot**

58. For the type of plot select With Regression. This option will add the line of best fit onto the plot.

59. Click OK

60. Under Y variable select Feed C and under X variable select Feed D.

61. Click OK to produce the chart.

	Y variables	X variables
1	'Feed C'	'Feed D'
2		

The general pattern of the dots is in a cloud that is going diagonally upwards. This indicates that the variables are correlated. We would use the equation for the line of best fit if we wanted to mathematically explain how Feed D and Feed C were related.

5 CORE STATISTICS

5.1 Introduction.

We know Six Sigma uses the DMAIC methodology to solve problems. As the team goes through the DMAIC process decisions have to be made. A lot of these decisions involve statistics so we use Minitab to ensure our decisions are sound and based on statistics rather than our own opinions. Minitab changes our data into information so we can make decisions.

In this book we don't cover the mechanics of statistical calculations. However, there is a requirement to understand some very basic statistics as this will help the reader to

1) Understand the limits and assumptions of the tools.
2) Communicate with peers.
3) Understand what the tests are telling you.
4) Understand the risk of being wrong.

I think of the understanding of core statistics being similar to owning and driving a car. You don't need to know exactly how the engine works but having an idea will probably help.

5.2 Types of Data

What is data? It is any information we care to collect about a system. As Six Sigma Practitioners we probably expect our data to be numerical but there is categorical data as well. Categorical data is pieces of information that are not numerical e.g. the product names used in the main example of chapter 3, Low Fat, Organic, Herbal & Sugar Free.

Statistical value refers to the number of data points required to make a statistically significant decision. In terms of statistical value per unit of data, continuous data has the most value. We will be covering both continuous and attribute data in the book and you can make a rough comparison of the number of data points required to make the same sort of decisions using the different types of data.

If you are working with modern technology you will more than likely be working with numerical data. However, if you have a system that uses attribute data then try to convert your attribute data system into a numerical one. As you will experience a leap in the statistical value from your data.

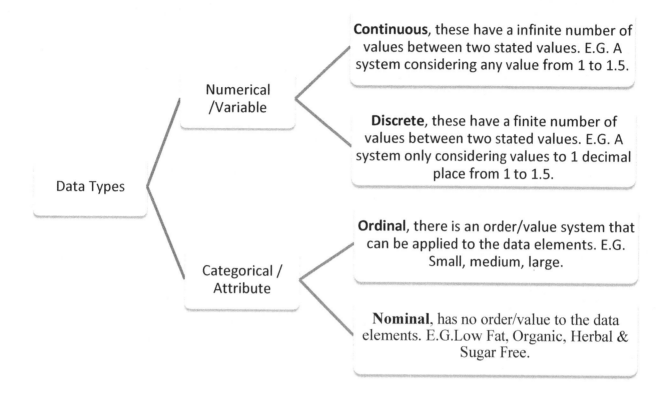

5.3 Measuring the Centre of a Data Sample

For illustration purposes we are going to use the 8 number list, shown on the left, as our population of data.

When we want to examine a data set we often want to know what the central value is in that data set and also the spread of the data. There are 3 very common measures for measuring the central value. These are the mean, the mode and the median.

Mean is the most useful measure of the central value, it is the sum of the data set divided by the number of elements in the data set.

5.5
7.3
6.1
4.2
6.2
7.5
5.5
6.7

$$Mean = \frac{5.5+7.3+6.1+4.2+6.2+7.5+5.5+6.7}{8} = 6.125$$

The mode is the data element that occurs the most often. In this case it is 5.5, as it occurs twice in the list and no other data element is repeated.

The median relates to the number in the central position if we were to order our list from the smallest value to the largest.

Order   1st 2nd 3rd 4th 5th 6th 7th 8th
Value   4.2 5.5 5.5 6.1 6.2 6.7 7.3 7.5

As we have an even number of elements in our data set we don't have one value at the centre. Therefore we must take the mean of the two central values, 6.15 (As 6.15= (6.1+6.2)/2).

In summary depending on which method of calculating the average that we choose we may get three different values.
For our data set,
    the mean is 6.125
    the mode is 5.5
    the median is 6.15

5.4 Measuring the Variation of a data sample

There are a number of ways we can look at the variation within our data set. The most common methods use the mean as the centre point and consider the spread of data around the mean. There are methods which take the median as the centre point and there are methods which use no centre point at all. Range returns the difference between the highest value in the data set and the lowest value in the data set.

Range= 7.5-4.2= 3.3

The interquartile range (IQRange) is the difference between the first quartile (Q_1) and the third quartile (Q_3) . The second quartile being the median. Q_1 is the value which is equal to or greater than 25% of your data, or the 25th percentile. The calculation gets messy as it usually involves interpolation. If we look at our ordered data again where we have 8 elements, n=8.

Order   1st 2nd 3rd 4th 5th 6th 7th 8th
Value   4.2 5.5 5.5 6.1 6.2 6.7 7.3 7.5

If we want to calculate IQRange then we must first calculate an interim value which I am going to call R.
        $R(Q1)=(1+n)/4= (1+8)/4=2.25$
I am going to split R into its integer value and decimal value, I am going to call these I & D respectively, where I=2, D=0.25.

Our formula for finding Q1 is
        $Q1= X_I + D(X_{I+1} - X_I)$
Where $X_{(2)}$ is the 2nd element in our data series.
        $Q1= X_2 + D(X_3 - X_2)$
        $Q1= 5.5 + 0.25(5.5 – 5.5)$
        $Q1= 5.5$
Our method for finding Q3 changes slightly
        $R(Q3)=3(1+n)/4= (1+8)/4=6.75$ now I=6 & D=0.75

$$Q3 = X_I + D(X_{I+1} - X_I)$$
$$Q3 = X_6 + 0.75(X_7 - X_6)$$
$$Q3 = 6.7 + 0.75(7.3 - 6.7)$$
$$Q3 = 7.15$$

We can now calculate the Interquartile range.

$$IQRange = Q3 - Q1 = 7.15 - 5.5 = 1.65$$

When a boxplot of our data set is displayed we see that the box is the Q1 to Q3 values with the line in the middle as the median value. So the IQRange is the length of the box. The whiskers at the end of the box extend to the minimum and maximum values in the data set as long as they are within 1.5 x IQRange from Q1 or Q3 respectively. If not they are shown as '*' and deemed to be outliers.

It is worth being aware that as the calculations for the median and IQRange will not use outliers they are a better measure of central tendency and spread for highly skewed data than the mean and standard deviation.

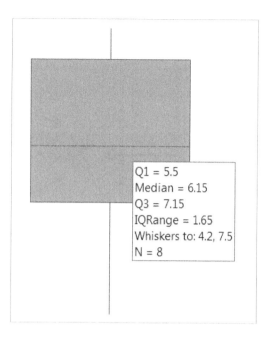

Variance and Standard Deviation are both expressions of variation about the mean value. We are now going to look at how they are both derived. By the way I hate typing out Standard Deviation so you will see it abbreviated to StDev throughout this book.

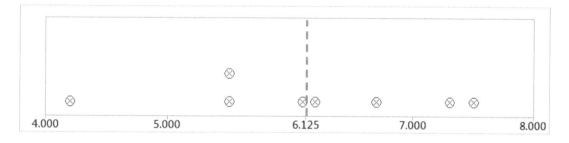

Let's start by looking at how our data sits around the mean. We can take each point in turn and have a look at its distance from the mean value.

The distance from the first point to the mean is 4.2-6.125 = -1.925. This is called the deviation. If I wanted to add up all the deviations I would write

Sum of Deviations= $(X_1 - \mu)+ (X_2 - \mu)+ (X_3 - \mu)+ (X_4 - \mu)+ (X_5 - \mu)+ (X_6 - \mu)+ (X_7 - \mu)+ (X_8 - \mu)$

Where μ is the population mean. For convenience we write the above equation in the following form.

$$\text{Sum of Deviations}= \sum_{i=1}^{N}(Xi - \mu)$$

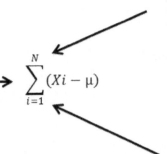

N is the symbol for the number of elements in the population. In our case it is 8. Meaning there will be 8 terms in the series.

The capital Sigma means add up the repeated terms in the series.

$$\sum_{i=1}^{N}(Xi - \mu)$$

This means that you start the series from i=1, the first data element.

If we compute our Sum of Deviations we will get zero. If you don't that means the mean is wrong. In order to get some value from deviations we can take the sum of deviations squared. As an equation this looks like

$$\text{Sum of Deviations Squared}= \sum_{i=1}^{N}(Xi - \mu)^2 =8.095$$

Dividing the Sum of Deviations squared by N, the number of elements in the population, gives us the population variance.

$$\text{Variance}= \frac{\sum_{i=1}^{N}(Xi-\mu)^2}{N} =8.095/8 = 1.0119$$

Finally, the Variance square rooted is the population standard deviation, σ. You now know how we calculate the variance and StDev of a set of numbers.

$$\sigma = \sqrt{\left(\frac{\sum_{i=1}^{N}(Xi - \mu)^2}{N}\right)} = 1.0059$$

You might have noticed that we talked about the population variance and StDev. However, on most occasions you won't have the complete population you will only have a sample from the population. Minitab will actually calculate sample statistics by default. There is more about population and samples in the next section.

The main difference between population variance and population StDev and their sample equivalents is that the denominator is changed to n-1 for the sample parameters. This makes the calculated parameter larger when the sample size is small but makes little difference when the sample size is large.

$$\text{Sample Variance}= \frac{\sum_{i=1}^{N}(Xi - xbar)^2}{n - 1}$$

$$\text{Sample StDev} = \sqrt{\left(\frac{\sum_{i=1}^{N}(Xi - xbar)^2}{n-1}\right)}$$

This is where I need to apologise and say that I am using 'Xbar' to represent $\bar{x}$, the sample mean.

5.5 Populations and Samples

The next two topics are strongly linked. They are also the key to understanding the statistics we do at this level and why we do it. The population is the data set from which we are going to be drawing our sample data. The term population represents all the possible data elements related to a parameter. It may even be the case that not all of the data regarding the population has been recorded. As populations can be so large we usually try and take a smaller and more manageable data sample. And of course when taking a sample we try and take a random sample so we don't influence our results.

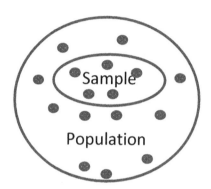

In order to help explain the issues surrounding samples and populations I am going to use an example Excel macro that I have written within a macro enabled spreadsheet. The worksheet is called 'Multiple Processes' and it is within the Excel spreadsheet called '05 Core Stats.xslm' .The data for the remainder of this chapter is also in this spreadsheet.

Exercise 5.5.1 Multiple Processes

Your boss has given you the task to purchase a factory and your boss has shortlisted three possible candidates for you to consider. As the price is the same for all three factories you are only going to consider the yield from each factory. The three factories have submitted their last 500 batch yields. These are listed in the spreadsheet. As your career is in the balance you wisely decide to hire a consulting firm to analyse the data. Rather than make the decision for you they provide you with a macro. When you press the button the macro takes 10 random data samples and gives you the mean. Using the means of the samples you must make the decision as to which factory should be purchased.

1.   Open the spreadsheet '05 Core Stats.xlsm'
2.   Ensure you have the Multiple Process tab selected.
3.   Press the *Take Sample* button for each factory. Note, if there is an error please press 'end' on the dialog box and continue as normal.
4.   Use the macro buttons to take repeat

Factory A	Factory B	Factory C
72.8	87.2	73.6
76.5	61.9	88.4
64.2	74.2	67.6
76.9	84.4	72.4
62	63.9	68.3
79.2	61.1	60.9
61.2	75.3	63.8
68.9	60.8	63.7
80.8	83.5	74.6
87.5	76.3	84
70	76.5	66.4
83.7	60.9	88.9
88.4	84.2	70.5
78.4	80.9	79.1
61	61	70.4
69.3	82.5	83
88.8	61.9	60.2

Factory A
Take Sample
Mean of Factory A=

Factory B
Take Sample
Mean of Factory B=

Factory C
Take Sample
Mean of Factory C=

samples until you are happy with your conclusion.

The consultants have also submitted their own data. They have found that Factory B delivers the highest mean yield and this is the factory that should be purchased.

Note-this macro used 'sampling with replacement'. This means that if an element was selected to make up the mean it was immediately replaced into the population giving it the chance to be selected again.

| Factory A |
| Take Sample |
| Mean of Factory A= 70.67 |

| Factory B |
| Take Sample |
| Mean of Factory B= 78.54 |

| Factory C |
| Take Sample |
| Mean of Factory C= 74.52 |

Once you start taking more repetitive samples for each factory it becomes very hard to make the decision as to which factory is the best. However, this is a process that we do every day without thinking about whether our sample mean matches the population mean. And this process of sampling not only applies to means but it can be applicable to medians & standard deviations (StDev) etc. In summary, when we analyse a sample in order to infer a property of the population there is a chance that we will be wrong. I am referring to the 500 pieces of data as the population as this is the data set that we are going to be drawing our sample from.

Incidentally, we are going to discuss making the wrong conclusion about the population in the next chapter called Hypothesis Testing.

The answer to Exercise 5.5.1 is that all three factories are the same.

32.8	Take random
38.7	samples &
35.5	calculate means
50.6	
43.8	
40.6	
55.2	
41.1	
59.9	
48.2	

Sample Size	Mean of Sample	Mean of Population
1		44.926
2		44.926
5		44.926
10		44.926
30		44.926
100		44.926
200		44.926
400		44.926
500		44.926

Example 5.5.2 Single Process

The next example is on the 'Single Process' tab of the 05 Core Stats.xlsm spreadsheet, please go to that tab now. On this worksheet we have a data set from a different factory which also happens to contain 500 elements, the mean of the population is 44.926 to 3 decimal places (dp). When the macro is executed it will randomly take a sample and calculate the mean of the sample. The sample size is shown in the first column of the table. The other difference is that this macro samples without replacement so that the same element is never used repeatedly.

Give it a go and click on the 'Take random samples…' button. I have shown the results that I obtained, however, your results will be slightly different. In my results we see that as the sample size

Sample Size	Mean of Sample	Mean of Population
1	59.500	44.926
2	50.300	44.926
5	38.900	44.926
10	51.990	44.926
30	42.963	44.926
100	43.186	44.926
200	44.762	44.926
400	44.914	44.926
500	44.926	44.926

increases the sample mean converges on the population mean. When the sample size is the same as the population the means must match.

I will summarise the key learnings from 5.5.1 & 5.5.2.

1) When we analyse a sample in order to infer a property of the population there is a chance that we will be wrong.

2) As we increase the sample size we will converge on the population parameter.

3) The only way to calculate the population parameter exactly is to analyse the entire population.

What we need to do is manage the risk of the sample parameter not reflecting the population parameter. This is where confidence intervals come in.

5.6 Confidence Intervals

As seen in the last section we want to manage the risk of the sample parameter not reflecting the population parameter. And I said this is where confidence intervals come in. We are not going to learn how to calculate confidence intervals as we want Minitab to do the maths for us. We need to appreciate what they mean to us in terms of samples and populations. We are going to do this by producing a Graphical Summary, which is a really useful starting point for most statistical analysis.

Example 5.6.1 Confidence Intervals on a Graphical Summary.

1. Open the spreadsheet '05 Core Stats.xlsm'.
2. Ensure you have the Single Process tab selected.
3. Copy the first 20 cells from column A and transfer them to a Minitab worksheet.
4. Label the column as **Factory.**
5. Click *Stat<<Basic Stats<<Graphical Summary.*
6. In the menu box that opens select the Factory column as the Variable to be investigated.
7. Click OK to produce the Graphical Summary.

↓	C1
	Factory
1	32.8
2	38.7
3	35.5
4	50.6

Let's have a look at the data table within the Graphical Summary, shown on the page below. We are going to look at the Normality Test next so I will leave section 1 alone for now.

In section 2, we are given sample parameters so we know the actual sample of 20 data points has a mean of 43.85 and sample StDev of 9.07. Skewness is a measure of how much a distribution is leaning to one side, skewed. Kurtosis is a measure of how sharp or flat a distribution is compared to the normal distribution.

In section 3, we are given data related to the range and median of the sample data.

In section 4, we get to the Confidence Intervals. In section 2 we were told that the sample had a mean of 43.85 and here we are told that Minitab is 95% sure that the population mean is between 39.605 & 48.095. If you remember back to the spreadsheet the population mean was listed as 44.926. Minitab got it right that time but remember 95% confidence means being wrong 1 in 20 times.

1	Anderson-Darling Normality Test	
	A-Squared	0.43
	P-Value	0.280

2	Mean	43.850
	StDev	9.070
	Variance	82.269
	Skewness	0.39293
	Kurtosis	-1.03810
	N	20

3	Minimum	31.900
	1st Quartile	35.775
	Median	42.450
	3rd Quartile	50.125
	Maximum	59.900

4	95% Confidence Interval for Mean	
	39.605	48.095
	95% Confidence Interval for Median	
	36.671	48.582
	95% Confidence Interval for StDev	
	6.898	13.248

The confidence interval is made up by adding & subtracting half the confidence interval width to the sample mean. The confidence interval width is a function of the following
1) The confidence level that you want to state, usually 95%.
2) The sample StDev, S.
3) The reciprocal of the square root of the sample size.
If the following actions were all carried out independently they would increase the width of the confidence interval
1) increasing the confidence level
2) increasing the sample StDev
3) reducing the sample size.

Exercise 5.6.2 Confidence Intervals

Here's one for you to do. Go back to 05Core Stats.xlsm and go to the Multiple Processes tab. Take the top 20 data elements, cells A2:A21, for Factory A and produce a Graphical Summary. What is the 95% Confidence Interval (CI) for the mean? Is the population mean likely to be 80.

Answer. We see that the 95% CI for the population mean is from 70.169 to 78.421. The population mean is unlikely to be 80. Using confidence intervals we are putting forward a best guess as to the population parameter whilst stating that there is a chance that we could be wrong using our sample data.

95% Confidence Interval for Mean	
70.169	78.421
95% Confidence Interval for Median	
68.994	79.012
95% Confidence Interval for StDev	
6.705	12.877

5.7 The Normal Distribution

Knowing the normal distribution is foundational knowledge for statistics. Understanding the normal distribution helps us further our knowledge of the assumptions that were made when the statistical test we use were developed. However, we now know the having normal data for many of the tests we use is not that important as long as the sample size is sufficient and we don't have special causes acting on our data. You can read about this yourselves in the development papers for Minitab 17. The normal distribution plotted on a frequency plot can be described by a number of generic rules.

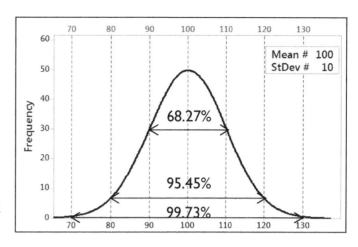

- 68.27% of all data appear 1 StDevs from the mean
- 95.45% of all data appear 2 StDevs from the mean
- 99.73% of all data appear 3 StDevs from the mean
- It can be described by its mean and standard deviation.
- The tails extend to ± infinity.
- All observations appear under the curve.
- The Curve is symmetrical.
- The mean, mode & median are almost equal.

Bernoulli...
Binomial...
Geometric...
Negative Binomial...
Hypergeometric...
Discrete...
Integer...
Poisson...

Chi-Square...
Normal...
F...
t...
Uniform...
Beta...
Cauchy...
Exponential...
Gamma...
Laplace...
Largest Extreme Value...
Logistic...
Loglogistic...
Lognormal...
Smallest Extreme Value...
Triangular...
Weibull...

Although we spend the majority of our time discussing the normal distribution we must remember that many other distribution models exist. Minitab can model 8 different discrete distribution models and 17 different continuous distribution models.

In order to test for normality we use the Anderson-Darling (AD) Normality test. The AD test starts by assuming that your data was normally distributed and then checks for a lack of normality. Again, we are analysing a sample in order to make the normality assumption about the population. Therefore, in order for the test to be reliable we must have more than 20 data points otherwise the test can indicate normality incorrectly.

Example 5.7.1 Testing for Normality

1.   Open worksheet Normality and transfer the data into a new Minitab Worksheet. This file contains two columns of data. Column 'Example1' has a sample size of 25 which is above our safe limit and Column 'Example2' which has a sample size of 100.

2.   Click *Stat<<Basic Stats<<Normality Test.*

3.   For the variable to be tested enter **Example1**.

4.   Note the radio buttons for the type of Normality test we are going to be using. The Anderson-Darling test is selected by default.

5.   Click OK and the Probability Plot is produced.

6.   Find the P-value for the AD test, if it is above 0.05 we can assume that the sample came from a normally distributed population.

7.   Another very rough and ready test is called the 'Fat Pencil Test' which is primarily used to test residuals. If you can cover the data points on the Probability Plot with a fat pencil you can assume normality. Remember the Fat Pencil test mainly applies to residuals and you will learn more about testing residuals for normality in later chapters.

Example 5.7.2 Testing for Normality

In this example we are going to look at the AD P-value on the Graphical Summary again and also look at the very limited case where the AD normality test doesn't work very well.

1.   Click *Stat<<Basic Stats<<Graphical Summary.*

2.   For the variable to be tested enter **Example2.**

3.   Then click OK and examine the results. The P-value of the AD Normality test indicates that there is sufficient evidence to conclude the population is not normally distributed. When we look at the histogram and the fitted curve it looks as though we

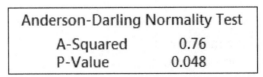

Anderson-Darling Normality Test
| A-Squared | 0.76 |
| P-Value | 0.048 |

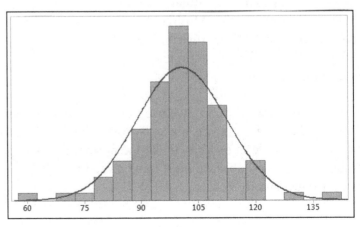

have a normally distributed sample. However, it is known that the AD test does not work very well when there are outliers extending the tails of the distribution. This can be seen in the histogram but more so in the boxplot. We can use one of the other normality tests that is better suited to this type of sample, the Kolmogorov-Smirnov (KS) test.

4. Click *Stat<<Basic Stats<<Normality Test.*

5. For the variable to be tested enter **Example2**.

6. On the radio buttons for the type of Normality test select the KS test.

7. Click OK and the Probability Plot is produced.

The P-value for the KS test is >0.15 and therefore indicates that the sample came from a normally distributed population. As good Six Sigma practitioners we should be thinking about the outliers that are visible on the Probability Plot and why they were generated.

Occasionally, our data will try to trick us. One particular trick that I want you to be aware of is the bi-modal distribution. This is when something changes in the process while we are collecting data and we end up collecting data from two separate distributions thinking they are one. Take a look at the histogram it is actually made of two distributions but this only really becomes apparent when we look at the control chart on the Diagnostics Report, if using the Assistant. The problem is that results of any hypothesis test that we are conducting becomes useless when we treat two separate distributions as a single distribution.

If you are not using the Assistant always check your process stability using a control chart. Bi-modal distributions are much harder to spot on histograms than they are on control charts.

5.8 The Central Limit Theorem

The Central Limit Theorem, CLT, states that if you repeatedly take a sample and build up a distribution of means, let's called that the child distribution. Then the child distribution will be more normally distributed and have a narrower distribution than the parent. Even if you start with a very non-normal distribution and repeatedly take a set sample size and calculate the mean of the sample. Then build up a distribution of those means that will result in a more normal and narrower distribution. It has been stated that setting the sample size at 40 will ensure the child distribution is normal. Another benefit is that the child distribution will have the same mean as the parent.

The equation shown below supports the CLT. It shows that the StDev of the child distribution will be reduced by a factor of $\sqrt{N}$, where on this occasion N is the size of the sample that you are going to repeatedly take.

$$S = \frac{\sigma}{\sqrt{N}}$$

Where S=sample StDev, σ= population StDev
Let's take a look at a demonstration of the Central Limit Theorem.

I have generated a random population of 250 elements and called it 'Original'. My σ (population StDev) is 28.44 and you can see that the distribution is fairly flat.

Now I am going to start taking 2 random samples from 'Original' (N=2) and calculating their mean. I am using sampling with replacement because I want to conduct my calculation many times. I actually do it 150 times in order to build a distribution.
You can see from the 'N=2' distribution that it is more normal looking and narrower than Original. Let's now look at increasing N and see how that changes the look of the distribution.

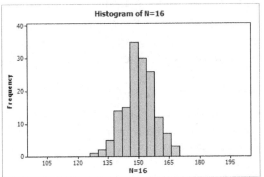

As a reminder, N is the number of samples I am taking and using to calculate their mean.
As I increase N the distribution displays a lower variance and becomes more normal looking.

The table shows the numbers generated by the equation and in practice by the demonstration. There is a slight difference between the calculated and actual S values which is probably due to my deliberate limit of taking 150 sets of samples.

N value	$\dfrac{\sigma}{\sqrt{N}}$	Calculated S	Actual S from example	AD P-value
1	28.44			<0.005
2	$\dfrac{28.44}{\sqrt{2}}$	20	19.1	0.25
4	$\dfrac{28.44}{\sqrt{4}}$	14.2	13.1	0.39
8	$\dfrac{28.44}{\sqrt{8}}$	10.1	11.5	0.467
16	$\dfrac{28.44}{\sqrt{16}}$	7.1	7.5	0.892

6 AN OVERVIEW OF HYPOTHESIS TESTING

6.1 What is Hypothesis Testing.
6.2 Understanding the Procedure

6.1 What is Hypothesis Testing

In a Six Sigma project we are usually trying to understand a loss so that we can reduce or eliminate it or we are trying to make something better. If it is a data driven project we want to be able to use data to make decisions that will improve our understanding and will eventually help us achieve an improvement. At its simplest level Hypothesis Testing (HT) is a method that is generically used to help us make decisions about our data.

Hypothesis Testing (HT) is a formal procedure used when we want to solve a statistical problem. As a Green Belt you need to have a good understanding of the procedure and be able to use it. However, as you become more experienced you conduct the procedure by reflex rather than formally. This chapter is written to teach you the formal way so you can start using the statistical tests. Before this starts to sound tiresome know that the rest of the book assumes you will conduct the procedure by reflex.

There are two parts to HT, the procedure and the statistical test. We will be focusing on the procedure in this chapter. The statistical tests start from the next chapter onwards. There is a lot of terminology in hypothesis testing and you need to understand all of it.

6.2 Understanding the Procedure

| 1. Define the investigation statement | | Is it one sided or two sided? |

| 2. Define our Hypotheses |

| 3. Assess the risk of being wrong |

The procedure for HT can be broken down into a number of generic steps.

I used to call step 1 'The Problem Statement'. However, I now feel that 'problem' is not the right word and probably more negative than it needs to be. I now call it an 'investigation statement'.

| 4. Conduct the test procedure and obtain |

| 5. Accept the null or alternate hypothesis. |

To start the process off we should have a clear idea in our minds what the information is that we are looking for. Ideally, there should be one investigation statement for one hypothesis test. Note, some statistical procedures in Minitab will have more than one hypothesis test associated with them. Being able to formulate this investigation statement helps us to focus on the problem at hand and it should make us ask 'if this information is really going to help with the project?'. But only you can answer that.

The investigation statement should be a single line question that has the following properties
    1) It should only have two possible results to the investigation
    2) It should indicate to a Six Sigma practitioner which test is applicable
    3) It should be concise.

We don't need to include data types even though this would have a bearing on the test used. It is inferred that the data type will be known.

Let's have a look at an example investigation statement.

Is the mean of Group Carb the same as the mean of Group Protein or is it different?

Let's go through our check-list.

    1) The answers can only be Carb has the same mean as Protein or Carb has a different mean to protein.
    2) A Green Belt should be able to conclude that the test is comparing the means of two groups of data. Therefore, a 2 sample T test is required.
    3) The statement is concise and to the point.

In order that we learn the terminology let's consider if our test is going to be one sided or two sided. For our example investigation statement 'Is the mean of Group Carb the same as the mean of Group Protein or is it different?' we use the word 'different'. 'Different' means that it can be 'less than' or 'greater than' and we are not really bothered. As 'different' has two outcomes we call this a 'two sided test'.

However, we may only be interested in knowing if the mean of carb is greater than protein. We now have two choices in terms of test options. Choice 1 is to use the standard two way test and then interrogate the data and graphs to figure out if it was actually greater than. Choice 2 is to use a one way test. For this we need to modify our investigation statement.

Is the mean of Group Carb equal to or less than the mean of Group Protein or is it greater than the mean of Group Protein?

As we are now only interested in 'or is it greater than' as the alternative this is called a one sided test. The benefit of opting for a one sided test is that it is better at spotting the difference between your two investigation statement options than a two sided test, when a difference exists.

> ## 2. Define our Hypotheses

In this step we state which of our two outcomes of our investigation statement is the null hypothesis, H_o, and which is the alternate hypothesis, H_a. The null is always given to the outcome which implies 'no change', ' difference' or even 'the population is normally distributed' for the AD normality test. The alternate is given to the outcome which implies 'there is a difference' or 'something has changed'.

Let's look at our two sided example again,

Is the mean of Group Carb the same as the mean of Group Protein or is it different?

The null hypothesis would be 'there is no difference between the means of Carb and Protein populations'
Mathematically, $H_o : \mu_{carb} - \mu_{protein} = 0$.

The alternate hypothesis would be 'there is a difference between the means of Carb and Protein populations'
Mathematically, $H_a : \mu_{carb} \neq \mu_{protein}$

And our one sided example again,

Is the mean of Group Carb equal to or less than the mean of Group Protein or is it greater than the mean of Group Protein?

The null hypothesis would be 'the population mean of Group Carb is equal to or less than the population   mean of Group Protein '
Mathematically, $H_o : \mu_{carb} \leq \mu_{protein}$

The alternate hypothesis would be 'the population mean of Group Carb is greater than the population mean of Group Protein'
Mathematically, $H_a : \mu_{carb} > \mu_{protein}$

Remember, if we wanted we could set up the H_a to be based around 'less than'.

> ## 3. Assess the risk of being wrong

We learned in the Core Statistics chapter that as we are taking a sample and then making inferences about a population then there is always a chance that we are going to be wrong. In this section we are going to discuss how to handle the risks involved. The risks are there because our sample size is smaller than the population size. And if it were the same then there would be no point using Minitab for hypothesis testing. We could just use a calculator to make decisions.
We are going to start to put together a hypothesis testing truth table. On the Y-axis we are going to put reality. As we don't know reality there are two possible states for reality; there is 'No Difference' or that

there is a 'Difference'. To make things easier to understand we are just going to look at 'No Difference' to start with.

At the end of the test procedure we will learn how to make our decision about whether there is a difference or not. And in the next chapter we will learn about selecting the appropriate test so don't worry about that now.

If my decision is 'No Difference' and in reality there is no difference then I will be correct.

Unfortunately, as I will never know reality I will never truly know if I am right or wrong. All I can do is calculate the risks to start with and try to ensure the odds are sufficiently in my favour before I start the process.

My Decision		
	No Difference	Difference
Reality No Difference	Correct ☺	☹ Wrong

The other way things can work out is if in Reality there is a difference. My decision will still have the same options but I will only be correct if the test detects a Difference.

My Decision		
	No Difference	Difference
Reality Difference	☹ Wrong	Correct ☺

Now we bring the two halves of the table together. In terms of my decision there are only two things that I can decide. But there are four outcomes when we bring Reality into the table as well. We know already that if I have a larger sample size I can improve my chances of being 'Correct'. There may be other factors that can help me be 'Correct' as well.

		My Decision	
		No Difference	Difference
Reality	No Difference	Correct ☺	☹ Wrong
	Difference	☹ Wrong	Correct ☺

'Null Hypothesis' was the name we gave the state when there was no change or there was no difference. Therefore, if we want we can substitute the word 'Reality' for Null Hypothesis. This does not change the table at all but improves our statistical terminology.

My Decision now relates to whether I 'Failed to Reject' or 'Rejected the Null Hypothesis. Notice the term 'Failed to Reject' is being used instead of Accepted, this will be explained later in this chapter.

		My Decision	
		Failed to Reject	Rejected
Null Hypothesis	TRUE	Correct ☺	☹ Wrong
	FALSE	☹ Wrong	Correct ☺

I have added the names of the different types of risk we associate with the matrix. I have split the matrix back up again as I want to look at the two states of reality separately.

If we are just looking at the case when there is no difference (or the null hypothesis is true) the probabilities of me deciding 'No Difference' added to probability of me deciding 'Difference' will equal 1 or 100%.

1=Confidence + Significance

1=(1-α) + α

We call the probability of correctly saying there is no difference the Confidence. You have probably heard that we use 0.95 or 95% as the default value for confidence. We call the probability of incorrectly saying there is a difference when there is none the Significance, α. This can also be called the producer's risk or a Type I error.

My Decision		
	No Difference	Difference
Reality **No Difference**	Correct ☺ Confidence, (1-α)	Wrong ☹ Significance or producer's risk, α Type I error

Let's now look at the other state of reality, when there is a difference. We call the probability of correctly saying there is a difference the Power. You may have heard of that term. Most practitioners will want a Power of typically between 80-90%. There are a number of factors that affect the power of a test and it is important to have sufficient power in any procedure you carry out.

The probability of incorrectly saying there is no difference is called the Consumers Risk or β. It is also known as a Type II Error.

My Decision		
	No Difference	Difference
Reality **Difference**	Wrong ☹ Consumers Risk, β Type II Error	Correct ☺ Power, (1-β)

Let's say that we conducted a HT test and concluded that there was no difference without establishing the Power prior to conducting the test. Well, was there really no difference or did we incorrectly conclude there was no difference when there really was? Without knowing the power we have no idea which is more likely. But if we have the right conditions to obtain a Power of 90% and then we concluded 'no difference' we know we can be much more confident of our conclusion.

Therefore, before we start any procedure we want to know that we have sufficient Power and Confidence. The Confidence is set by default at 95% but can usually be changed in the options settings of the test menu's. Power can be calculated in a separate process known as Power & Sample Size (PSS) or it is calculated within the Assistant. There are probably quite a few occasions where you would want to know you have sufficient Power before you conduct a test e.g. when getting a large enough sample size is an issue. In those instances, using a separate procedure prior to the Assistant becomes necessary. During Minitab courses I have found that a fair number of beginners like to skip over this step but for the reasons explained above that could lead to disaster. We are now going to learn how to use the PSS procedure. At this point we need to know the type of HT test we would be using but we don't need to know anything further about the test at this point.

Example 6.2.1 PSS for 1 Sample t test.
Curran Cycles make a 50cm frame. They want to test whether the mean of the 50cm frame is actually 50cm and for this they know that they need to conduct a 1 sample t test. They know that the difference that they are interested in being able to detect is 0.3cm and they know that historically they get an StDev=0.45cm in the 50 cm cycle frames. Explore the Power that would be obtained if they sample 20, 25 & 30 frames for a two sided test and then a one sided test.

No data file is required for this example.

1.   Click ***Stat<<Power and Sample Size<<1 Sample t***

2.   For this test we must specify our estimate of the population Stdev. Enter '0.45' for this in the menu.

Specify values for any two of the following:

Sample sizes:	20 25 30
Differences:	0.3
Power values:	
Standard deviation:	.45

3.   We want to know the Power so we will leave that section blank. Enter all three samples sizes that we are interested in. Leave a space between each number.

4.   Enter the difference we are interested in.

5.   Click OK to execute the procedure. Examine the Power curve graph.

On the Power curve graph we have Difference as the X-axis and Power as the Y-axis. We actually have 3 curves displayed one for each sample size. For each of the curves we can see how changing the detectable difference would change the Power, or vice versa. Hovering the mouse pointer over each of the dots displays the exact value of Power.

6.   Navigate to the Session window and find where the Powers are listed against each of the sample sizes.

Difference	Sample Size	Power
0.3	20	0.807292
0.3	25	0.892017
0.3	30	0.941576

For the two sided 1 sample t Test with 20 samples and this particular set of conditions
- Estimated population Stdev of 0.45
- Detectable difference of 0.3
- 95% Confidence

We get a power of 80.7%. This means that if the population mean of the 50cm cycle frames was different by 0.3cm we would have a 80.7% chance of detecting a difference. You can see that increasing the sample size increases the Power.

We are going to change to a one sided 1 sample t Test and assess the Power that results for the same conditions. In the actual test our H_a would change from the two – sided test to a one sided alternate hypothesis.

7. Click *Stat<<Power and Sample Size<<1 Sample t*

8. If it is not already there enter the data as shown.

9. Click on the *Options* button.

10. Under Alternative Hypothesis select the radio button for 'Greater than'. As you can see we can also change the Significance level within this menu.

11. Click OK twice. Examine the Power curve graph. The Power curves are now one-sided.

12. Navigate to the Session window and find where the Powers are listed against each of the sample sizes.

For the one sided 1 sample t Test with 20 samples we get a power of 89.0%. This has increased by around 8% from the two sided test.

Difference	Sample Size	Power
0.3	20	0.890246
0.3	25	0.944343
0.3	30	0.972541

The next graphic shows the factors that affect the Power of a HT Test.

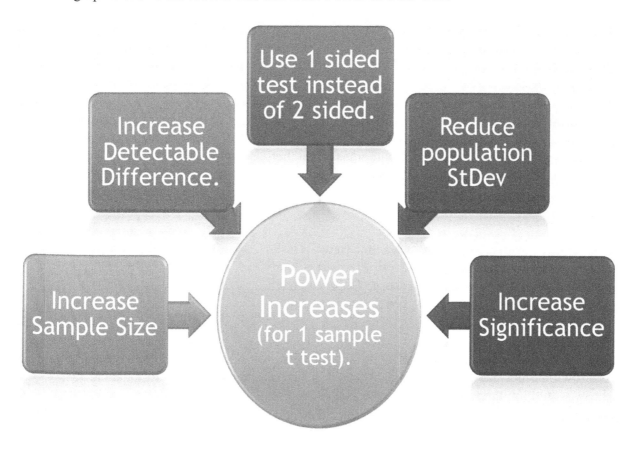

Exercise 6.2.2 PSS for 1 Sample t test.

For a two sided 1 sample t Test with a StDev of 4 and a difference of 1 how many samples would you need to get a Power of 90%?

Note when entering Power into the menu it is entered as a decimal.

```
1-Sample t Test

Testing mean = null (versus ≠ null)
Calculating power for mean = null + difference
α = 0.05   Assumed standard deviation = 4


                Sample   Target
Difference       Size    Power   Actual Power
         1        171      0.9       0.901594
```

4. Conduct the test procedure and obtain

5. Accept the null or alternate hypothesis.

HT procedures are going to be taught in the next chapter using the Assistant. The Assistant actually interprets the analysis for you in order to provide you with a conclusion regarding the data. If we use the classic method we must run the test and then find the P-value in the session window. We then make the decision to Reject or Fail-to-Reject the null hypothesis based on the P-value. Most people learn the rhyme 'If the P is low the null must go'. This means that if the P-value is below the significance level then reject the null hypothesis.

If that is all you want to know then skip the rest of this section. If you want to know more about what we are actually doing when we decide to Reject or Fail-to-Reject the null then read on.

Let's start with the P-value. What is the P-value?

'It is the probability of getting your sample results, including results that are more extreme, given that the null hypothesis is true'.

Therefore, we need a method of working out probabilities for getting certain samples (or events) if the null hypothesis is true, or when there is no effect/change. To do this we use something called a null distribution which gives us a distribution of outcomes when there isn't any effect i.e. the null is true. Let's see how we might put together our own null distribution.

Example 6.2.3 P-value.

Develop a method for testing whether a single dice (note, it is permissible to call a single die a dice in modern English) is likely to have been tampered with to give a high score. Once you have developed your test method you will be given 3 dice to test.

For my method of testing I am going to work out the null distribution for the cumulative score of a single dice thrown 4 times. I am using four throws as this increases the resolution of the data. Just having 1 throw would limit me to the score 1 to 6.
With 4 dice the probability of scoring a 4 or 24 is the same and is

$$\frac{1}{6} \times \frac{1}{6} \times \frac{1}{6} \times \frac{1}{6} = \frac{1}{1296} = 0.000772 \quad \text{or } 0.0772\%$$

Working out the values in between 4 & 24 is a bit harder. However, I am not going to calculate the probabilities because I have run a simulation in Excel 10,000 times. Below are my results in graphical form.

Cumulative Score of Throwing Four Dice Vs Probability of Score.

As you can see from the graph, I obtained a probability of getting a score of 24 as 0.0005 in my simulation. And I got a probability of getting a score of 4 as 0.0012. Both of these scores are different to the theoretical value of 0.000772 but we will still go with the simulation. We see that rolling a score of 14 has the highest probability of 0.1153, meaning a score of 14 would be expected 11.53% of the time. If we wanted to we could work out the probability of getting a range of scores by adding the individual probabilities together. The probability of getting a score of 10, 11 or 12 is 0.0641+0.0759+0.0973 = 0.2373 or 23.7%.

Similarly we could ask what is the probability of getting a score of 7 or less. The probability of getting a score of 7, 6, 5 or 4 is 0.0162+0.0082+0.003+0.0012 = 0.0286 or 2.86%.

Carrying on with the example, I now need to set a cut-off for when I am going to conclude that the dice has been tampered with. I decide to consult my youngest daughter, who is a prolific cheat at every game. She suggests that I should use 3% as my significance level for this test, I go with that. I am now ready to start testing the dice and as I am demonstrating hypothesis testing I will use the procedure.

Investigation Statement – Will the test dice deliver a higher score over four rolls than a normal dice? As we are only interested in a higher score we know that this is a one sided test.

Hypothesis - H_o = The test dice delivers the same score or less than a normal die.
H_a = The test dice delivers a greater score than a normal die.

Assess the Risk- I have set my significance to 0.03 or 3% on advice from my daughter.

Conduct the Test –
For Dice 1, I get a score of 12. This gives me a P-value of 0.7623, these are the cumulative probabilities from 12 to 24.
For Dice 2, I get a score of 20. This gives me a P-value of 0.0544, these are the cumulative probabilities from 20 to 24.
For Dice 3, I get a score of 21. This gives me a P-value of 0.0282, these are the cumulative probabilities for 21 to 24, 0.00156 + 0.009 + 0.0031 + 0.0005.

Accept the null or alternate.

We can only reject the null if we have 'sufficient evidence'. The 'evidence' is that the results we obtained are extremely unlikely given the null is true i.e. the P-values. Sufficient means the level of evidence exceeds our significance level in terms of improbability.

For Dice 1, we have a P-value of 0.7623 in terms of improbability it does not exceed α=0.03. Therefore, we do not have sufficient evidence to reject the null. Which means we accept dice 1 as a good dice.

For Dice 2, we have a P-value of 0.0544 in terms of improbability it does not exceed α=0.03. Again, we do not have sufficient evidence to reject the null. Which means we accept dice 2 as a good dice.

For Dice 3, we have a P-value of 0.0282 in terms of improbability it does exceed α=0.03. On this occasion we have sufficient evidence to reject the null and accept the alternate hypothesis.

We can see that there is a cut off when getting a score of 20 and 21. With 20 we deem the dice to be fair but a score of 21 and the dice is deemed unfair. However, on occasion we may want to have a zone for 'undecided' as there can be grey areas. Also, we never really know if the dice was unfair we just assume that the event was so unlikely that the alternate hypothesis has to be true. This was a demonstration, in real life we would have a larger sample i.e. more than 4 throws and would have used a test where we could have used Minitab to calculate the Power of the test.

This whole exercise is basically something similar to what Minitab is doing when it calculates a P-value in any test.

7 HYPOTHESIS TESTING

7.1 Introduction to Hypothesis Testing.

Tests Comparing One Sample to a Target
7.2 1 Sample T
7.3 1 Sample Stdev
7.4 1 Sample % Defective
7.5 Chi-Square Goodness of Fit

Tests Comparing Two Samples with Each Other
7.6 2 Sample T
7.7 Paired T
7.8 2 Sample Stdev

Tests Capable of Comparing more than Two Samples
7.9 Chi-Square % Defective
7.10 Chi-Square Test for Association

7.11 Hypothesis Testing Exercises

7.1 Introduction To Hypothesis Testing.

Previously it was said that there are two parts to Hypothesis Testing, the procedure and the tests. In chapter 6, you covered the procedure in detail. If not, please go back and cover the chapter as you really need to know terms like Confidence, Power, Null, Alternate, one sided test & P-value.

In this chapter we are going to start learning how to use these tests via the Assistant. You will see how these tests take your sample data and give you information about your population. They will be predominantly used in the Analyse phase of DMAIC but could also be used in control for showing that a change has been achieved.

The way the Assistant carries out HT is much more accessible to beginners than the classic menu's. Additionally, some of the test procedures have also been changed to remove complexity. However, there are still general prerequisites for the tests. For instance, if sample size is sufficient the normality of the data is not an issue. Also, you will see the warning repeatedly that 'unusual data points can have a strong influence on the results'. This means that if there is a lot of special cause variation acting on your data the results may not be repeatable. Therefore, checking that your process is in control prior to hypothesis testing is always wise.

One advantage of the Assistant is that everything is in one place. Unlike the Classic methods you don't have to go between the Graphic and Session windows to look at your results.

Note that all the data for this chapter is in Excel file 07 Hypothesis Testing.xlsx which can be downloaded from WWW.rmksixsigma.com. The answers for the exercises are also available from the same site.

1. Click *Assistant<<Hypothesis Tests*
This will open up the main page for hypothesis testing. There are 3 boxes that contain the tests and these have been sub divided by your objective; compare one sample with a target, compare two samples with each other and compare more than two samples. Clicking on any of the tests will take you to the test menu. However, if you click on 'Help Me Choose' above any of the boxes it will take you to a decision tree.

2. Click '*Help Me Choose*' above the 'compare one sample with a target' box.

The decision tree asks two questions in order to help you decide which of the four tests to use. The first question is about data type. Do you have Continuous or Attribute data?

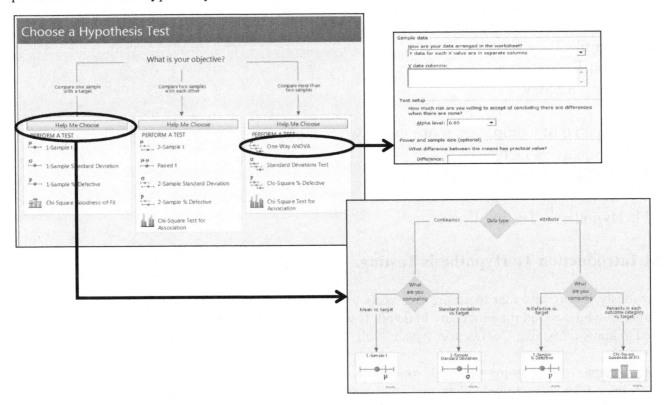

If you need further information to answer the question you can click on the diamond.
3. Click on the diamond for '*What are you comparing*'.

This opens up another page which informs us about the differences between the two tests. There is even an example on how the test could be used.

4. Click on the *Back* button. Then click on '*more*' which is below the button for the 1-Sample StDev Test. This opens up a page which gives the requirements for the test conditions. Each one of the sub menus can be opened to obtain more details on the data requirements.

Now that we understand a bit more about the menu system we are going to start looking at how to use the tests.

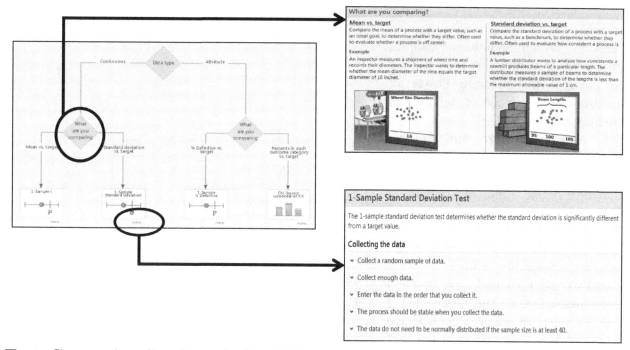

Tests Comparing One Sample To A Target
7.2   1 Sample t test

1 Sample t test	
Function	Tests whether the mean of a population is at a target level given a sample of data.
Sample Size	20 data points are required for the normality of the population that the sample is drawn from not to be an issue. More samples may be required to obtain a reasonable power (<80%) depending on the difference you wish to detect.
Data type & Format	Continuous data which is time ordered from a uni-modal distribution.
Considerations	The process must be stable.

Example 7.2.1 Bursting Discs

Bursting Discs Specialists (BDS) make the Raptor bursting disc which is rated at 15bar. A bursting disc is a safety device that is added to a pressure vessel. If the pressure in the vessel gets too high the disc will rupture and the pressure will be relieved to a safe area.

BDS want to check whether their Raptor Discs actually burst at 15 bar pressure. But as the discs are expensive they want to limit the number they use for testing. They feel they want to be able to measure a difference of 0.15 bar. From tests conducted previously they know that they can use 0.2 bar as an estimate for the population StDev. What is the minimum number of discs they must sample to get a power of 90%?

Then test the sample data provided in worksheet Bursting Disc to establish whether BDS can claim that the population bursting pressure of the Raptor Disc is correctly rated.

As we need to know the number of samples we require prior to conducting the t test we need to conduct the separate Power & Sample Size (PSS) procedure within the classic menus.

1. Click *Stat<< Power and Sample Size<<1 Sample t*

2. We need to establish the sample size so leave that box blank. Enter the remaining data, that was given in the question, then click OK.

3. Check the Power graph and also check the results in the Session window.

We see that we need a sample size of 21 to achieve a Power of 90%. This means that if there is a difference of greater than 0.15 we will have a 90% chance of detecting it. If you remember the Confidence is set within the test menu usually at a default value of 95%.

Let's have a look at the second part of the question using our Hypothesis Testing Procedure that we learnt in chapter 6. After all there was a reason we did a whole chapter on it.

Our Investigation Statement is ' Is the mean of the population bursting pressure of the Raptor disc 15bar or is it different?

From the Investigation Statement we can form our Null & Alternate Hypothesis.

H_o : Mean bursting pressure is 15 bar for the Raptor.

H_a : Mean bursting pressure is not 15 bar for the Raptor.

We have already assessed the PSS and we are happy with the Power achieved so we can conduct the test.

BDS actually take a sample of 25 discs over a period of time and check the bursting pressure. The data is recorded in time order in spreadsheet 07 Hypothesis Testing.xlsx in the worksheet Bursting Disc.

4. Transfer the single column of data into Minitab. Remember to copy the title row of the data into Minitab's title row.

5. Click *Assistant<<Hypothesis Tests*

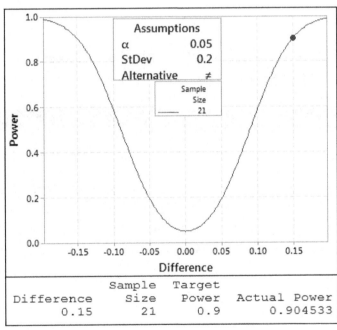

Specify values for any two of the following:	
Sample sizes:	
Differences:	.15
Power values:	.9
Standard deviation:	.2

Assumptions
α   0.05
StDev   0.2
Alternative ≠

Sample Size: 21

Difference	Sample Size	Target Power	Actual Power
0.15	21	0.9	0.904533

6. Click on the *1 sample t Test* box within the **Compare one sample with a target** group.

7. The test menu opens. Select 'Burst_Press' as the sample data. We are testing to see if your population is different to 15 so enter '15' as the target. Below the Target section you will see the radio buttons used to select whether we use a 'one sided' or 'two sided' test. Select the bottom radio button for the 'two sided' test.

8. At the bottom of the menu we tell Minitab the difference between the mean and the target that has implications for us. Minitab will use this and the sample StDev to calculate the power. Enter '0.15'as the Difference.

9. Click OK to run the test.

The Assistant produces a page report that is within the Graph window. The pages of this report are essentially treated as Graphs. They are the Report Card, Diagnostic & Summary Report. We will go through each of these in turn and look at the important areas.

Please navigate to the Summary Report. In the top left corner we get the answer to our Investigation Statement. The question ' Does the mean differ from 15?' is asked and the answer is given on the sliding scale as 'No'. We see that we have a P-value of 0.346 and as this was above our Significance level of 0.05 we did not have enough evidence to reject the null. We can see that the Assistant has a zone for P-values between 0.05 and 0.1. The Assistant deems a P-value in this zone to be inconclusive. Our P-value is far outside the marginal zone so we don't have to worry about that.

Below that we see our sample data displayed on a histogram. The calculated 95% confidence interval for the population mean is shown and we see that the value 15 sits within the confidence interval. Therefore, we cannot say that the population mean is different to 15.

Also check the actual distribution. The test only works if it is a single distribution not two distributions joined together. Refer

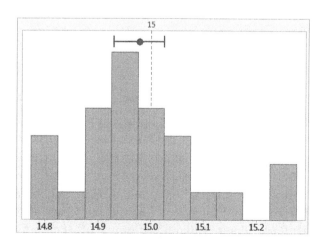

back to module 5.7 to see the discussion on bi-modal distributions.

On the top right of the Summary Report we have our sample statistics. We see the sample mean and the upper and lower limits of the confidence interval. Note, that the sample StDev is calculated to be 0.116. The Assistant uses this value for its Power calculations. Previously, we used 0.15 as our population estimate.

Statistics	
Sample size	25
Mean	14.978
95% CI	(14.930, 15.026)
Standard deviation	0.11616
Target	15

Please navigate to the Diagnostic Report.
At the top we see a basic control chart showing our sample data. We have no unusual data points that need to be explored.
At the bottom of the Diagnostic Report we get the analysis of Power. We actually get a power that is rounded up to 100.0%. This is much higher than our estimate as the sample size is higher and the StDev used here is from the samples and lower than our initial value.

Finally go to the Report Card. This gives us a summary on the validity of our test. We are told

1)   That there were no unusual data points that could make our test results unreliable.

2)   Normality of our data was not an issue due to our sample size.

3)   Due to our sample size there was a high Power value for the test. This was important as the test concluded there was 'no difference'. Therefore, the high Power value reduces our chances of getting a Type II error.

Example 7.2.2 Tablet

Parky wants to measure the power draw from his new quad core tablet and compare it to the power draw figure supplied by the manufacturer. It's the best time to do this as the tablet has only just come out of the box. Parky sets up his power measuring system to take a reading every minute and sets up the tablet so it doesn't go into a screen saver mode. Help Parky work out if the actual population of the power draw of this tablet is different to 12.4 watts. For the purposes of calculating the Power (1-β) Parky decides that a difference of 0.4 watts would be the smallest significant difference to him.

Parky actually takes 142 data samples. The data is recorded in time order in spreadsheet 07 Hypothesis Testing.xlsx in the worksheet Tablet.

1. Transfer the single column of data into Minitab.
2. Click *Assistant<<Hypothesis Tests*
3. Click on the *1 sample t Test* box within the **Compare one sample with a target** group.
4. The test menu opens. Select 'Tablet' as the sample data. We are testing to see if the population mean is different to 12.4 so enter '12.4' as the target.
5. Select the radio button for the 'two sided' test.
6. At the bottom of the menu we tell Minitab the difference between the mean and the target that has implications for us. Minitab will use this and the sample StDev to calculate the power. Enter '0.4'.
7. Click OK to run the test.

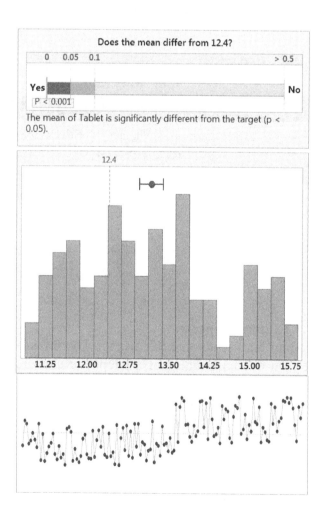

Minitab produces a three page report.

Please navigate to the Summary Report. In the top left corner we get the answer to our Investigation Statement. The mean of the population is likely to differ from 12.4.

Below that we see our sample data displayed on a histogram. The calculated 95% confidence interval for the population mean is shown and we see that the value 12.4 sits below the confidence interval for the population. The shape of the distribution does not look great. There could be issues that need further investigation.

On the Diagnostic Report we see the control chart of our data. It does not show any unusual data points but it does show a shift in the mean level of the data.

Click on any data point in the chart. This highlights all the data points. Then hover over the first data point where the level increases. It will reveal the position of that data point, it is observation 78 out of 142.

Parky wonders what could have changed on the tablet and then asks his son if he had used the tablet. He replies that he installed the Candy Squash app and left it running.

That explains why the power usage changed. It also demonstrates that the histogram we saw earlier was indeed a bi-modal distribution. As demonstrated, it is far harder to spot on a histogram than a control chart.

Don't' feel bad if you didn't spot it the Report Card did not spot it either. It just shows that even though the Assistant is doing a lot of the work you always need to be on your toes.

If Parky still wants to test his tablet he must repeat the whole experiment again or isolate the relevant data.

7.3 1 Sample StDev

1 Sample StDev	
Function	Test whether the StDev of a population is at a target level given a sample of data.
Sample Size	The results of this test could be invalid if there is more data in the tails of the population distribution than expected in a normal distribution. A sample size of at least 40 is required to test for this condition. More may be required to obtain a reasonable power or if the distribution you took your sample from has heavy tails.
Data type & Format	Continuous data which is time ordered from a uni-modal distribution.
Considerations	The process must be stable.

Example 7.3.1 Internet Speeds

Compo is telling his friends that the average UK broadband internet speed is reported to be 8.5Mbps when exactly on a 2 mile radius of a telephone exchange. Additionally, the StDev of the broadband speeds is reported to be 0.6Mbps ±0.2Mbps.

We have collected the relevant data, is Compo's statement about StDev true?

To be able to complete this test with a relatively small sample size, 40, and the requirement to have a reasonable power we need to set a limit in our difference of interest that is a fairly large proportion of our target.

If we were to set the difference of interest to 0.1 instead of 0.2Mbps the sample size requirement would increase dramatically.

We have Compo's sample data which consists of 40 data elements. The data is recorded in time order in spreadsheet 07 Hypothesis Testing.xlsx in the worksheet called 'Mbps'.

1. Transfer the single column of data into Minitab.

2. Click *Assistant<<Hypothesis Tests*

3. Click on the *1 sample StDev* box within the **Compare one sample with a target** group.

4. The test menu opens. Select 'Mbps' as the sample data. We are testing to see if the population is different to 0.6 so enter '0.6' as the target.

5. Select the bottom radio button for the 'two sided' test which tests for a difference whether higher or lower than the target level.

6. At the bottom of the menu we tell Minitab the difference between the mean and the target that has implications for us. Enter '0.2'.

7. Click OK to run the test.

Minitab produces a 3 page report. We will go through each of these pages in turn and look at the important areas.

Please navigate to the Summary Report.
In the top left corner we get the answer to our Investigation Statement. 'Does the standard deviation differ from 0.6?' is asked and the answer is given as 'Yes'.
We see that we have a P-value of <0.001. As this is below our Significance level of 0.05 we have strong evidence to reject the null. The probability of getting the results that we did given that the null hypothesis was true are deemed to be very low.

Below that we see the calculated 95% confidence interval for the population StDev against the target value. The population of Broadband speeds will likely have a higher StDev than our target.

On the top right we have our sample statistics. We see the sample mean and StDev. We are given the upper and lower limits of the confidence interval for StDev. This test tells us that Compo was wrong with his statement about broadband speed StDev. You could use the 1 sample t Test to check if he was right about the mean level.

Please navigate to the Diagnostic Report.
On the top we see a basic control chart showing our sample data. We have no unusual data points that need to be explored.

At the bottom of the Diagnostic Report we get the analysis of Power. We have two different Power values. If the difference we wanted to explore was greater than the target by 0.2 our Power would be 85%, which it was for our data.

Go to the Report Card. This gives us a summary on the validity of our test. We are told
1)   That there were no unusual data points that could make our test results unreliable.
2)   The results of this test could be invalid if there were more data in the tails of the population distribution than expected in a normal distribution. A sample size of at least 40 was required to test for this condition. Our sample did not show this condition.
3)   Due to our sample size we had a good Power for the test.

7.4 1 Sample % Defective

1 Sample % Defective	
Function	Test whether the defect rate of a population is at a target level given a defect rate from a sample of data.
Sample Size	The sample size must be sufficient to give a reasonable Power when trying to detect the difference that is meaningful to the user.
Data type & Format	Counts of attribute data.
Considerations	The sample must be representative of the process. Each item tested must have the same chance of being defective as any other item. Samples must be randomly selected.

Example 7.4.1 Blades

Hannan works for a company that produce directionally casted single crystal turbine blades for supersonic engines. The internal trigger level for defective blades is 27%, if above this value the casting department would be required to start an improvement initiative to reduce the defect rate. Up to now the department has always reported that the defect rate is not greater than 27%.

Hannan, reviewed the reporting guidelines and found that the company check 100 blades every month. Last month they found 30 defective blades but again they reported that the defect rate was not greater than 27% to the Operations Director.

Help Hannan assess whether the casting department are using the correct methodology when reporting to the Operations Director. If it is not correct assess the data using the correct methodology.

This example does not require us to use a data set.

Hannan looks at last months data and wonders if the assessment is correct as initially 30 defects in 100 samples is 30% and 30% is higher than the target of 27%. However, Hannan understands Six Sigma Statistics and decides to run the 1 Sample % Defective test in Minitab.

1. Click *Assistant<<Hypothesis Tests*
2. Click on the *1 sample % Defective* box within the **Compare one sample with a target** group.
3. The test menu opens. We are going to name the item that we tested as 'Blades'. We also have the option of using the generic name 'Test Items'.
4. Enter '100' as the number of items tested and '30' as the number found to be defective.
5. We enter our target of '27' as the percentage defective parts we wish to test against. On this occasion we want to use a one-sided test as we are only interested in finding out if our %defective within the

Sample data

Name of items tested: Blades

Total number of items tested: 100

Observed number of defectives: 30

What target do you want to test the % defective against?

Target: 27 %

What do you want to determine?

◉ Is the % defective of Blades greater than 27?

population is greater than 27%. To do this ensure the top radio button is selected under 'What do you want to determine?'.

6. On this occasion we have not been told what difference the company wants to be able to detect so we will assume it is 1%. Enter '1' for Difference.

7. Click OK to run the test.

Please navigate to the Summary Report.

In the top left corner we get to see why the casting department are reporting that their defect rate is not greater than 27%. It is because the P-value does not provide sufficient evidence to reject the null hypothesis.

Below that we see the confidence interval for the population defect rate and the target value is well within the confidence interval.

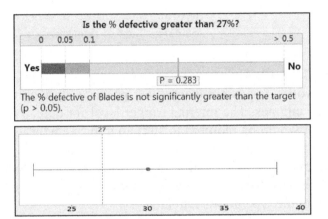

In the Diagnostic Report we see the analysis of the Power of the test. For this test we wanted to detect a difference of 1 but for a sample size of 100 we only get an 8% Power. This means that if a difference did exist we only had an 8% chance of detecting it. This suggests that we could easily suffer from a Type II error.

Hannan realises that he needs to increase the sample size and uses the table on the diagnostic report to decide on the sample size required. He opts for a sample size of 15,000 which should give him a Power between 80 & 90%.

| What sample size is required to detect a difference of 1? | |
Sample Size	Power
7124	60%
9326	70%
12280	80%
17048	90%

Hannan finds that there were 4150 defective blades in the 15,000 that were used as his sample.

8. Run the test again but this time use '15,000' as the number of items tested and '4150' as the number of defectives.

Please navigate to the Summary Report.
On this occasion we see a different answer. We have a P-value of 0.034 and this does

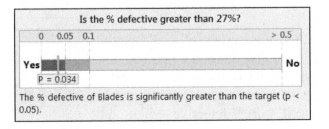

provide sufficient evidence to reject the null hypothesis. We can say that the population defect rate is greater than 27%.

We see the confidence interval for the population defect rate is greater than the target value.

In the Diagnostic Report we see that the Power achieved was 86.5%. This is a much more reasonable value to use than the 8% Power they had before.

Additionally, the Report Card indicates that the sample size was adequate for the test.

Hannan must now advise the casting department that they need to begin an improvement initiative to reduce the defect rate.

7.5 Chi Square Goodness of Fit

Chi Square Goodness of Fit	
Function	Data is categorised into three or more categories. The split of the data is compared to a target split. Categories that are different to their target value are identified.
Sample Size	There must be a minimum 5 samples in each category. However, as sample size increases the accuracy of the test will increase.
Data type & Format	Counts of attribute data.
Considerations	Samples must be randomly selected. Samples must be easily categorised without any overlap between categories.

Example 7.5.1 Budget

The Government has published figures on a national survey they conducted where they asked a number of households to state what was the single most difficult item to purchase for their monthly household budgets. The results were 12% said Food, 20% said Council Tax, 24% said Motoring, 34% said Mortgage and 10% said Energy.

A local council decided to check if their constituents felt the same way. They received the results of 339 questionnaires and checked the local results against the national results.

Are there any difference between the local and national results?
If there are any differences in which categories are they?
The data is recorded in spreadsheet 07 Hypothesis Testing.xlsx in the worksheet called 'Budget'.

1.   Transfer the three columns of data into Minitab. The Counts column represents the survey results received by the council. The Proportions column is the split we are testing the council results against, in this case the national results.

2.   Click *Assistant<<Hypothesis Tests*

3.   Click on the *Chi-Square Goodness-of-Fit* box within the **Compare one sample with a target** group.

4.   The test menu opens. We have the option of using the generic name for our process but we are going to use the name **Budget**.

5.   We have 5 categories so change Number of Outcomes to '5'.

6.   We have the option of entering our data manually into the menu or we can ask Minitab to pick up the data from the Worksheet Window by selecting the column headings. The second way is far easier so we will use that.
Use the drop down icon next to Outcome Name and select column 'C1 Household Budgets'.
Use the drop down icon next to Sample Count and select column 'C2 Counts'.
Use the drop down icon next to Target Percent and select column 'C3 Proportions'.

The final frame shows the complete table within the test menu.

7.   Click OK to run the test.

Please navigate to the Summary Report.
In the top left corner we are given the answer to our Investigation Statement, do any of the local categories differ from the national results? As the P-value is less than the significance level we have sufficient evidence to reject the null hypothesis. Therefore, at least one of the local categories is different to the national result. At this time we do not know which category is different.

Also on the Summary Report we see a Bar Chart showing the percentages of each category with the sample against the target. The greatest difference is in the categories of Food and Mortgage. The sample for Food was greater than the target but it was the other way round for Mortgage. However, we do not know if the categories are statistically significant.

On the top right of the Summary Report we are told which Categories differed from the targets. We are told that the Food Category and Mortgage Category did differ from the targets and we are told in which direction they differed.

Outcome	Sample Percent	Target Percent	Differ
Food	17.7	12	Higher
Council Tax	20.6	20	No
Motoring	25.7	24	No
Mortgage	25.7	34	Lower
Energy	10.3	10	No
	Total count = 339		

Please navigate to the Diagnostic Report.
At the top we see a chart which shows the magnitude of difference between sample and target and the direction of difference. We see that the Food category has the greatest percentage difference. That chart is not shown here.

At the bottom of the Diagnostic Report we get a table showing the summary of results. We can see confidence intervals for each category.

Outcome	Target Percent	Sample Percent	Individual 95% CI
Food	12	17.7	(13.6, 21.8)
Council Tax	20	20.6	(16.3, 25.0)
Motoring	24	25.7	(21.0, 30.3)
Mortgage	34	25.7	(21.0, 30.3)
Energy	10	10.3	(7.1, 13.6)

Go to the Report Card. This gives us a summary on the validity of our test. We are told that our sample size was sufficient to ensure the validity of the test and the confidence intervals.

Check	Status
Validity of Test	✓
Validity of Intervals	✓

The next section is the compare two samples with each other group. We cover the 2 sample t test, paired t test and the 2 StDev tests but we are not going to cover the attribute tests in this sections. This is because in terms of test set-up and interpretation of results they are very similar to tests for comparing more than two groups and those tests are covered later.

Tests Comparing Two Samples With Each Other
7.6   2 Sample t Test

2 Sample t test	
Function	Test whether the means of two populations differ given a sample of data from each population.
Sample Size	15 data points are required for the normality of the population that the sample was drawn from not to be an issue. More samples may be required to obtain a reasonable Power (<80%) depending on the difference you wish to detect.
Data type & Format	Continuous data which is time ordered from a uni-modal distribution.
Considerations	The process must be stable. Unlike the classic method the method used within the Assistant does not need to know if the groups have equal variances.

Example 7.6.1 Factory Outputs

Iqra works for a famous chocolate bar manufacturer and wants to find out which of two factories has the highest sugar yield. She takes 62 random samples from each factory and analyses them for sugar content and then knowing the sugar that went into each bar she can work out the sugar yield. Help Iqra work out which factory has the highest sugar yield.

The 2 Sample t test is probably the most commonly used test in hypothesis testing as it covers the comparison of the means of two populations. It is therefore used to measure whether a change of state has occurred or whether two populations are different. In this example we must establish if the two factories are different from each other.

The data is recorded in time order in spreadsheet 07 Hypothesis Testing.xlsx in the worksheet 'Sugar yield'.

1.   Transfer both columns of data into a new Minitab project file.
2.   Click *Assistant<<Hypothesis Tests*
3.   Click on the *2 sample t Test* box within the **Compare two samples with each other** group.

4.   We need to tell Minitab how the data is arranged in the worksheet. In our case the two samples are in two separate columns, this is known as 'unstacked'. If the data were 'stacked' the data would be in one column and there would be a column carrying the data headers. Select 'Each sample is in its own column' and then select the column names.

5.   We want to determine only if there is a difference between the two factories so select the bottom radio button.

Sample data

How are your data arranged in the worksheet?

Each sample is in its own column

Sample 1: Phobos

Sample 2: Demios

What do you want to determine?

○ Is the mean of Phobos greater than the mean of Demios?

○ Is the mean of Phobos less than the mean of Demios?

● Is the mean of Phobos different from the mean of Demios?

6. At the bottom of the menu we tell Minitab the difference between the two means that has an implication for us. We don't have a value for this but after consulting with Iqra we will use a value of 1.

7. Click OK to run the test.

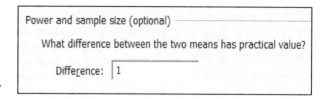

Please navigate to the Summary Report. In the top left corner we get the answer to our Investigation Statement. The question ' Do the means differ ?' is asked and the answer is given on the sliding scale as 'Yes'. The P-value is 0.019 which means we have sufficient evidence to reject the null.

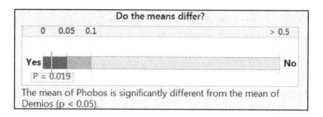

Below that we see the 95% confidence interval for the difference between the means. This can be positive or negative depending on which order we selected our samples in the test menu. We also see that zero is not within the confidence interval. This indicates there is a difference between the groups.

Below that we see our sample data displayed on two histograms with the calculated 95% confidence interval for the population means overlaid. It is interesting to note that the two confidence intervals overlap very slightly and yet Minitab has detected a difference.

On the top right we have our sample statistics. We see the sample mean and the upper and lower limits of the confidence interval. We are given -1.27 difference based on the mean values but the real difference between the populations could be anywhere between -2.32 and -0.21.

Please navigate to the Diagnostic Report.
At the top we see two basic control charts showing our sample data, I have only shown one of them here. Any unusual data points would be marked in red on this chart.

If a data point stands out from the rest of the data by a long way it should be investigated. It is possible to get 2-3% of data points shown as unusual and it would be nothing to worry about.

The Assistant identifies a data point as unusual if it is more than 1.5 times the interquartile range beyond the lower or upper quartile of the distribution. The lower and upper quartiles are the 25th and 75th percentiles of the data.

At the bottom of the Diagnostic Report we get the analysis of Power. We are told that with our present sample with a requirement of detecting a difference of 1 we would only have a 46.0% chance of detecting a difference if one existed. But we know that we detected a difference so we don't have to worry. It would have been a different story if we had conducted the Power test on its own prior to conducting this analysis in the Assistant.

For α = 0.05 and sample sizes = 62:
If the true means differed by 1, you would have a 46.0% chance of detecting the difference.

We are also given examples of the sample size required in each group to obtain a specific Power. We can see that if we wanted a Power of 90% then we would require 187 samples in each group.

What sample sizes are required to detect a difference of 1?	
Each Sample	Power
88	60%
110	70%
140	80%
187	90%
Your Samples	
62, 62	46.0

Observed difference = -1.2716

Please go to the Report Card. This gives us a summary on the validity of our test. We are told
1) That there were no unusual data points that could make our test results unreliable.

2) Normality of our data was not an issue due to our sample size.

3) The sample size was sufficient to detect a difference between the means.

4) We are told that as the Assistant uses a different calculation method to the classic menu's we do not need to worry whether the groups have equal variances or not.

7.7   Paired t Test

Paired t test	
Function	Test whether changing a specific condition on a population has an effect. Changing a specific condition results in dependant observations.
Sample Size	20 data points are required for the normality of the population that the sample is drawn from not to be an issue. More samples may be required to obtain a reasonable Power (<80%) depending on the difference you wish to detect.
Data type & Format	Continuous data which is time ordered.
Considerations	The process must be stable. As each element is tested under two conditions the data for each element must be in the same row.

Example 7.7.1 Darts

Aman Darts Specialists want to demonstrate the improvement that there new spinning titanium shaft gives over standard nylon shafts. They run a demonstration with 50 volunteer darts players of varying abilities who use standard nylon shafts. After allowing them to warm up they take their total score using 9 darts. The players are then given the new titanium rotating shafts which they fit into their darts replacing the nylon shafts. After another warm-up period their scores from 9 darts are recorded again. Establish if the titanium shaft is better than the nylon shaft. A difference of 9 is deemed to be the minimum difference of interest to Aman Darts.
The two scores for each player are recorded in a separate row of the spreadsheet.

A Paired T test is different to a 2 Sample t test as it is used for two dependent populations whereas a 2 Sample t test is used for two independent populations. Let's take the example of the darts demonstration. Aman Darts could have scored the nylon darts with one set of players and then tested the titanium shafts on a second set of players and then compared the scores. This would be two independent populations. However, there might be a problem if most of the good players went into one of the groups. To get round the possibility of all the good players going into one group only one group is used and they test both types of shaft. This gives us the two dependent populations.
A Paired t test is the same as calculating the difference of the dependent values and then using a 1 sample t test against a target difference of zero.
The data is recorded in time order in spreadsheet 07 Hypothesis Testing.xlsx in the worksheet 'Darts'.

1.   Transfer both columns of data into a new Minitab project file.
2.   Click *Assistant<<Hypothesis Tests*

3.   Click on the **Paired t** box within the **Compare two samples with each other** group.

4.   Enter the sample data in the order shown. As we only want to know if Titanium is better this is a one-way test. We

Sample data

Measurement 1: Titanium

Measurement 2: Nylon

select the appropriate radio button under Test set-up.

5. At the bottom of the menu we tell Minitab the difference between the two means that has implications for us. Enter '9' for the difference.

6. Click OK to run the test.

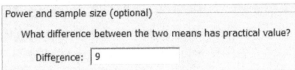

Please navigate to the Summary Report.
In the top left corner we are told the answer to the question 'Is Titanium greater than Nylon ?' and the answer is 'Yes'. The P-value means we have sufficient evidence to reject the null that there is no effect. This means the players did get a statistically significant better score with the Titanium shafts.

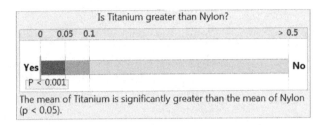

Below that we see a histogram showing the values of the actual differences between the scores for each person. We see how some people had a worse score, others stayed the same but mostly there was an increase in scores. We can see the Confidence Interval (CI) for the mean difference in the score and how this was greater than zero.

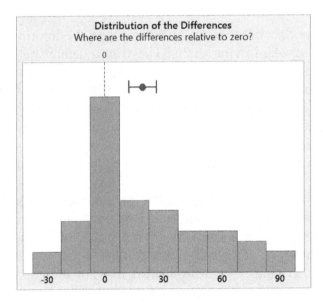

On the top right of the page we have our sample data. We see that the mean difference in scores was 19.56. You might also notice that Minitab is using a 90% CI where a 95% CI is expected. This is because Minitab uses a 90% CI for a one-way test.

Please navigate to the Diagnostic Report.
At the top we see a control chart showing both sets of data and the associated difference. Unusual data points would be shown in red and these might affect our results. Luckily we don't have any in this study.

At the bottom of the Diagnostic Report we get the analysis of Power. We are told that with our present sample with a requirement of detecting a difference of 9 we would only have a 68.2% chance of detecting a difference if one existed. But we know that we detected a difference so we don't have to worry.

Please go to the Report Card. This gives us a summary on the validity of our test. We are told
1) That there were no unusual data points that could make our test results unreliable.
2) Normality of our data was not an issue due to our sample size.
3) The sample size was sufficient to detect a difference between the means.

What is the chance of detecting a difference of 9?
< 40%   60%   Power   90%   100%
68.2%
8.0645   Difference   12.434

For α = 0.05 and sample size = 50:
If the true mean of Titanium were 9 greater than Nylon, you would have a 68.2% chance of detecting the difference.

Check	Status
Unusual Data	✓
Normality	✓
Sample Size	✓

7.8 2 Sample StDev

2 Sample StDev test	
Function	Test whether the StDevs of two populations differ given a sample of data from each population.
Sample Size	20 data points are required for the normality of the population that the sample is drawn from not to be an issue. More samples may be required to obtain a reasonable Power (<80%) depending on the difference you wish to detect.
Data type & Format	Continuous data which is time ordered.
Considerations	The process must be stable. The method of calculation used within the Assistant differs from the classic method. This means that normality is not an issue as long as the sample size is at least 20.

Example 7.8.1 Feeders

Woody wants to settle the age old argument regarding which type of feeder gives less feeder variation, The corimass feeder or the belt feeder. He collects feed rate data from both feeders when running at the same feed rate. Woody wants to be able to detect a difference of 10%. Even though this sounds quite large Woody knows that a lot of data points will be required to achieve a good Power for this test. Collecting a lot of data is not an issue as the control system logs all the required information.
Help Woody settle the age old question and calculate if there is a difference between the two types of feeder in terms of feedrate StDev.

The data is recorded in time order in spreadsheet 07 Hypothesis Testing.xlsx in the worksheet 'Feeders'.

1. Transfer both columns of data into a new Minitab project file.
2. Click *Assistant<<Hypothesis Tests*
3. Click on the *2 sample StDev* box within the **Compare two samples with each other** group.

4. Select 'Each sample is in its own column' and then select the column headers.

5. We want to determine only if there is a difference between the two feeders so select the bottom radio button. This is a two-way test.

6. At the bottom of the menu we tell Minitab that Woody is interested in detecting a difference of 10%. This is the value that would have practical implications in selecting new feeders in the future.

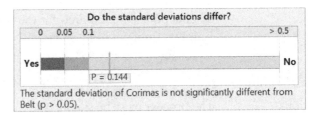

7. Click OK to run the test.

Please navigate to the Summary Report. In the top left corner we get the answer to ' Do the standard deviations differ ?' and the answer is 'No'. The P-value is 0.144 which means we do not have sufficient evidence to reject the null that there is no effect. This means that Woody must conclude that there is no difference in terms of variation between the two types of feeder.

Below that we see a plot showing 95% confidence intervals for the two StDevs. As the confidence intervals overlap and the P-value is 0.144 we can conclude there is no difference between the StDevs.

Below that we see our sample data displayed on two histograms. It is interesting to see the type of distributions that we get. This may become relevant in a future project.

On the top right we have our sample statistics. We see that both feeders are operating at almost the same mean level of 540. The average level of StDev for Belt is lower than that for the Corimas but remember there is insufficient evidence to say this difference was not created by anything other than chance.

Statistics	Corimas	Belt
Sample size	705	750
Mean	540.64	540.48
Standard deviation	10.147	9.6572
Individual 95% CI	(9.738, 10.60)	(9.185, 10.18)

Please navigate to the Diagnostic Report.
At the top we see two basic control charts showing our sample data, I have only shown the one for the Belt feeder. This is because it contained some unusual data points. Looking at the 5 data points in question they are not that far from the main body of data. I have 5 unusual data points in 750 which is 0.67%. As this is a very low percentage and the points are not that far out I am not going to take any action.

At the bottom of the Diagnostic Report we get the analysis of Power. We are told that with our present sample with a requirement of detecting a difference of 10% we had an 87.5% chance of detecting a difference if one existed. Our Power is above 80% but not quite 90%. The question is are we satisfied that we had sufficient Power to detect a difference? My answer would be yes, 87.5% is a fairly good Power level.

For α = 0.05 and sample sizes = 705, 750:
If the true standard deviation of one sample were 10% smaller than the other, you would have a 87.5% chance of detecting the difference.

Please go to the Report Card. This gives us a summary on the validity of our test. We are told
1) There were unusual data points that might make our test results unreliable. However, we discounted them.
2) Normality of our data was not an issue due to our sample size.
3) Due to our sample size being greater than 20 the P-value should be valid for the test.
4) Finally, we are warned that our sample size was not sufficient to obtain a Power of 90%. We would have needed 789 samples in each group to achieve a Power of 90%.

There are two additional tests in the 'Compare two samples with each other' group but we will not cover these two tests in this section. We will cover similar tests in the next section, 'Compare more than two samples'. The reason for not covering these in this section is that test set-up and interpretation is virtually identical between the two sections.

Tests Capable Of Comparing More Than Two Samples
7.9   Chi-Square % Defective

Chi-Sqaure %Defective (for more than 2 groups)	
Function	Tests whether the populations of more than 2 defect rates are significantly different from each other.
Sample Size	The sample size must be sufficient to give a reasonable Power when trying to detect the difference that is meaningful to the user. There must be at least 5 observed defects in each group and Minitab will state whether the expected number of defectives in each group was sufficient.
Data type & Format	Counts of attribute data.
Considerations	The sample must be representative of the process. Each item tested must have the same chance of being defective as any other item. i.e. if it is known that one operator produces products with a lower defect rate then products should not be mixed when analysing. Samples must be randomly selected.

Example 7.9.1 Distributors

Kaley works for Nile, a major online retailer. She has been tasked to investigate how their third party distribution companies are performing in terms of delivery times. Nile processes all orders within 2 days so that they are ready for pick-up at local warehouses within 2 days. The distributors then have a further 2 days to deliver the orders to customers. Any delivery which is completed outside of the 4 day deadline is deemed to be a miss or defective. All four of the distributors operate out of all the warehouses and Kaley takes all of the data for March, which is known to be a representative month. When asked Kaley says that a difference of 3% would be a significant difference for her investigation. Help Kaley do an initial investigation to establish if any of the distributors are operating significantly differently to any of the others.

The data is recorded in spreadsheet 08 Hypothesis Testing.xlsx in the worksheet 'Distributors'.

1.   Open the file and transfer the data into a new Minitab project file. We have 3 columns of data, Distributors, Late and Total.

2.   Click *Assistant<<Hypothesis Tests.*

3.   Click on the *Chi-Square % Defective* box within the **Compare more than two samples** group.

4.   The test menu opens. We are going to name the item that we are testing as 'Deliveries'.

5.   Type in the X variable name as 'Distributors'.

6.   As we have 4 companies we need to set 'Number of distinct X values' to '4'.

7.   In the middle of the menu we enter all our data by selecting the column names from the drop down menus. From the first drop down menu select 'Distributors' to auto-populate the data. For the Total Number tested drop-down select 'Total' and finally for the Number of Defectives drop-down select 'Late'. Alternatively, type all the data in by hand if that pleases you.

Distributors ▾	Total Number Tested ▾
Khanage Ltd	1500
Walks	1800
Fence	1700
SEL	1650

Number of Defectives ▾
52
72
85
40

8.   Kaley told us that she wants to be able to detect a difference of 3% so we will enter '3' for 'Difference'.

Power and sample size (optional)

What difference between the % defectives has practical value?

Difference: 3

9.   Click OK to run the test.

Please navigate to the Summary Report.
In the top left corner we are told that the % defectives differ. This means that at least one of the populations is different to the others.
We have to go to the % Defectives Comparison chart to find out which groups are actually different. We are told that 'Red intervals that do not overlap differ'. For Kaley this means that SEL differs from Fence. We cannot say that SEL differs from Khanage or Walks and we cannot say that Fence differs from Walks or Khanage.

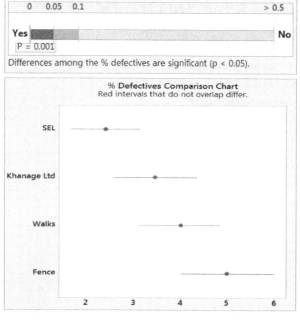

In the top left we see the Grouping Information table and that helps clarify which groups differ. These tables are invaluable when there are many groups which differ greatly. The table confirms that the only distributors that differ are SEL and Fence.

		Which % defectives differ?
#	Distributors	Differs from
1	SEL	4
2	Khanage Ltd	
3	Walks	
4	Fence	1

In the Diagnostic Report we see the number of Observed and Expected items for the successful and failed deliveries. Below the table we are told that the expected number of items in each group should be 1.5 to ensure the validity of the test.

Number of Defective and Nondefective Items

	Defective		Nondefective	
Distributors	Observed	Expected	Observed	Expected
Khanage Ltd	52	56.2	1448	1444
Walks	72	67.4	1728	1733
Fence	85	63.7	1615	1636
SEL	40	61.8	1610	1588

- To ensure validity of the test, the expected number of defectives and nondefectives should be at least 1.5.
- To ensure validity of the comparison intervals, the observed number of defectives and nondefectives should be at least 5.

To ensure the validity of the comparison intervals the observed number of items should be at least 5 in each group.

In the Power Report we are given a Confidence Interval for our power which is 97.26% to 98.44% for detecting a difference of 3.

What is the chance of detecting a difference of 3?

Based on your samples and α level (0.05), the chance of detecting a difference of 3 ranges from 97.26% to 98.44%.

We are also given a table of Powers that can be achieved with differing sample sizes and the Confidence Intervals for each group. Those tables are not shown here.

Finally, in the Report Card we are told are test and intervals were valid, as also shown in the Diagnostic Report. And our sample size was sufficient to detect a difference.
This information tells Kaley that there is a performance difference between SEL and Fence which could be investigated and used to improve SELs performance.

Check	Status
Validity of Test	✓
Validity of Intervals	✓
Sample Size	✓

7.10   Chi-Square Test for Association

Chi-Square Test for Association	
Function	Tests whether values of categorised components of different items are likely to have differing populations, where there are three or more category's for each item.
Sample Size	Minitab will state whether the expected number of items in each category was sufficient to ensure validity of the results.
Data type & Format	Counts of categorical data.
Considerations	Data must be collected randomly for each item. If the data is measured it must be allocated to only one category. There is no Power assessment for this test.

A number of the hypothesis tests associated with categorical data have similar sounding names and functions. To avoid confusion let's review the function of this test and the Chi-Square Goodness of fit test. The Goodness of fit test worked on a single item such as the grade boundaries in a single department and compared the calculated percentages to a target value. The test for association works for more than one item and assesses whether the populations of categories within those items contain differing percentages.

Example 7.10.1 Grades

Mahwish is checking the results of a local school across a number of broadly defined departments. She wants to check if the percentages of Pass, Fails and Distinctions is the same across the departments of Humanities, Science, Technical and Languages. She obtains data which gives counts of categorical data from the department heads. Help Mahwish analyse the data to establish if any of the categories are likely to have differing populations.
The data is recorded in spreadsheet 07 Hypothesis Testing.xlsx in the worksheet 'Grades'.

1.   Open the file and transfer the data into a new Minitab project file.
2.   Click *Assistant<<Hypothesis Tests*
3.   Click on the *Chi-Square Test for Association* box within the **Compare more than two samples** group.

4.   The test menu opens and we are asked 'How will you enter your data?'. As we are efficient we will get Minitab to pick up the data from the worksheet window by selecting 'Get from current worksheet'.

5.   We then need to tell Minitab that our 'Outcomes are columns' as the data for our categories, Distinction, Pass and Fail, are listed in columns.

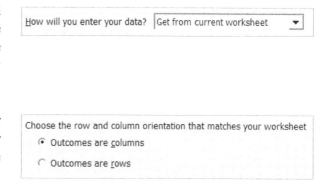

6. Minitab asks us the 'Y name'. 'Y' refers to the response, which is the variable we are measuring as we change our inputs. Inputs are typically called 'X'. Our response is 'Grade' so we enter that against 'Y name'. We have 3 categories or outcomes of grade.

7. The X variable are our departments and we have 4 of those. Enter '4' for Number of X values.

8. Minitab will draw the empty table for us. We then need to select the appropriate column headings for Minitab to input the data.

9. Once you have entered the column headings and the data has been automatically populated click OK to run the test.

Subject	Distinction	Pass	Fail
Technical	700	3960	280
Humanities	500	2880	160
Languages	960	4240	500
Science	720	3500	120

Please navigate to the Summary Report.
In the top left corner we get the answer to the Investigation statement. The percentage profiles differ. This means that at least one pair of our category breakdowns differ.

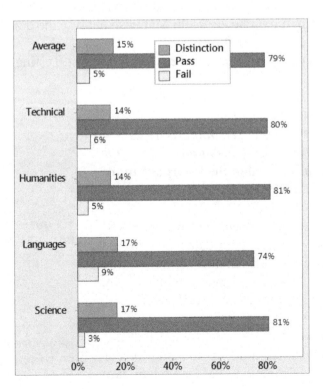

In the Percentage Profiles chart we are shown how the percentages of the outcomes vary between the departments and we are shown the average levels at the top.

We see that each department had a similar profile with the number of passes being the highest outcome in each category. The fail grade was less than 10% in each department and there was an average of 15% distinctions in each department.

%Difference between observed and expected counts is a graph showing exactly what the title explains. Each bar shows the %difference between the observed and expected difference. For example, Science-Fails has a value close to -50%, this means that the observed fails were close to 50% less than expected. Conversely, Languages had almost 50% more observed fails than expected. These values appear to be high so I can make an educated guess and assume that they are categories that differ. The next greatest difference is Humanities-Fails which are at -21%. Without having a separate P-value I can't say if Humanities-Fails is statistically significant.

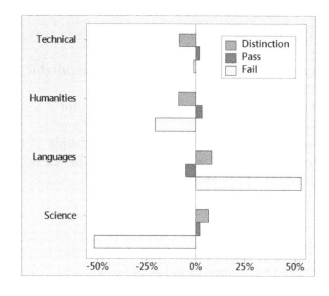

I apologise if I am pointing out the obvious, the term 'Observed' means the value from the sample data, whereas, 'Expected' is calculated for each combination of Grade Vs Subject.

On the Diagnostic Report, we are given the actual breakdown of Observed and Expected values in a table. It can be seen that even though the percentage difference of Science and Language Fails was high the real difference value was not that high.

Below the table we are told that the expected value in each category must be at least 1 for this test in order for the P-value to be valid. We have met this condition.

In the Report Card we are told that are results were valid as we had sufficient values in each of the expected count categories.

	Technical		Humanities		Languages		Science	
	Obs	Exp	Obs	Exp	Obs	Exp	Obs	Exp
Distinction	700	768	500	550	960	886	720	675
Pass	3960	3889	2880	2787	4240	4487	3500	3417
Fail	280	283	160	203	500	326	120	248
Total	4940		3540		5700		4340	

Expected counts should be at least 1 to ensure the validity of the p-value for the test.

Check	Status
Validity of Test	✓

This concludes the chapter on Hypothesis Testing. You should repeat the examples until you can complete them without looking at the book. Once you can do that try the exercises. Model answers for the exercises are available at www.rmksixsigma.com.

7.11 Hypothesis Testing Exercises

Detailed answers to all of the exercises are available from www.rmksixsigma.com
Exercise 7.11.1 PSS
Establish the sample size that you would need for a 1 sample t test where you had a Power of 90% under the following conditions
1) A one-way test where you are interested only if the alternate is greater than the null hypothesis
2) You are interested in being able to detect a difference of 3
3) The historical StDev has been 5.

Exercise 7.11.2 PSS
Establish the Power that you achieve with a 2 sample t test under the following conditions
1) A two-way test where you are only considering if the alternate is different to the null hypothesis
2) You have a sample size of 60 in each group.
3) You are interested in being able to detect a difference of 1
4) The historical StDev has been 3.
Before running the procedure try and estimate the power value that would be achieved and then compare your guess to the answer.

Exercise 7.11.3 Conduct a 1 Sample t
Analyse the data in File 07Hypothesis Testing.xlsx worksheet Ex 7.11.3 and answer the questions shown below. The data was collected randomly and is recorded in time order.
1)   Is the sample data within Column Pressure likely to have come from a population where the mean was different to 77?
2)   What is the confidence interval for the mean of the population?
3)   Have the requirements of the test that you have used been met?
4)   What was the Power of the test when you want to detect a difference of 2?
5)   Are there any issues associated with this level of Power ?
6)   Does the Report Card generate any warnings?

Exercise 7.11.4 Conduct a 2 Sample StDev
Analyse the data in File 07Hypothesis Testing.xlsx worksheet Ex 7.11.3 and answer the questions shown below. The data was collected randomly and is recorded in time order.
1)   Is the sample data within Column Pressure likely to have come from a population where the StDev was different to 5?
2)   What is the confidence interval for the StDev of the population?
3)   Have the requirements of the test that you have used been met?
4)   What was the Power of the test when you want to detect a difference of 1?
5)   Are there any issues associated with this level of Power ?
6)   Does the Report Card generate any warnings?

Exercise 7.11.5 Conduct a 1 sample t

Analyse the data in File 07Hypothesis Testing.xlsx worksheet Ex 7.11.5 and answer the questions shown below. The data was collected randomly and is recorded in time order.

1)   Is the sample data in columns TempA and TempB likely to have come from different populations?
2)   If the populations are different, which population mean is greater?
3)   Have the requirements of the test that you have used been met?
4)   What was the Power of the test when you want to detect a difference of 5?
5)   Are there any issues associated with this level of Power ?
6)   Does the Report Card generate any warnings?

Exercise 7.11.6 Conduct a 2 sample t

Analyse the data in File 07Hypothesis Testing.xlsx worksheet Ex 7.11.6 and answer the questions shown below. The data was collected randomly and is recorded in time order.

1)   Is the sample data in columns Freq_A and Freq_B likely to have come from different populations?
2)   If the populations are different, which population mean is greater?
3)   Have the requirements of the test that you have used been met?
4)   What was the Power of the test when you want to detect a difference of 3?
5)   Are there any issues associated with this level of Power ?
6)   Does the Report Card generate any warnings?

Example 7.11.7 Conduct a chi-sq % defective 2 groups.

Analyse the data in File 08Hypothesis Testing.xlsx worksheet Ex 7.11.7 and answer the questions shown below.

A questionaire is sent to a large number of companies. In one of the questions the companies are asked to select which sector their business would come under. This is then compared with the national average.

1)   Are any of the population sectors different from the target samples?
2)   Which population sectors are different from their target samples?
3)   Have the requirements of the test that you have used been met?
4)   Does the Report Card generate any warnings?

8 ANOVA

8.1 Introduction to ANOVA

The problem is that ANOVA stands for Analysis of Variance. However, it's easier to call this chapter ANOVA because it is an all encompassing title for everything that we are going to be covering. You might remember that I left out two techniques from the Assistant's Hypothesis Testing menu. We are going to be covering 'One-Way ANOVA' and the 'Standard Deviations Test' using the Assistant in this section.

We are then going to be leaving the Assistant for a short amount of time and we are going to be looking at the ANOVA General Linear Model (GLM). This will be an introduction to the GLM for Green Belts and hopefully in the Black Belt edition we can take a deeper look at the GLM. I did consider leaving out the GLM procedure from the Green Belt edition but it is such a useful tool I did not want Green Belts to be without it.

Note that all the data for this chapter is in Excel file 08 ANOVA.xlsx which can be downloaded from WWW.rmksixsigma.com. The model answers for the exercises are also available from the same site.

8.2 The theory behind ANOVA

If we had two different materials and we tested 50 samples of each for breaking strength we might get the Individual Value Plot (IVP) shown. We could then calculate the mean strength of each material using the sample data. We have a continuous response variable which is strength and we have two different materials that we are testing. We could say that the property 'Material' has two levels, material A and material B.

And as you have already completed chapters 6 & 7 I don't need to tell you that we would use the sample data to make a 95% confidence interval of the mean of the populations using a 2 sample T test for both materials. We would then compare the confidence intervals to say if one material was different to the other.

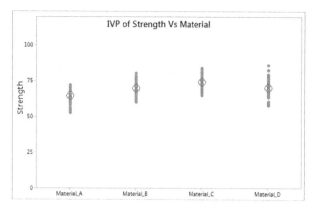

If we had more than two levels we could still make the IVPs and then to assess if the levels were different we could use a number of 2 Sample T tests to establish which of the groups were different from each other. Luckily, Minitab is here to make our lives easy and has given us the One-Way ANOVA test.

Let's go back to our example, we have 4 levels of material and we have plotted the response variable for each level. Our Investigation Statement would be 'Does changing the material of construction have an effect on strength?'. Our null hypothesis is 'There is no difference in mean levels between any of the populations' and our alternate hypothesis is 'There is a difference in mean levels between at least one pair of populations'.

Basically, we want to know if any of our groups are different from each other in terms of mean strength.

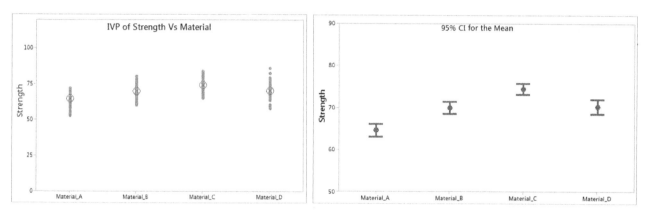

To establish if the levels of material are different we could plot the 95% Confidence Interval (CI) for each level. We know that if the intervals don't overlap then we have sufficient evidence to say that the groups are different. We can see that Material A & B are different, A & C are different, B & D are not different etc.

To explore how One-Way ANOVA works let's ask ourselves what if the mean levels of each material where the same as in the diagram but there was more variability in the results. Look at the IVP and try to imagine that the variability in the groups is increasing but the mean levels are staying the same.

When the level of variability in the groups is increased the confidence intervals begin to overlap and we cannot say that the groups are different. This means that in our example there are two factors which affect our ability to state whether we can say there is a difference between the groups, one is the difference in mean levels between the groups and the other is the variability within the groups.

The One-way ANOVA procedure actually calculates the between mean to within group variation ratio and calls it the F statistic.

$$\frac{Between\ Group\ Variation}{Within\ Group\ Variation} = F\ Statistic$$

Let's take it back to the Material Vs Strength example and consider what is happening to the F-Statistic when we change the Within Group Variation.

$$\frac{Between\ Group\ Variation}{Low\ Within\ Group\ Variation} = High\ F\ statistic$$

Just doing the calculation in relative terms with a low within group variation will result in a high F statistic.

And now if we can use our imagination again and increase the within group variation.

$$\frac{Between\ Group\ Variation}{High\ Within\ Group\ Variation} = Low\ F\ statistic$$

If you have a dynamic imagination and you have been imagining that the within group variation has been changing value and the F Statistic has been changing value you may be thinking 'okay, when will I have sufficient evidence that the value of my F-statistic will tell me that there is a difference between at least one pair of the groups?'

Minitab will calculate the F statistic and then compare that to the null distribution for this test, which happens to be called the F distribution. It will then generate a P-value and the definition of the P-value is 'It is the probability of getting your sample results, including results that are more extreme, given that the null hypothesis is true'. If our P-value exceeds the limit we have set ourselves to say this event is beyond random chance then we reject the null hypothesis.

The simple answer is that our P-value will tell us if we have sufficient evidence to reject or fail to reject the null hypothesis.

The above theory was discussed to give you a deeper understanding of the methods used for One-Way and GLM ANOVA methods used within the classic menus. The Assistant actually uses something called Welch's method which does not use the F-test. The advantage of Welch's method is that it does not require the groups to have equal variances.

Let's do some examples and see One-Way ANOVA in action.

8.3. One Way ANOVA

One Way ANOVA test	
Function	Tests whether the population means of three or more levels of a single predictor differ given a sample of data from each population.
Sample Size	When there are up to 9 levels at least 15 data points are required at each level for normality, of the population that the sample is drawn from, not to be an issue. 20 samples are required when there are 10 or more levels. More samples may be required to obtain a reasonable power (<80%) depending on the minimum difference you wish to detect.
Data type & Format	The response data is randomly selected continuous data which should be time ordered from uni-modal distributions.
Considerations	The process must be stable. Unlike the classic method the method used within the Assistant does not require that the groups have equal variances.

Example 8.3.1 Material Breaking Strengths

Zee is checking the breaking strength of 5 different materials in a standardised test. Zee does around 25 tests on each of his samples and reports the breaking strengths in time order. Can you help Zee establish if any of the materials have differing breaking strengths? Can the materials be categorised into groups? For the Power and sample size calculation Zee feels 4 is the minimum difference that he would wish to detect between groups.

We have Zee's sample data recorded in time order in spreadsheet 08 ANOVA.xlsx in the worksheet called 'Materials'.

Material_A	Material_B	Material_C	Material_D	Material_E
68.68	67.15	77.06	79.12	69.88
67.25	66	74.86	82.72	76.16
63.63	73.19	70.9	86.82	68.2
68.54	75.67	74.31	86.99	71.98
72.22	66.37	76.2	77.89	67.15
63.38	63.87	77.29	84.57	69.3

1. Transfer the data into Minitab.
2. Click *Assistant<<Hypothesis Tests*
3. Click on the *One-Way ANOVA* box within the **Compare more than 2 Samples** group.
4. The test menu opens. We have to tell Minitab how our data is arranged. The X data for the 5 levels is in 5 columns with the level title at the top of each column. This is traditionally called 'Unstacked Data'. Ensure 'Y data for each X value are in separate columns' is selected. The other format is stacked data where there would be only two columns. The level title would be in one column and the response data in the other column.

How are your data arranged in the worksheet?

Y data for each X value are in separate columns

Y data columns:

'Material_A'-'Material_E'

5. Select the 5 columns of data, Material_A to Material_E.
6. At the bottom of the menu we tell Minitab the minimum difference between groups that has implications for us. Enter '4'.
7. Click OK to run the test.

Please navigate to the Summary Report.
In the top left corner we get the answer to our Investigation Statement 'Do the means differ?' and the answer is given as 'Yes'.
We see that we have a P-value of <0.001. As this is below our Significance level of 0.05 we have strong evidence to reject the null.

Below that we see the Means Comparison Chart. We are told that 'Red intervals that do not overlap differ'. This really means that if an interval is red it is different to at least one other interval. In this case it's not that much of a problem that they are all red as it is fairly easy to evaluate how you would split the groups using the comparison chart.

To help us understand the structure of the groups we have the Grouping Information Table (GIT) on the top left. This tells us that A, B & E are different to C & D. Material C is in its own group as is material D.

In order to visualise the groups I have put rings surrounding the materials that can be considered within the same group on the means comparison chart.

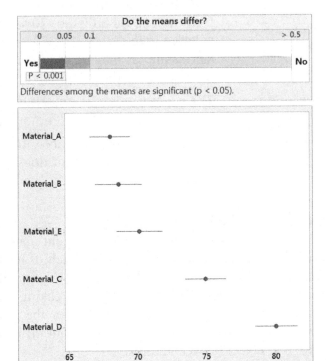

#	Sample	Differs from
1	Material_A	4 5
2	Material_B	4 5
3	Material_E	4 5
4	Material_C	1 2 3 5
5	Material_D	1 2 3 4

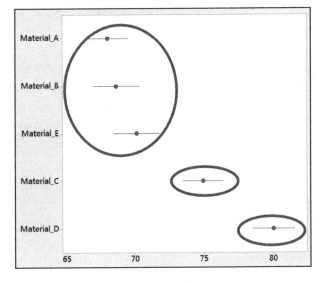

The Diagnostic Report contains histograms and SPC charts so that we can evaluate trends in time ordered data, look for unusual data points and also look for bimodal distributions.

The SPC chart for Material C looks unusual and I would personally make a note to check the results from Material C again. Minitab does not give us any warnings about the data.

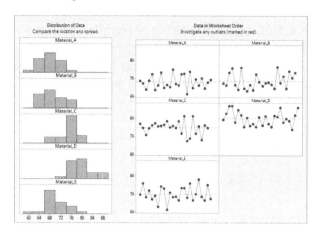

On the Power Report we are told that we had a Power of somewhere between 73.98% to 85.66% in this test. This figure is slightly low but the test managed to detect a difference.

Finally on the Report Card we are given a summary on the validity of our test. We are told

1)   That there were no unusual data points that could make our test results unreliable.

2)   The sample size was sufficient to detect a difference between means.

3)   Normality was not an issue as we had a sample size of at least 15 within the groups.

4)

For information we are told that the test within the Assistant does not require the data groups to have equal variances.

8.4.   Standard Deviation Test

Standard Deviation test	
Function	Tests whether the population StDevs of three or more levels of a single predictor differ given a sample of data from each population.
Sample Size	20 samples are required in each group for non-normality not to be an issue.
Data type & Format	Randomly selected continuous data which should be time ordered from uni-modal distributions.
Considerations	The process must be stable. Power is not reported within this procedure.

Example 8.4.1 Material Breaking Strengths

Zee has established which of his materials belong in groups when it comes to the mean breaking strength. He then decides that he would like to know if any of the materials have different variances of breaking strengths. Help Zee evaluate his data and establish if any of the populations have differing variances?

We are using the same sample data recorded in the worksheet called 'Materials', as used in the previous example.

1. Transfer the data into Minitab, if it is not there already.
2. Click *Assistant<<Hypothesis Tests*
3. Click on the *Standard Deviations Test* box within the **Compare more than 2 Samples** group.
4. The test menu opens. We have to tell Minitab how our data is arranged. Ensure 'Y data for each X value are in separate columns' is selected.
5. Select the 5 columns of data, Material_A to Material_E.
6. This test does not provide a Power calculation so we do not enter the difference we are interested in being able to detect.
7. Click OK to run the test.

Please navigate to the Summary Report.

In the top left corner we are told that our standard deviations do not differ. This means that we must accept our null hypothesis that there are no pairs of groups that have a differing standard deviation.

In the Standard Deviations Comparison Chart we are told that 'Blue indicates no differences'.

And the Grouping Information Table (GIT) tells us that no differences have been identified.

The Diagnostic Report is identical to that shown in the previous example. The graphs and charts do not show any unusual patterns or data points.

There is a table of data within the Descriptive Statistics Report that we may find useful. And the Report Card reports that there were no issues with our test that could lead to inaccuracies with the results.

		Which standard deviations differ?
#	Sample	Differs from
1	Material_A	
2	Material_C	
3	Material_D	None Identified
4	Material_B	
5	Material_E	

Example 8.4.2 Khansini Space Probe

The Khansini probe recently gathered gravitational data on 10 of Saturn's moons. Firstly establish whether any of the moons are likely to have populations which have differing gravitational variances? Then establish if the moons can be grouped in terms of gravitational variance.

For the last part establish whether any of the moons have different levels of mean gravity and whether they can be grouped in terms of their gravitational means. The minimum difference between groups that has implications for us is 0.3.

We will be using the sample data recorded in the worksheet called 'Saturn'. This data is recorded in time order.

1. Transfer the data into Minitab.
2. Click *Assistant<<Hypothesis Tests*
3. Click on the *Standard Deviations Test* box within the **Compare more than 2 Samples** group.
4. The test menu opens. We have to tell Minitab how our data is arranged. Ensure 'Y data for each X value are in separate columns' is selected.
5. Select the 10 columns of gravitational data from columns Rhea to Albiorix.
6. Click OK to run the test.

How are your data arranged in the worksheet?

Y data for each X value are in separate columns

Y data columns:

Rhea-Albiorix

On the top left corner of the Summary Report we are told that our standard deviations differ. This means that we must accept the alternate hypothesis that there is at least one pair of groups that have a differing standard deviation. We can examine which moons are different on the remainder of the Summary Report.

The best way to look at the group structure is to use the Grouping Information Table to establish the groups and then display the different groups on the Comparison Chart.
Sitting in the middle we have Kiviuq and Skathi. I have called them A on the Comparison chart. We cannot say that either of them differs from any of the other moons.
Then we have Hyperion, it only differs from Albiorix, Titan and Pheobe. On the Comparison chart we would say that B differs from E.
Paaliaq cannot be said to differ from Hyperion, Kiviuq or Sakthi but it does differ from everything else. On the Comparison chart C differs from D & E.
Sometimes we get caught in a paradox if we start doing inferences e.g. If D& E don't differ why does B differ from E but not D. The way to think about it is to use pair-wise comparisons only. For example, we have sufficient evidence to say that B is different to E. We don't have sufficient evidence to say that B is different to D. Similarly, we don't have sufficient evidence to say that D is different to E.
The Diagnostic Report does not highlight any unusual data. And the Report Card does not give us any warnings that our results may be inaccurate.

We will now use the One-Way ANOVA procedure to check if any of the planets have differing mean levels of gravity.
7.   Click *Assistant<<Hypothesis Tests*
8.   Click on the *One-Way ANOVA* box within the **Compare more than 2 Samples** group.

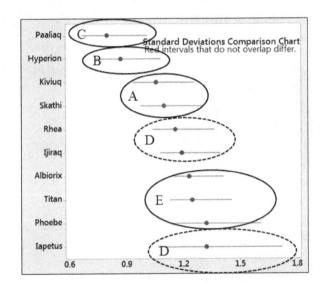

9. The test menu opens. We have to tell Minitab how our data is arranged. Ensure 'Y data for each X value are in separate columns' is selected.
10. Select the 10 columns of gravitational data from columns Rhea to Albiorix.

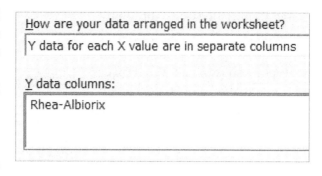

11. At the bottom of the menu we tell Minitab the minimum difference between groups that has implications for us. Enter '0.3'.
12. Click OK to run the test.

Please navigate to the Summary Report.

On the top left of the Summary Report we are told that the 'means differ' which tells us that at least two of the planets have differing population means of gravitational force.

The grouping for means are very different to standard deviations. Before we had Kiviuq and Skathi which could not be differentiated from any other group but this time we have Titan and Phoebe. I call this group A on the Means Comparison Chart.

		Which means differ?	
#	Sample	Differs from
1	Paaliaq	2 5 6 7 8 9 10
2	Kiviuq	1 10
3	Titan	
4	Phoebe	
5	Skathi	1
6	Albiorix	1
7	Rhea	1
8	Ijiraq	1
9	Iapetus	1
10	Hyperion	1 2

Kiviuq is only different to both Paaliaq and Hyperion. Paaliaq is different to every other group apart from Group A. Group D is only different to C.

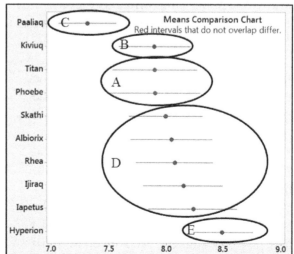

The Diagnostic Report does not show any unusual data points.

The Power Report shows that the Power that we had to actually spot a difference was very low. However, the test found a difference so we don't need to worry about the low Power.

The Report Card gives us the all clear.

This completes the section on One-way-ANOVA and the Standard Deviations Test. Both of which will prove to be very useful tools. In the next section is one of my favourite tools and it is called the ANOVA General Linear Model. Unfortunately, they have not put it into the Assistant yet so we have to learn it using the classic menu's.

8.5 ANOVA General Linear Model

In the last section we saw One-Way ANOVA in action. We saw that if we had one predictor variable with fixed levels against a continuous response variable we could use One Way ANOVA to establish if there was a difference in at least one pair of the levels. We also used the Grouping Information tables to group the levels of the predictor variables. The General Linear Model (GLM) gives us much more functionality and allows us to explore whether the difference between levels of multiple predictor variables are significant. The GLM can do much more but it only makes sense to look at the more common uses in this volume. As far as we are concerned the GLM can do pretty much everything the Balanced ANOVA and Two Way ANOVA procedures can do.

Two guys who work in the same office as me, Mr Steve Griffiths and Mr Frank Gleeson, insisted that I put a zombie example into the book, you have them to thank for this example that I am going to use to explain GLM.

In this example we are going to be looking at the data gathered on a zombie survival horror game. The response is 'Survivability' as a percentage and this is defined as the number of gamers that manage to survive the first 10 levels of The Strolling Dead survival horror game. Let's say that I manage to keep all the variables that affect Survivability constant and only vary Skill Level and I get the results shown in the Individual Value Plot (IVP) shown. There are 9 results at each level of Skill Level. The chart appears to indicate that as you

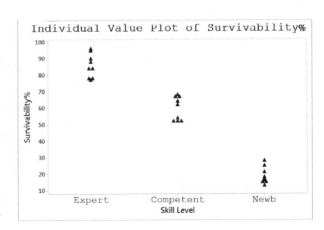

100

develop from Newb to Competent to Expert your chances of surviving the first 10 levels increases. I say 'appears' as we do not know if the populations are actually different or we are seeing this variation due to random sampling. We need to conduct a One-Way ANOVA to confirm our hypothesis.

Again, if I keep all factors that could affect Survivability constant but this time change the players weapon of choice we will get the IVP shown. This time it appears going from knife to a sword to a gun will increase Survivability%. To know if the populations are really different I would again use One-Way ANOVA.

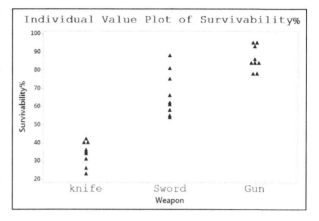

Let's say that there are only two factors that affect Survivability in this game and they are Skill Level and Weapon. I arrange play testing and I collect data for these factors together. The selection of data shown is every combination of the factors. As there are 3 levels of each factor we get 9 runs. However, when I arranged the play testing I ran 3 repeats of every combination making 27 runs in total.

The reason for collecting the data for both factors together might be due to efficiency in terms of time but there is a better reason and it is called 'Interaction'. We have seen that for each factor on its own changing the level gives a fairly straight line result in terms of Survivability. Yet there is a chance that when two factors work together, at a particular level, they produce a spark in the response variable giving an unexpected increase. This is called an Interaction and you can't find it when you are working with only one variable. Interactions can also work the other way as well and can cause a sharp decrease in the response. We will look at interaction plots and how to spot if interactions are significant a bit later.

Before we go into the GLM we need to understand some of the terms that are used.

We have two factors that we think are predictors for Survivability; these are Skill Level and Weapon. We must decide if our factors are Fixed or Random because the calculation of effects is handled differently for both. This means our conclusions may be incorrect if we do not specify Fixed and Random Factors correctly when setting up the procedure.

A factor is Fixed when data has been collected from

Weapon	Skill Level	Survivability%
knife	Expert	68
Sword	Expert	94
Gun	Expert	91
knife	Competent	52
Sword	Competent	61
Gun	Competent	82
knife	Newb	28
Sword	Newb	37
Gun	Newb	53

all the levels of interest in the study. The results obtained when using Fixed factors only apply to the levels within the study.

A factor is Random if there is a range of possible levels but only a random sample of levels is included in the data. The results can then be applied to all possible levels, even those not included in the study. We also need to know that having Fixed and Random factors will change what we are investigating with the GLM.

If you have Fixed factors then you will be investigating how changes in the mean level of the factors will affect levels within the response.

However if you have Random factors they will tell you whether the variance within the factors is significant to variance within the response.

Now lets go back to our zombie game study and decide what type of factors we have. Weapon is a Fixed factor, there are other weapons in the game but we used data from the 3 that interested us. Also, we know that the results of the GLM will only apply to knife, sword and gun. For similar reasons Skill Level is also a Fixed factor.

Now let's pretend we had 'Player Age' as a factor and we randomly selected levels of 19, 26 & 42 to use in the study. We have not included other player ages but we will want to apply what we have learnt to ages that have not been included, like say 30. This means that Player Age would be a Random factor. Also, if we used Player Age as a Random Factor then we would find out whether the variation in player age was significant to the variation in Survivability when we ran the GLM.

You also get Covariates within a GLM but in order to keep things simple while you get to grips with GLM we are only going to consider Fixed factors.

There's a couple of other bits of terminology that are worth learning at this time. The design of GLM that we have employed is called a 'Crossed' design, the other option is 'Nested'. These terms are much easier to explain in diagrams. A Crossed design is where all combinations of factors have at least one experimental run. Not all combinations of factors are run in a Nested design.

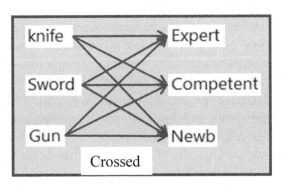

Take a look at the diagrams and you can see how easily the terms are explained in a diagram.

In practice, the nested design is rarely used but it is experimental conditions that dictate whether you use a crossed or nested design.

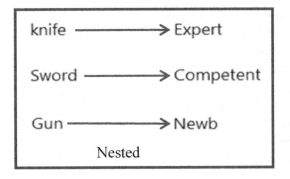

With respect to the whole design rather than factors, another couple of terms that are worth learning are 'Balanced' and 'Unbalanced'. A balanced design contains the same number of runs for each combination of terms. In the Zombie Game example we have 3 runs for every combination of factors, therefore, our design is balanced.

In order to validate our model we must check something called 'Residuals'. In order to explain how we generate the Residuals and explain what we check I will use the Zombie Game example

Weapon	Skill Level	Survivability%
knife	Expert	68
Sword	Expert	94
Gun	Expert	91
knife	Competent	52
Sword	Competent	61
Gun	Competent	82
knife	Newb	28
Sword	Newb	37
Gun	Newb	53

Finally, there are a number of Graphs which provide helpful analysis before we go into the GLM. We will learn how to generate these and how we interpret them using the example. The graphs are

1) Main Effects Plot
2) Interaction Plot
3) Multi-Vari Chart

The Main Effects Plot will show us the isolated effects of the factors and their levels. But it won't tell us if they are significant.
The Interaction Plot will show us if interactions are present but won't tell us if they are significant.
The Multi-Vari Chart delivers the data so we can see both main effects and interactions but again we don't know if anything is significant.
And as a review, 'significant' means beyond what we would expect to see just from chance.

8.6 General Linear Model Examples

General Linear Model	
Function	It is used to build a model of significant terms that have an effect on a response variable.
Sample Size	There is no Power and Sample size procedure associated with the GLM. However, there must be sufficient data across the factors for Minitab to solve the necessary simultaneous equations.
Data type & Format	The response must be a continuous variable. Factors can use discrete, numeric or continuous data, although continuous factors are not covered here. Factors can be Fixed or Random.
Considerations	The design can be Crossed or Nested, Balanced or Unbalanced. I recommend graphical examination of the data prior to analysis. The model is validated using Residuals.

Example 8.6.1 The Strolling Dead

A software house want to examine the Survivability of the first 10 levels of their new survival horror game, The Strolling Dead. They recognise that two factors are important to model, Skill Level of Player and the Weapon used. They have collected the data and want you to firstly present conclusions from the Main Effects & Interaction Plots and also a Multi-Vari Chart. They then want you to use the GLM procedure to tell them which factors and interactions are significant to the response, Survivability.

The first part of the question requires us to produce the Main Effects plot and then interaction plots. We will start with the Main Effects plot which shows us how the mean for each level of the factor varies. In order that our plots look the same we are first going to set the order of appearance of the categorical levels on the X-axis. We covered how to do this in chapter 4 section 8.

1.   Transfer all the data from Worksheet 'Zombie' into a new Minitab Project file.
2.   Place the active cursor in the Weapon column, C1, anywhere you wish.
3.   Click *Editor<<Column Properties<<Value Order*
4.   Using the radio buttons at the top of the menu select 'Order of occurrence in worksheet'.
5.   Click OK.
6.   Repeat steps 2 to 5 for the Skill Level column, C2.

7.   Click *Stat<<ANOVA<<Main Effects Plot*
8.   The graph menu opens. Under Response enter Survivability% and under Factors enter Weapon and Skill Level.
9.   Click OK to produce the Main Effects Plot.

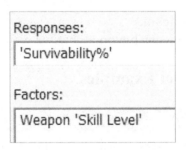

The Main Effects plot is useful as it isolates what each of the factors is doing to Survivability%. Within the plot each factor has its own panel. The data points represent the mean value for each level of the factors. The Y-axis represents our continuous response, Survivability%. You will notice that the Y-axis scale is common to both factors. As the 3 data points for Skill Level have a greater range on the Y-axis they are having a greater effect on the response.

The dashed horizontal line represents the 'Observed Mean' or the mean of all the

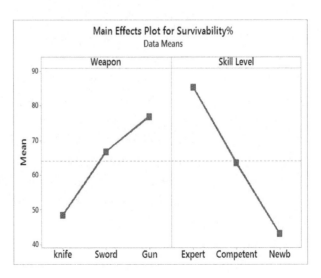

Survivability% data.

Changes in levels of Weapon do appear to be markedly different in terms of Survivability%, but as we have no P-values we cannot say that the factor is significant.

We could also say that in terms of the factor 'Weapon' the level 'Sword' is not very different to the observed mean.

And we could make similar conclusions about the factor 'Skill Level'. We see the 'Competent' level is right on the Observed mean.

In summary, looking at the main effects plot my conclusions would be

1) Changes in level for both Factors appear to affect the response.

2) Changes in Skill Level appear to have a slightly greater effect on the response.

We will now produce the Interactions plot. This tells us if any combination of our factors or levels combine to produce a spark to change the response more (or less) than we otherwise would have expected.

10. Click   *Stat<<ANOVA<<Interaction Plot*

11. The graph menu opens. Under Response enter Survivability% and under Factors enter Weapon and Skill Level. The order that we enter the factors does not really matter. Also, we don't need to see the full interaction matrix.

12. Click OK to produce the Interactions Plot.

Interpretation of the Interactions Plot is very simple. If the lines are parallel then there will probably not be any interactions present. If the lines are not parallel then there is probably an interaction present. The lines do not necessarily have to cross.

My interpretation of this plot would be that there may well be statistically significant interactions present. The interaction is between Sword and Expert. With the data presented here, if you are at Expert level your Survivability% is almost as high as if you had a gun. This is not true of the other two skill levels.

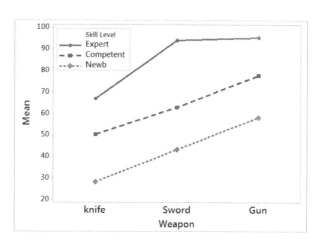

Finally, we have the Multi-Vari Chart. I think of this one as a cross between the Main Effects Plot and Interaction Chart. Drawing and interpretation of Multi-Vari charts is a skill in itself and we will develop it more in the next example.

13. Click *Stat<<Quality Tools<<Multi-Vari Chart*

14. The graph menu opens. Under Response enter Survivability% and enter Skill Level as Factor 1 and enter Weapon as Factor 2.

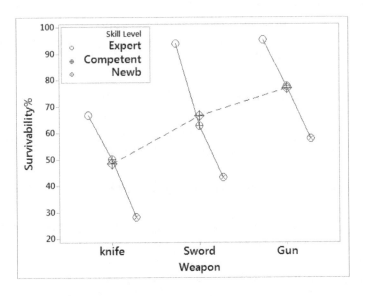

15. Click OK to produce the Multi-Vari Chart.

Something that I believe to be a useful rule in life is 'You don't get something for nothing'. I bring that up here because it is also true of the Multi-Vari chart. Although you can see both factor effects and factor interactions within the same chart you have to do a bit of work to spot them.

We entered Skill Level as Factor 1, therefore, the mean levels of Skill Level are shown within the groupings of Weapon, which is displayed on the X-axis. The dashed line shows how the means of Skill Level within Weapon Groups are joined.

The Sword*Expert interaction can be spotted but I wonder if I am only seeing that because I already know it is there.

We have now produced the required graphs and have attempted to interpret how the factors interact and how they affect the response. We think both the factors are significant and there may be an interaction present. We can only find out if our guesses are correct and statistically significant by conducting the ANOVA GLM procedure. We then need to validate the results by checking residuals.

It is worth noting that the set-up menus for ANOVA and Regression have changed considerably from the previous version of Minitab.

16. Click **Stat<<ANOVA<<General Linear Model<<Fit General Linear Model**

17. The GLM menu opens. Under Response enter Survivability% and under Factors enter Weapon and Skill Level.

18. Now here is the change. To enter the Interaction click the **Model** button. The Model menu will open. In the top left you will see our factors. Hold down the **Ctrl** key and click on the factors to highlight them both. If you did this correctly the **Add** button in the top right will become enabled. Left click on the **Add** button to include the interaction term into the model. Note: that interactions are listed as Factor1*Factor2 for a 2 way interaction. Higher order interactions are possible when there are more than 2 factors in the study.

19. Click OK. If we wanted to change our factors from Fixed to Random we would click on the **Random/Nest...** button at this point. Click OK to execute the procedure.

Please navigate to the Session Window.
Under the **Factor Information** section we are given key attributes of our two factors.

```
Factor Information

Factor        Type    Levels  Values
Weapon        Fixed        3  knife, Sword, Gun
Skill Level   Fixed        3  Expert, Competent, Newb
```

Under the **Analysis of Variance** section you will find the terms that we wish to model along with their P-value. We can actually answer the questions posed within this example using the information given here.

```
Analysis of Variance

Source               DF    Adj SS   Adj MS  F-Value  P-Value
  Weapon              2    3736.9  1868.44   127.72    0.000
  Skill Level         2    8024.9  4012.44   274.27    0.000
  Weapon*Skill Level  4     239.6    59.89     4.09    0.016
Error                18     263.3    14.63
Total                26   12264.7
```

For our Fixed Factors a P-value below our significance level tells us that mean levels of that factor are different in some way.

For our Interaction term a P-value below our significance level tells us that combinations of certain factors have different effects.

We now know that there will be some difference in Survivability% between the different levels within Weapon. The same can be said for Skill Level.

We also know that the interaction is significant, so if we want to calculate Survivability% we will have to account for the interaction as well as the separate factors.

Under **Model Summary** we are told how well our model fits the data. There are four metrics here with the last one being new to Minitab 17.

```
Model Summary

      S    R-sq  R-sq(adj)  R-sq(pred)
3.82487  97.85%     96.90%      95.17%
```

Think of S as a measure of error between the fitted line and your data. The lower the S the better.

R-sq is the amount of variation in the response explained by the predictors. The issue is that for larger models the more terms you add the better value you will get. Although, this may appear to be a fair compromise you may be encouraged to add non-significant terms into your model, which is not a good thing.

R-sq(adj) is similar to R-sq but it is **adjusted** for the number of predictors in the model. This encourages you not to keep adding non-significant terms.

R-sq(pred) gives us a measure of how well our model will fit new data points. As it is a measure of prediction for new points it is useful for comparing different models.

Under **Coefficients** we are given more details regarding the levels within our Factors. The first thing that we need to look at is our VIF or Value Inflation Factors. They should be less than 5. They are a measure of stability in our model. If they are above 5 we need to start over as our model will not be stable. You can think of the VIFs as a measure of health of the simultaneous equations used in forming the model.

You will have noticed that not all the levels for each factor are shown, there is one missing for each. For the next part of the explanation it would be helpful to have the full table.

Coefficients					
Term	Coef	SE Coef	T-Value	P-Value	VIF
Constant	64.111	0.736	87.10	0.000	
Weapon					
knife	-15.56	1.04	-14.94	0.000	1.33
Sword	2.67	1.04	2.56	0.020	1.33
Skill Level					
Expert	21.33	1.04	20.49	0.000	1.33
Competent	-0.44	1.04	-0.43	0.674	1.33
Weapon*Skill Level					
knife Expert	-2.89	1.47	-1.96	0.065	1.78
knife Competent	2.22	1.47	1.51	0.149	1.78
Sword Expert	5.89	1.47	4.00	0.001	1.78
Sword Competent	-3.33	1.47	-2.26	0.036	1.78

20. Press Ctrl+E, for Edit Last or Click **Stat<<ANOVA<<General Linear Model <<Fit General Linear Model** to open the GLM root menu.

21. Click on the **Results** button.

22. Then select 'Full set of coefficients' from the drop-down menu next to coefficients.

Full set of coefficients ▼

23. Then Click OK until the test is executed. Then navigate to the Session Window and find the Full Coefficients. I'm not showing the full table on this occasion.

Term	Coef	SE Coef	95% CI	T-Value	P-Value
Constant	64.111	0.736	(62.565, 65.658)	87.10	0.000
Weapon					
knife	-15.56	1.04	(-17.74, -13.37)	-14.94	0.000
Sword	2.67	1.04	(0.48, 4.85)	2.56	0.020
Gun	12.89	1.04	(10.70, 15.08)	12.38	0.000
Skill Level					
Expert	21.33	1.04	(19.15, 23.52)	20.49	0.000
Competent	-0.44	1.04	(-2.63, 1.74)	-0.43	0.674
Newb	-20.89	1.04	(-23.08, -18.70)	-20.07	0.000

The P-values for the levels of the factors now tell us if the level was significant compared to the observed mean. If you think back, or even look back, at the main effects plot you will recall that the Competent level was dead on the observed mean level. The P-value, like the Main Effects plot, is telling us that this level of the factor is not significant compared to the observed mean.

After Coefficients we arrive at the **Regression Equation**. In this example we have been lucky and we have not needed to reduce or change our model and this means that we can use the regression equation to predict values of survivability. However, please bear in mind that we have not validated our model by checking Residuals at this point. I have changed the layout of the regression equation in order to improve clarity. Let's say we want to calculate Survivability% for an Expert using a Sword. Any algebraic term containing the level Sword or Expert would become a 1, and everything else would be zero. The same applies for the interaction terms but the only term to be non-zero would be Sword*Expert (1x1=1) every other combination would be zero, for example Sword*Newb (1*0=0).

The equation for an Expert using a Sword becomes
Survivability%=64.111+2.67+21.33+5.89 = 94.001% .

If you go to your Multi-vari chart and click on the point corresponding to an Expert using a sword you will see that the actual mean of the data was 94%, which is excellent considering I didn't set it up. The actual error of our regression equation will be higher than this as indicated by our R-sq(pred)=95.17%.

Finally, we are told that one of our points was deemed to be unusual. Observation 8 had a value of 37 and the prediction equation thought it should have been 43.33.

```
Survivability% = 64.111
 - 15.56 Weapon_knife
 + 2.67 Weapon_Sword
 + 12.89 Weapon_Gun
 + 21.33 Skill Level_Expert
 - 0.44 Skill Level_Competent
 - 20.89 Skill Level_Newb
 - 2.89 Weapon*Skill Level_knife Expert
 + 2.22 Weapon*Skill Level_knife Competent
 + 0.67 Weapon*Skill Level_knife Newb
 + 5.89 Weapon*Skill Level_Sword Expert
 - 3.33 Weapon*Skill Level_Sword Competent
 - 2.56 Weapon*Skill Level_Sword Newb
 - 3.00 Weapon*Skill Level_Gun Expert
 + 1.11 Weapon*Skill Level_Gun Competent
 + 1.89 Weapon*Skill Level_Gun Newb
```

```
Fits and Diagnostics for Unusual Observations

Obs   Survivability%    Fit   Resid   Std Resid
  8            37.00   43.33   -6.33       -2.03  R
```

We may want to refer back to our data collection and check if something unusual occurred. However, on this occasion there is only one unusual point and it is not too far out so no action is required.

Did you notice that '**Actual Value - Fit = Resid**'? 'Resid' is short for Residual and this is important as we use Residuals to validate our model.

In this section we are going to find out how to form the full set of Residuals and the four graphs of the Residuals that we need to examine in order to validate our model.

24. Press Ctrl+E, for Edit Last or Click *Stat<<ANOVA<<General Linear Model<<Fit General Linear Model* to open the GLM root menu.

25. Click on the *Graphs* button.

26. Under Residual Plots click the radio button for 'Four in One'. This will generate our Residual Four in One plot, which is something you will use quite often as you advance in Minitab. Click OK to step back to the GLM root menu.

27. Click on the *Storage* button.

28. Select the tick boxes for 'Fits' and 'Residuals'. This action will calculate the Fits and store them in the Worksheet

Residuals plots
- ○ Individual plots
  - ☐ Histogram of residuals
  - ☐ Normal probability plot of residuals
  - ☐ Residuals versus fits
  - ☐ Residuals versus order
- ● Four in one

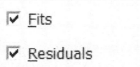

Window. Remember 'Fits' means the data points as calculated by the Regression Equation. It will also store the Residuals in the same place where **Actual Value-Fit = Residual.**

29. Click OK and OK again to execute the procedure.

Please navigate to the Worksheet Window. You will see that Minitab has stored our Fits and Residuals in Column C4 & C5, respectively. The Fits actually repeat every 9 points as they are based on the repeating combination of the levels of the Factors. The Residuals should not repeat in the same way because the values of the response don't repeat.

Please navigate to the Residuals Four-in-One Plot. As the name suggests the Four-in-One Plot is a graph made up of 4 sub plots of Residuals. In our example we had 27 separate data points which each generate a residual, even though some of the residuals share the same value. The 27 data points are then plotted on the four plots. In order to validate our GLM the residuals must comply with the following rules

• They must be close to being normally distributed

• They must not be extremely skewed.

• They must show roughly equal variance.

• If the variables have been recorded in time order they must not show any patterns.

We will now breakdown the Four-in-One plot and have a look at each of the sub plots in turn and check if our model complies. When we look at the Normal Probability Plot we want our Residuals to be close to being normally distributed. They definitely pass that test. When checking residuals we should not be as strict as we are when we are checking primary data for normality. If we can cover the points with a fat pencil then that is good enough.

↓	C1-T	C2-T	C3 ☑	C4	C5
	Weapon	Skill Level	Survivability%	FITS	Res
1	knife	Expert	68	67.0000	1.00000
2	Sword	Expert	90	94.0000	-4.00000
3	Gun	Expert	91	95.3333	-4.33333
4	knife	Competent	52	50.3333	1.66667
5	Sword	Competent	61	63.0000	-2.00000
6	Gun	Competent	82	77.6667	4.33333
7	knife	Newb	28	28.3333	-0.33333
8	Sword	Newb	37	43.3333	-6.33333
9	Gun	Newb	53	58.0000	-5.00000

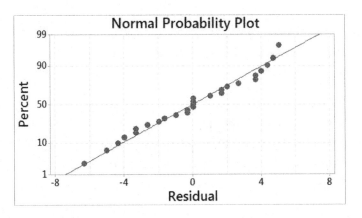

In the Histogram of Residuals we want to see that the Residuals are not severely skewed. We can see a slightly skewed distribution but it is nothing to worry about.

In the Versus Fits plot we are looking for patterns and we are looking to see that residuals are equally spaced around the zero line. The Assistant within its Regression routines gives us some useful pointers on spotting patterns and what they mean.

Clusters may indicate that a term is missing from the model, Strong curvature may indicate a higher order term is missing.

Unequal variation would indicate a poorly fitting model.

Our Versus Fits plot does not show any issues.

The Versus order plot is only applicable if the data was recorded in the order that it was taken but not if any kind of sorting has taken place. In this plot we want to see a random pattern. If we were to see patterns such as two high points then two low points this would indicate a missing factor.

Example 8.6.2 Shift Pattern

Jules is doing a human factors study at his factory. He wants to find out if the percentage defect rate changes with factors relating to tiredness and where in the factory the teams are working.. The factory works Monday to Friday and there are three shifts during each working day. The factory teams actually work a pattern where the Night shift will move to Afternoons in their second week and then Mornings in their third week. In this way each team will go around the pattern every three weeks. Jules collects 3 weeks worth of data so that each team has had a chance to work every shift. Jules does not want to cause ill feeling between the shifts so he does not enter a factor for shift code.

The factors he takes into consideration are

Shift- This can be Morning, Afternoon or Night.

Area- Preparation, Production or Packaging.

Day- Monday, Tuesday, Wednesday, Thursday or Friday.

Before Jules conducts Analysis of Variance help him by creating a Multi-Vari Chart. Examine the chart, can you make any conclusions as to which factors may be significant to the defect rate?

Once you produced the Multi-Vari chart carry out a test to determine if any of the Factors and Interactions are significant? If the factors are significant then establish which level of the factors are different from each other. Can you make recommendations to say where Jules' improvement activities should be focused

Worksheet: Shift Pattern

Initially, we are going to look at the data using a Multi-Vari Chart.

1.   Transfer all the data from Worksheet 'Shift Pattern' into a new Minitab Project file.

2.   To produce the Multi-Vary Chart click **Stat<<Quality Tools<< *Multi-Vari Chart.***

3.   Select Defect Rate % as the response. Select the factors in the order shown.

4.   Click OK to produce the chart.

The MVC shows our response on the Y-axis. Our data is then broken down into groups in order to represent our factors. Our factors are displayed in the following order: The values for Days are represented by patterned circles. (Remember, each circle represents the mean of 3 weeks worth of data points.) These can be thought of as the primary cluster, where each circle is joined by a black line.

The means of the primary clusters are represented by a red square. The means are joined ,within the panels, by red dashed lines and it can be seen how these vary within the secondary factor, Shift.

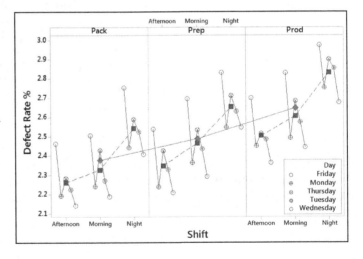

The means of the 3 'Shifts' are compared between panels. They are shown as green diamonds and joined by a green solid line.

Incidentally, the tie lines can be removed by clicking on the *Options* button in the previous menu.

We could start to make conclusions about our data, however, we would be less likely to make mistakes if our data was ordered correctly. At present the data is displayed in alphabetical order, which is the default for Minitab. However, we would prefer 'Day' to be displayed in day-order. Also, we want 'Shift' to be ordered as Morning, Afternoon & Night and the flow through the factory is Preparation, Production and then Packaging.

We will correct the order of the data first and then look at the chart again.

5. Navigate to the active worksheet and move the active cursor anywhere into column C1, which contains the 'Day' data.

6. **Click Editor<< Column Properties<< Value Order.** Note, it is the action of placing the active cursor that sets the value order for a particular column.

7. The default is Alphabetical order but we want to change this. Click on the radio button for 'Order of occurrence in worksheet'.

8. Then click OK.

9. Repeat this for the remaining factors but not the response column.

Note, we could also have used the option for 'User Specified Order' and made use of the predefined lists for 'Day'.

10. Produce the chart again by clicking **Stat<<Quality Tools<< Multi-Vari Chart.** Then click OK.

With less chance or making silly mistakes we can start to make conclusions about our data.

*   The defect rate appears to be higher in the production department.

*   The defect rate appears to be higher towards the end of the week but lower on a Wednesday.

*   The defect rate is higher on Nights.

Let's just see if our conclusions can be seen any more clearly if we enter the factors in a different order.

11. Click on the Edit Last button or press Ctrl+E.

12. Enter the factors in the following order, Shift, Area and then Day.

13. Then click on OK.

It may be a personal preference but I prefer how the data is presented in the new MVC. I like the way the variation in defect rate for the most complex factor can be examined across the panes. I can't see any interactions but I think my previous conclusions are correct.

*   The defect rate is highest on a Friday and then Thursday. It is probably lowest on a Wednesday.

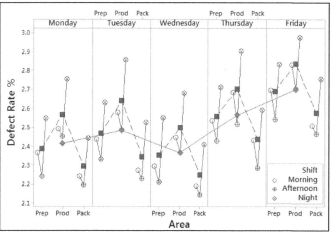

*   The night shift in any particular area has the highest defect rate.
*   The Production area has the highest defect rate then Preparation.

We will now use the GLM to establish which factors are significant and check if there are any interactions present

14. Click **Stat<<ANOVA <<General Linear Model <<Fit General Linear Model** to open the GLM root menu.

15. Under Response enter Defect Rate % and under Factors enter Day, Shift and Area.

16. Click on the **Results** button. Remove the tick next to Regression Equation. For this study we don't require this information in the session window.

17. Click OK once to return to the root GLM menu.

18. Click on the **Model** button. Hold down the Ctrl key and highlight all three factors.

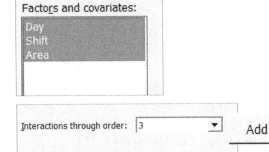

19. From the drop down menu for 'Interactions through order' select '3'. Then click on the **Add** button.

20. When you click add the terms in the model will change as shown. We now have our factors in the model, two way interactions and the single three way interaction in the model.

21. Click OK and OK again to execute the model.

22. Go to the Session window and find the Analysis of Variance table to establish which of the factors and interactions are significant. We see that none of the interactions are significant but the three main effects are significant. We should modify our model to only include the significant terms.

```
Analysis of Variance

Source              DF    Adj SS    Adj MS    F-Value   P-Value
  Day                4   1.88095   0.47024    209.62     0.000
  Shift              2   2.19759   1.09880    489.80     0.000
  Area               2   1.65003   0.82502    367.76     0.000
  Day*Shift          8   0.02636   0.00329      1.47     0.180
  Day*Area           8   0.01015   0.00127      0.57     0.803
  Shift*Area         4   0.01588   0.00397      1.77     0.142
  Day*Shift*Area    16   0.03070   0.00192      0.86     0.621
Error                90   0.20190   0.00224
Total               134   6.01357
```

23. Click **Stat<< ANOVA << General Linear Model <<Fit General Linear Model** to open the GLM root menu or press Ctrl+E.

24. Click on the **Model** button to go to the Model menu.

25. Highlight each of the interaction terms by holding down the Ctrl key and then clicking each term in turn. Then click on the red cross button. The terms in the model should be reduced to the default terms.

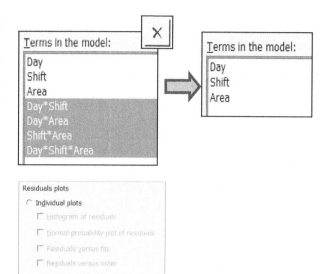

26. Click OK to return to the main GLM menu and then click on the **Graphs** button. Select the radio button for the four-in-one Residual plots. As we know we will not be modifying the model any further we should produce the residual plots at this point.

27. Click OK and OK again to execute the procedure.

28. Go to the Session window and find the Analysis of Variance table. We see that only the main factors remain in the model as significant terms. We also have a Lack-of-Fit test appearing for our model. The null hypothesis for this test is that our data fits our model. With a P-value of 0.444 we do not have sufficient evidence to reject this model.

```
Analysis of Variance

Source          DF    Adj SS    Adj MS   F-Value   P-Value
  Day            4   1.88095   0.47024    207.90     0.000
  Shift          2   2.19759   1.09880    485.80     0.000
  Area           2   1.65003   0.82502    364.76     0.000
Error          126   0.28499   0.00226
  Lack-of-Fit   36   0.08309   0.00231      1.03     0.444
  Pure Error    90   0.20190   0.00224
Total          134   6.01357
```

29. The model summary indicates that we have a good model with a large amount of the variation explained and the model can be used for making future predictions.

```
Model Summary

        S     R-sq   R-sq(adj)   R-sq(pred)
0.0475587   95.26%      94.96%       94.56%
```

30. We also need to check the table of Coefficients and ensure that the VIFs are below 5. It may be tempting to ignore this step but remember VIFs are a measure of health of the simultaneous equations used to form the model.

```
Coefficients

Term           Coef   SE Coef   T-Value   P-Value    VIF
Constant    2.50503   0.00409    612.00     0.000
Day
  Monday    -0.09044   0.00819    -11.05     0.000   1.60
  Tuesday   -0.02262   0.00819     -2.76     0.007   1.60
  Wednesday -0.14030   0.00819    -17.14     0.000   1.60
  Thursday   0.05889   0.00819      7.19     0.000   1.60
Shift
  Morning   -0.03863   0.00579     -6.67     0.000   1.33
  Afternoon -0.13332   0.00579    -23.03     0.000   1.33
Area
  Prep      -0.01547   0.00579     -2.67     0.009   1.33
  Prod       0.14247   0.00579     24.61     0.000   1.33
```

The Lack-of-Fit test told us that our model fitted our data well but we also need to check the residuals in order to validate the model before we proceed with the rest of the problem.

Navigate to the Residuals Four-in-One plot.

1- Residuals are normally distributed and will pass the 'fat pencil' test.

2- Histogram of residuals is not severely skewed.

3- Residuals are reasonably equidistant about the zero line. They don't show signs of clustering or forming a cone.

4- If the data was recorded in time order the residuals should look random and they do.

Our residuals fit the above criteria so we can be confident that we have a good model.

For the next part of the question we have been asked if any of the levels differ from each other. Although not part of the solution I have produced the Main Effects plot showing the individual factor effects on the response. For Day, can Monday and Tuesday or Monday and Wednesday be considered to be part of the same group or are they in separate groups. With One-Way ANOVA we would have asked Minitab to conduct pair-wise comparisons and produce a Grouping Information Table for us. The GLM can do something similar.

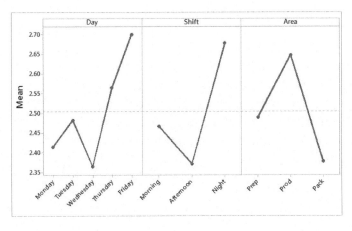

31. Click **Stat<<ANOVA<<General Linear Model<<Comparisons.**

32. Ensure the correct response column is selected and the 'Type of Comparison' is set to **Pairwise**. We have the option of selecting the type of comparison method we are going to use, we will stick with the default Tukey method. (I am planning a detailed explanation of the comparison methods in the Black Belt edition).

33. In order to select the factors that we will be comparing double click on each of the factors in turn or hold-down the left mouse key and click on each factor in turn and then press the '**C=Compare…**' button at the bottom. If done correctly a 'C' will appear adjacent to the factors.

34. Click OK and navigate to the Session Window and locate the Grouping Information Tables (GITs).

It's pretty clear that the GITs are telling us that the levels of all of the factors should be treated individually. The GITs have also ordered the levels starting with the worst, in terms of defect rate%, at the top.

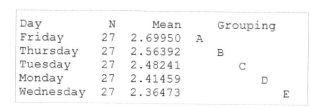

Day	N	Mean	Grouping			
Friday	27	2.69950	A			
Thursday	27	2.56392		B		
Tuesday	27	2.48241			C	
Monday	27	2.41459				D
Wednesday	27	2.36473					E

The last part of the question was to make recommendations for improvement. My recommendations would be to look at the Production area and establish why they are causing the most defects. I would also link tiredness into causes of defects as they are occurring towards the end of the week and mostly on night-shift. We might want an education program on how to manage night-shifts and a changing shift pattern for the shift personnel.

Shift	N	Mean	Grouping		
Night	45	2.67698	A		
Morning	45	2.46640		B	
Afternoon	45	2.37171			C

Area	N	Mean	Grouping		
Prod	45	2.64750	A		
Prep	45	2.48956		B	
Pack	45	2.37803			C

That wraps up the Green Belt level chapter on ANOVA. I wanted the GLM section to be an introduction into using the more complex classic menu's and that becomes a lead into the more complex techniques used in the Black Belt addition. In the Black Belt edition it is my hope to cover alternate comparison methods and also discuss and show how random factors and covariates are used in GLM.

8.7 ANOVA Exercises

Exercise 8.7.1 One Way ANOVA

Evelee golf balls monitors the golf ball weights produced by its 5 moulding machines. From capability tests they know that they are well below the max weight of 45.93 grams. They have hired you as a consultant and want to know if any of the moulding machines are producing golf balls at different mean weights. They feel that smallest difference that they would want to be able to detect between machines is 0.05g.

Analyse the data in File 08 ANOVA.xlsx worksheet Ex 8.5.1 and answer the questions shown below. The data was collected randomly and is recorded in time order.

1) Is there a difference in populations between the golf ball weights produced by any of the moulding machines?
2) Can the machines be grouped ?
3) Have the requirements of the test that you have used been met?
4) What was the Power of the test when you want to detect a difference of 0.05?
5) Are there any issues associated with this level of Power ?
6) Does the Report Card generate any warnings?

Exercise 8.7.2 Conduct a StDev Test

This time at Evelee golf balls someone has the bright idea that it might also be a good idea to find out if any of the moulding machines are producing golf balls at different standard deviations.

Analyse the data in File 08 ANOVA.xlsx worksheet Ex 8.7.1 and answer the questions shown below. The data was collected randomly and is recorded in time order.

1) Is there a difference in populations between the golf ball weights standard deviations produced by any of the moulding machines?
2) Can the machines be grouped ?
3) Have the requirements of the test that you have used been met?
4) Does the Report Card generate any warnings?

Exercise 8.7.3 Use the ANOVA GLM

Compo has got a new toy. It's an injection molding machine for making phone cases. Compo loads the machine with plastic granules and then sets the temperature and pressure and the molding machine forms the phone cases.

As Compo is prone to dropping things he wants to ensure the strength of the cases is maximised. He sets up an experiment where he varies three factors, the grade of the plastic granules, temperature of the heater and the pressure used for the extrusion. In this experiment **Strength** is the response and the factors are called **Temp**, **Press** and **Material**. The levels for Temp and Press are set using a dial which has fixed settings. This makes all the factors fixed. In the experiments Temp has 3 levels; 100, 110 &115 degc. Press has 3 levels; 7, 10 and 13 psi and there are two types of plastic granules called A & B.

Analyse the data in File 08 ANOVA.xlsx worksheet Ex 8.7.3 and answer the questions shown below. The data was collected randomly and is recorded in time order.

1) Form the Main Effects Plot and Interactions plot. Can you guess which factors and interactions are significant?
2) Which Factors and Interactions are significant when you use the ANOVA GLM ?
3) What is the Regression Equation for this model? And how much of the variation in Strength does it account for?

4) What settings would maximise the strength of the phone cases?
5) DO the VIFs indicate any problems with the model?
6) Do the residuals and Lack-of-Fit Test indicate any issues with your model ?

Exercise 8.7.4 Use the ANOVA GLM

A multi-media service provider wants to analyse some of their sales data. They have data on property size across 3 regions in a city. They want to know if sales are affected by property size and city region. Are there differences within the property size bands and sales? Also are there differences within the city regions and sales?

Analyse the data in File 08 ANOVA.xlsx worksheet Ex 8.7.4 and answer the questions shown above and additionally those shown below. The data was collected randomly and is recorded in time order.

In this procedure are Fixed Factor s are **Prop_size** and **Region.** The response is **Sales.**

1) Form the Main Effects Plot and Interactions plot. Can you guess which factors and interactions are significant?
2) Which Factors and Interactions are significant when you use the ANOVA GLM ?
3) How much of the variation in Sales does the model account for?
4) Which Property Size and Region will generate the highest Sales?
5) DO the VIFs indicate any problems with the model?
6) Do the residuals indicate any issues with your model ?

9 CONTROL CHARTS

9.1 Introduction to Control Charts

Control charts are one of the simplest tools that you will come across and yet they are an essential part of our Minitab tool kit. It's often the case that the simplest tools are very useful when used properly.

Control charts help us to decide whether our process is operating in a stable and predictable manner or whether there are forces acting on the process which will generate undesirable outcomes.

A single control chart monitors a single variable that we wish to track. We enter time ordered and independent data into the chart. Control limits are calculated and if our data goes beyond the control limits our process is unstable or out of control. If it remains within the control lines we say that it is stable or in control.

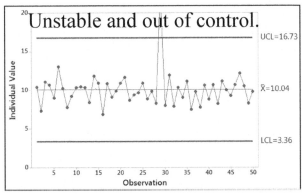

If our process lives within the control limits we say it is only exhibiting the natural random variation that we expect. However, you might argue 'isn't all variation due to something ?' and if you said that you would be right because it is a bit subjective. If we are within our specification limits for the process and the customer is happy we may not wish to find causes for these variations which are within the control limits

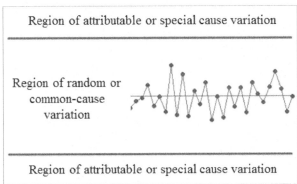

120

If our process continually crosses into the region of attributable variation we now say that something has been influencing the measured variable. For example

You weigh yourself every morning and record the weights on a control chart. You get a single out of control result that is low. It was because you accidentally held onto the towel rail while measuring your weight.

You take a sample from the product line and test it for weight and record the results on a control chart. The weight is low and after investigating you find that one of the feeders had become jammed.

You produce a control chart showing your fuel efficiency to work every morning. You find that on a particular day the fuel efficiency was worse and out of the control limits. It was the day you listened to the rock radio station instead of classical.

Process Capability is going to be the next module that we look at but I wanted to stress the link with control charts at this point. As a rule of thumb we should not display specification limits on a control chart as it often confuses people. However, I will break the rule to make a point. This chapter assumes that our control limits are always going to be inside our specification limits. A specification limit being a limit that an internal or external customer cares about. This is because the parameter being measured will result in defects when it goes beyond the specification limit.

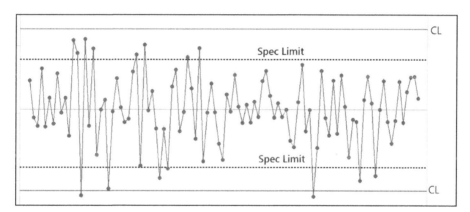

When you initially examine a process, if you find that the control limits are outside of the specification limits then you have major problems with process capability and you need to address those immediately using the appropriate tools such as a DMAIC project.
If you find that the control limits are well within the specification limits you can continue to use control charts to monitor/improve your process.

9 .2 When should we use Control Charts

There are a number of broadly defined occasions when we should use control charts and these are 1) When we want to know if our process is in-control or not, 2) When our process is out of control or 3) When our process is already in control and we are using control charts for monitoring.
For item 1) If you are conducting a DMAIC project you will want to establish if your process is stable late in the Measure phase. This is because even if the goal of your project is not to bring stability to the system if your system is out of control you will need to remove special cause variation before you proceed onto the main goal of the project.
If you worked through the book sequentially you will have already used control charts to determine whether your data was being influenced by special causes. Do you remember the Diagnostic Reports

when you were conducting hypothesis testing? The Assistant uses control charts to point out special cause variation in your data. If any out-of-control points were found it would tell you in the Report Card that 'unusual data can have a strong influence on the results, you should try to identify the cause of its unusual nature'.

For item 2) If the process is out-of control we will want to find out what is affecting our process and then apply ERIC to it and remove the parameter that is influencing the process. (ERIC = Eliminate, Reduce, Isolate, Control with a hierarchical preference).

For item 3) If the process is in control then we want to monitor it and ensure that nothing happens to our process/system. We will have already reduced our process variability so that our control limits are within our customers specification limits for the process. If an uncontrolled factor upsets our process and we get a result outside of the control limits we can then take action. Hopefully, this will still be before we make out of specification product.

9.3 False Alarms

False alarms are out of control points that are generated when the process is behaving as it should. For example, when Dr Walter A. Shewart first invented control charts he used 3 StDevs from the mean to set the control limits.

(We still use similar default values for control limits even now. The calculations can be reviewed within the Help<<Methods and Formulas menu of Minitab. As this book let's Minitab do the calculations we will not be reviewing the exact method of calculating the control limits.)

If you have a perfectly normal distribution and set the control limits at 3 StDevs then 99.73% of the points will be within the control limits; we know this from our early review of the normal distribution in Chapter 5. This works out to 1 in 370 points on average will be in the region of special cause variation. However, these are false alarms and are generated as probable events that are at the extremes of the distribution.

If we do get an out-of control point then we need to investigate if it was caused by an attributable factor or by being a legitimate point that was at the extremes of our distribution. As this takes time we need to ensure we don't get too many false alarms. If you are using the traditional drop down menu's to produce the control charts then you can increase the number of tests for special causes, going beyond 3 StDev's is not the only way to detect an attributable influence on your process. Also, when we start moving away from a normally distributed process we will get more false alarms.

We can protect ourselves from false alarms by using subgrouping and by reducing the number of tests we use to detect special cause variation. We will take our first look at subgrouping in the next section.

9.4 Subgrouping

Have you ever seen those TV programs where they show you how a fast moving consumer good is made? Where items like aerosol cans are flying down a conveyor in single file. And there is an operator at the side of the line and she takes four cans out of the moving line and then she would weigh each one to check for fill level. The operator is taking a subgroup from the main line. The reason for taking the subgroup is two-fold 1) It gives our control chart protection against false alarms and 2) It helps us to understand common cause and special cause variation that the process is experiencing.

A subgroup is a group of items that have been made under/exposed to similar conditions. They don't have to be consecutive items but they usually are. The sample should be taken over a relatively short time frame. We then set a longer time frame between subgroups samples.

We select a short time frame to sample the sub-group as we do not wish to capture any special cause variation within the subgroup. We want to be able to say that the subgroup variation is only made up of the random process variation. We also want to be able to say that the special cause variation will occur between subgroups.

9.5 Subgroup Size and Sampling Frequency

If we could sample everything we would not need to use sub-groups; our control charts would just consist of all the data plotted as individuals. However, we usually can't sample everything due to cost, time or the sheer number of samples available.

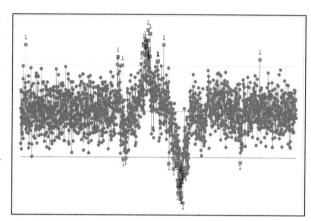

This first control chart shows 2000 data points which represent 2000 sequential items from a production line. We see two types of special cause variation. There are individual points that are out of control and there are shifts of the mean which cause out of control points. Let's take a look at how the control chart looks if I choose my subgroup size as 5 and decide that I will resample after 95 parts. So I am sampling the first five out of every 100.

This is an Xbar R Chart with my sampling regime of taking 5 parts as my sample and then leaving the next 95 parts. The bottom half of the chart represents the range within each subgroup and top half is the mean within each subgroup. The chart does pretty well at picking up the shifts in mean but not the single points where we get an instantaneous out of control point.

Adding more sampling points will improve our resolution. With the additional samples we may or may not hit one of the single out of control points and capture some special cause variation within the subgroups. This is not really a problem but it is a problem if we are systematically capturing special cause variation in the subgroup.

When thinking about your subgroup size and sampling frequency think about the following
1) How many samples can I analyse?
2) Will I continue to systematically capture special cause variation within my sub-group?
3) What type of unusual behaviour am I trying to capture?
Over what period will a shift in mean take place? This is probably the most important.

9.6 Detection Rules for Special Cause variation

You would be forgiven if you thought there was only one rule for detecting special causes. Within Minitab there are 8 rules for detecting special cause variation that can be used within the traditional drop down menu's. Each of these 8 tests is designed to alert us to a particular event occurring in our data. If the test activates it is deemed to be more likely to be due to an attributable cause rather than randomness.

Even though we are going to be focusing on using the Assistant, which only uses a couple of the rules, it's worth knowing what can be applied if required.

Perform selected tests for special causes ▼	K
☑ 1 point > K standard deviations from center line	3
☐ K points in a row on same side of center line	9
☐ K points in a row, all increasing or all decreasing	6
☐ K points in a row, alternating up and down	14
☐ K out of K+1 points > 2 standard deviations from center line (same side)	2
☐ K out of K+1 points > 1 standard deviation from center line (same side)	4
☐ K points in a row within 1 standard deviation of center line (either side)	15
☐ K points in a row > 1 standard deviation from center line (either side)	8

To access this option select the Chart options button, for example 'I-MR Options', at the root menu for any of the continuous data control charts and then click on the 'Tests' tab. Not only can the rules be switched on or off from this menu it is also possible to modify how they are applied. For example, if we wanted the particular chart to apply rule 2 but only look for 5 points on the same side of the centre line we would simply change the value of 'K' to '5' for test 2 instead of '9'. We would also ensure that the test was switched on.

Remember, the more tests we have switched on the more chance there is of generating false alarms but we also have more chance of detecting attributable special causes.

Let's graphically have a look at Minitab's detection rules with the default 'K' values. The graph that we will be displaying has been constructed and not all data points are shown. The Y-axis, is in units of StDev from the mean.

Test 1, 1 point more than 3 StDevs from the center line.

Test 2, 9 points in a row, all on the same side of the center line. Test 2 is very useful in that it detects for shifts in the mean of the process.

One point that can be a bit confusing is that for certain tests involving sequences of points Minitab will only report the last point that is out of control. This stops the chart from getting too messy. For example, if you produce a chart with test 2 activated and 9 points in a row meet the condition for special cause variation Minitab will only report the last point as having failed test 2.

111111111111111111111

Test 3, 6 points in a row all increasing or all decreasing

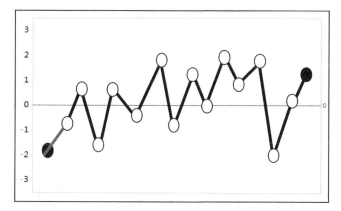

Test 4, 14 points in a row alternating up and down.

Test 5, 2 of 3 points more than 2 StDevs from the centre line on the same side.

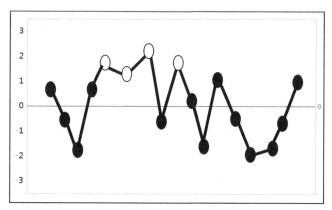

Test 6, 4 of 5 points more than 1 StDev from the centre line on the same side.

Test 7, 15 points in a row within 1 StDev of the centre line, either side.

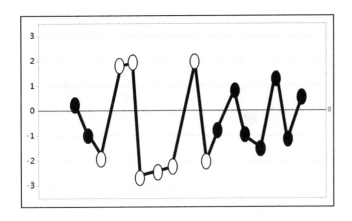

Test 8, 8 points in a row more than 1 StDev from centre line, either side.

9.7 Control Chart Selection for Continuous Data

Control chart selection can be very easy or fairly hard depending on how deep you want to start. If you are starting absolutely from the start of the process where you only have raw data then you need to think about your subgroup size and sampling frequency and answer the following questions.

1) What are my analysis limitations? How many samples can I take and how often can I analyse? Usually we can only sample a small fraction of the population. If it is at all possible we want to be analysing subgroups. Having individual data points is a fall-back position.

2) Will I continue to systematically capture special cause variation within my sub-group? You want to set your sampling frequency and sub group size so you don't get any special cause variation within the subgroups.

3) What type of unusual behaviour am I trying to capture? Ask yourself if tests 1 and 7 are sufficient or whether you want to check for one of the other 6 special causes within Minitab. If you do then you should not use the Assistant.

Once you have answered the above questions it is very easy to select the appropriate chart. If data was not collected in subgroups then we use the I-MR chart. If the data was collected in subgroups we select the appropriate chart depending upon the size of the subgroup.

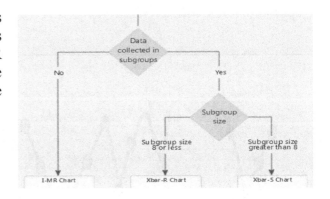

9.8 I-MR Chart

I-MR Chart using the Assistant	
Function	Tests whether a process is stable (in control). This chart is used when the only option is to take a single sample, which makes sampling in subgroups impossible.
Sample Size	The Assistant gives the choice of whether existing control limits are applied or whether control limits are estimated from the data. The recommendation is to have at least 100 data points when estimating control limits from the data.
Data type & Format	Continuous data which is captured at regular intervals is required. Ensure the data is captured frequently enough to capture process shifts but not so frequently that it overwhelms the process.
Considerations	The I-MR chart consists of two halves. At the top is a plot of the Individual (I) data within control limits which are estimated using the average Moving Range (MR) which is displayed on the bottom half of the chart. The points on the MR chart are the difference (or range) between successive data points. If Minitab detects a high degree of non-normality within the data it may recommend a transformation of the data. At Green Belt level you should seek advice from a Black Belt if this occurs. The Assistant will apply tests 1,2 on the I chart to detect special causes and test 1 only on the MR chart.

Example 9.8.1 Stock Accuracy Results

A company conducts a stock count every week at all of its store locations. The overall stock accuracy is recorded as a key performance indicator. Cooks has been asked to evaluate the stability of stock management at Store1 using a control chart. Due to the time taken to conduct a stock count it is not possible to take samples with subgroups so an I-MR chart must be used. All data for this chapter is in '9 Control Charts.xlsx' and the data for this example is in the worksheet called 'I-MR'.

The reason for not trying to collect data within subgroups is the time and resources taken to complete the stock count. It would mean too much time and resource allocation for the company to conduct multiple stock counts.

1. Transfer both columns of data into Minitab.
2. Click *Assistant<<Control Charts*

	Store1	Store2
1	67.80	76.3
2	88.00	77.4
3	75.00	88.1
4	78.80	83.0
5	76.00	81.7

3. Click on the *I-MR Chart* box which is used for continuous data which does not have subgroups.

I-MR Chart

4. The test menu opens. Initially, we are only going to examine data from Store1 so enter that as the Data Column. As we don't have historical control limits we will use Minitab to calculate control limits from the data by making the appropriate selection from the drop down list. As soon as we do that Minitab conducts a check on the data and will give us a warning if the data is unstable. We are given the option of excluding that data from calculations even though it will still be displayed on the chart.

5. Click OK to produce the charts.

Minitab does not do it in this example but it would be at this point that Minitab might offer us the option of transforming the data. This only happens if a transformation would reduce the number of out-of-control points. As a Green Belt I would advise that you seek advice from a Black Belt at this point as a transformation may not be beneficial in practice.

Please navigate to the Summary Report.
In the top left corner we are told that the process mean is not stable as 4.9% of the points on the Individuals chart are out of control, which is 5 points out of 102. There are no P-values associated with this statement.

At the bottom of the Summary Report we get to see the full I-MR Control Chart, shown below. The X-axis has the Observation number which is common to both halves of the chart. The left hand Y-axis are scaled to show the Individual values and Moving ranges respectively. The right-hand side shows the control limit values and the average moving range, MR bar. This is denoted as 'MR' with a line on top of it. MR bar is used to calculate the control limits for the individuals chart. The average MR or MR bar is an estimate of StDev used in I-MR charts. We can see which points are out-of-control as they are red squares but we don't know why they are out-of-control until we refer to the Stability Report.

The Stability Report tells us that Observation 59 failed as it was outside the control limits, Test 1, on both the I & MR charts. Observations 40-43 failed Test 2 on the I-Chart. Test 2 tells us if 9 points in a row were on either side of the center line, it is looking for shifts in the process. Remember, Minitab is only reporting the last point in the row of 9 each time. This means it's actually 12 points in a row that were on the same side of the centre line.

Chart	Test	Out-of-Control Points
I	Test 1: Outside control limits	59
	Test 2: Shift in mean	40-43
MR	Test 1: Outside control limits	59

I think it is worth remembering that on the left hand side of the Stability Report are examples of unusual trends. I would recommend that it is worth familiarising yourself with the trends shown and making it a habit to check the control chart for these trends.

Finally on the Report Card we are given a summary of the findings and some general information. For this control chart we are given a warning regarding stability. In particular, we are told that as one point was out of control on the MR chart it may affect the control limits that were calculated using the average MR on the I chart.

Exercise 9.8.2 Stock Accuracy Results

The company states that certain best practices in stock management have been used at Store2. The company invites Cooks to produce an I-MR chart of the Store2 stock accuracy results and check for stability. They also ask for pertinent differences in the Stock Accuracy results between the two stores. Help Cooks produce and I-MR chart for Store2 and check for Stability. In order to check for differences between the stores also use the Before/After control Chart menu within the Assistant.
All data for this chapter is in '9 Control Charts.xlsx' and the data for this example is in the worksheet called 'I-MR'.

On the Summary Report for the I-MR chart for Store 2 we are told that there are no points that are out-of-control. Using values shown on the I-MR chart we could compare the values for mean level and average moving range, however, the Before/After Control charts better display the differences.

On the Summary Report for the Before/After comparison we are shown hypothesis test for reduction in StDev and mean. There is a difference between the two stores. This can be seen in the side-by-side control charts for the two stores. Therefore, stock management practices used in Store2 have resulted in a higher stock accuracy score and lower variance in the stock accuracy.

9.9 Xbar-R Chart

Xbar-R Chart using the Assistant	
Function	Tests whether a process is stable (in control). This chart is used when the data has been collected in subgroups with sizes of between 2 and 8.
Sample Size	The Assistant gives the choice of whether existing control limits are applied or whether control limits are estimated from the data. The recommendation is to have at least 100 data points when estimating control limits from the data.
Data type & Format	Continuous data where the subgroup samples are captured at regular intervals is required. Ensure the data is captured frequently enough to capture process shifts but not so frequently that it overwhelms the process.
Considerations	The Xbar-R chart consists of two halves. The top is a plot of the average value of each subgroup. The bottom plot is the range within each subgroup. The control limits of the Xbar chart are calculated using the average range value. Therefore, always look at the range chart first as a high average range value may make it appear that you are in control on the Xbar chart. You can get a high average range value if you trap special cause variation within your subgroups. The Assistant will apply tests 1,2 on the Xbar chart to detect special causes, with test 7 also being applied if the control limits are estimated from the data. The Assistant will only apply test 1 on the R chart. There isn't a significant increase in the false alarm rate for non-normal data when using charts with subgroups. Once control limits for the process have been established they should be used when producing additional charts for that process. However, if a process change occurs then new control limits should be calculated.

Example 9.9.1 Cup Cakes

Mahwish's cup cakes are coming out of the continuous oven at 300 cakes per hour. Every hour four cakes are check weighed. Using an Xbar-R chart check that the cup cake weights are in control. The data for this example is in the worksheet called 'XbarR'.

1. Transfer the data into Minitab. There are five columns of data in 50 rows. Each row represents a subgroup sample taken every hour.

	Cake1	Cake2	Cake3	Cake4	Cake5
1	120.52	123.12	120.93	122.54	118.47
2	120.32	120.33	121.69	118.57	120.62
3	119.51	117.93	122.06	116.20	116.75
4	123.89	121.25	125.14	123.35	119.46
5	119.94	119.11	119.32	118.69	116.88
6	122.61	121.20	120.97	118.56	119.96
7	119.53	118.23	121.14	116.39	115.83
8	116.25	121.06	118.58	118.26	115.62
9	119.98	116.56	121.78	118.71	120.03

2. Click *Assistant<<Control Charts*
3. Click on the **Xbar-R Chart** box which is used for continuous data which has a subgroup size of 8 or less.

4. The test menu opens. Minitab asks us how our subgroups are arranged so in the drop-down menu we have to tell it that the 'Data is in multiple columns with one row for each subgroup'.
5. Select columns Cake1 to Cake5 as the Data Columns. As we don't have historical control limits we will use Minitab to calculate control limits from the data by making the appropriate selection from the drop down list. As soon as we do that we are given notification that one of the points on the chart is out-of-control and we get the option of omitting it from the chart.

6. Click OK to produce the charts.

Please navigate to the Summary Report. In the top left corner we are told that the process mean is stable. The Xbar portion of the chart displays the mean of each subgroup, which is stable.

At the bottom of the Summary Report we get to see the full Xbar-R Control Chart. We see that we have a single out-of-control point on the R chart and we are told on the Stability Report that it fails test 1 (the only test that the R chart uses). The average range value for the chart is 4.87. If I hover over the out-of-control point with my mouse I am told that the range for sample 20 is 14.81. We need to investigate this data point as it may have an impact on the control limits for the Xbar chart.

Finally, on the Report Card we get a warning regarding stability. It states that although the process mean is stable the process variation (R chart) is not. And because the average range is used to calculate the control limits in the Xbar chart we should not validate the Xbar chart as being stable until we have investigated the out of control point.

Chart	Test	Out-of-Control Subgroups
R	Test 1: Outside control limits	20

Check	Status
Stability	⚠

We will go back to the source data and check the subgroup for data point 20. The range is made up of the difference of the highest point and lowest point, Range=125.81-111=14.81.

19	119.48	117.68	121.10	118.02	116.17
20	118.62	125.81	116.95	119.95	111.00
21	119.69	125.04	120.43	125.94	117.81

Let's pretend that we investigated the operator's paperwork and found that there was a typo. 111 should have been 121.

19	119.48	117.68	121.10	118.02	116.17
20	118.62	125.81	116.95	119.95	121.00
21	119.69	125.04	120.43	125.94	117.81

7. Correct the data and run the Assistant with the new data. When using the Assistant we cannot use the 'Update Graph' facilities.
On this occasion, the new Summary Report indicates that the process mean is not stable.

When we look at the Control Charts we see that two points are out-of-control on the Xbar chart and the R chart is now in control. Our correction has resulted in a new average range value of 4.75 and when this is used to calculate the new control limits for the Xbar chart it was enough to make two of the points fail Test1 on the Xbar chart.

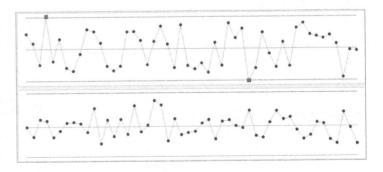

Finally on the Report Card we are told that the process variation (shown on the R chart) was stable but the process mean was not stable.

Check	Status
Stability	⚠

9.10 Xbar-S Chart

There are no differences between using Assistant procedures for the Xbar-R or Xbar-S apart from the recommended subgroup size. As it is more useful for Green Belts to experience the classic menu's for producing control charts this example has been written to show the features of control charts using the classic menu's.

Xbar-S Chart using the classic menu's	
Function	Tests whether a process is stable (in control). This chart is used when the data has been collected in subgroups with sizes of 9 and over.
Sample Size	The recommendation within the Assistant is to have at least 100 data points when estimating control limits from the data. There is no reason why this should be different for the classic method where the only option is to calculate control limits from the data.
Data type & Format	Continuous data where the subgroup samples are captured at regular intervals is required. Ensure the data is captured frequently enough to capture process shifts but not so frequently that it overwhelms the system.
Considerations	The Xbar-S chart consists of two halves. The top is a plot of the average value of each subgroup. The bottom plot is the StDev within each subgroup. The control limits of the Xbar chart are calculated using the average StDev value or Sbar. Therefore, always look at the Stdev chart first as a high average StDev value may make it appear that you are in control on the Xbar chart. You can get a high Sbar value if you trap special cause variation within your subgroups. There isn't a significant increase in the false alarm rate for non-normal data when using charts with subgroups.

Example 9.10.1 Wafer Biscuit Breaking Strengths

Snappy wafer biscuits use the snap of their wafer biscuits as a Unique Selling Point for their product. They ask Raeesa to establish if the snap strength of their wafer biscuits is in control, there are two types of biscuit, A & B. Initially, help Raeesa produce a control chart of Type A and assess stability.
The data for this example is in the worksheet called 'XbarS'.

1.   Transfer the data into a new Minitab project worksheet. There are 11 columns of data in 132 rows.   Column C1, 'Type' primarily tells us the wafer biscuit type that is being produced, for now we are only interested in Type A. 'Time' tells us the time that the subgroup sample was taken we then have 9 columns of data where each row contains subgroup data of the breaking strength.

2. Click **Stat<<Control Charts <<Variable Charts for Subgroups <<Xbar-S.** The root menu for the Xbar-S Chart opens.

3. Minitab asks us how our subgroups are arranged. In the drop-down menu we have to tell it that 'Observations for a subgroup are in one row of columns'.

4. Select columns Strength1 to Strenght9 as the Data Columns.

5. Click on the **Scale** button that is present on the root menu.

6. Under X Scale click on the radio button for Stamp. This gives us the option of using our own index for the data points. We can display up to three columns.

7. Enter Time and Type as labels to be used for the Index.

8. Click OK & OK again to produce the charts.

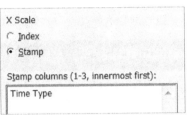

We can see patterns in both charts straight away. Type A and Type B wafers appear to have a differing mean level of strength although the within-group variation appears to be at the same level. However, the biscuits made during start-up and change-over are again at differing levels of mean and variation. As we need to check the stability of Type A wafers we need to eliminate the rest of the data from the chart. Note that this will break the rule of having regular time intervals between samples. However, we do have sacrificial change-over samples that should remove special variation between runs of Type A and Type B. We just need to check that this hypothesis holds true when the chart for Type A is produced.

9. Press Ctrl+E or click on the Edit Last icon to return to the Xbar-S chart root menu.

10. Click on the **Scale** button and remove Type as a Stamp Column. As we know all of the data will be for Type A we can save some space on the X-axis.

11. Click OK to return to the root menu.

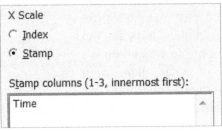

12. Click on the **Data Options** button. Within this menu we can set the data that is either going to be included in the chart or excluded from the chart by using the radio buttons at the top. We will leave the setting on 'Include'.

13. In order to tell the menu which rows we want to include we have a number of options. Select the radio button for 'Rows that match' and then click on the **Condition** button.

14. There are many ways to set the condition including logic operators such as AND & OR. All we need to do is specify the following condition TYPE="A", which means include any row of the specified data when the Type is A.

15. Click OK three times to produce the chart.

With data from Type B, Changeovers and Start-ups removed from the chart it looks much more like a control chart should. There were 4 runs of Type A wafer and it is not clear from the chart where the runs intersect so we can say we have not made an error by not collecting data at regular intervals.

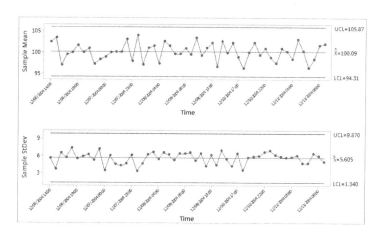

Can Raeesa conclude that the process is stable? Well by default the classic menu will only use Test 1 for special causes. In order to be thorough we should check for the presence of other types of special cause variation.

16. Press Ctrl+E or click on the Edit Last icon to return to the Xbar-S chart root menu.

17. Click on the **Xbar-S Options** button.

18. Click onto the **Tests** tab.

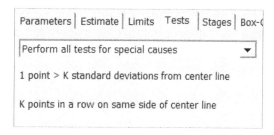

19. The drop-down menu can be used to set whether no tests, all tests or selected tests are conducted. Please select the option to 'Perform all tests...'.

20. Click OK and OK again to produce the Xbar-S chart again.

We see that two points on the S chart have failed Test2. The Session Window tells us that points 46 and 47 have failed because 9 points in a row were on the same side of the centre line.

Test Results for S Chart of Strength1, ..., Strength9

TEST 2. 9 points in a row on same side of center line.
Test Failed at points: 46, 47

Exercise 9.10.2
Help Raeesa check whether Type B wafer biscuits strengths are also stable by producing an Xbar-S chart. Use all the Tests for special causes.

The Xbar-S chart for Type B wafer biscuits is in control even when all of the tests for special causes are applied.

9.11 Control Charts for Attribute Data

We are going to be looking at two of the main control charts for counts of attribute data. These are the P & U charts and if these don't work we will switch to the Laney P' and U' charts, which were introduced by David B. Laney.

A P Chart only considers the number of fails or defectives within a subgroup. Subgroup sizes can vary but the items within the subgroup can only be graded as pass or fail, it does not matter if they have multiple faults.

Pass   Fail   Fail   Fail   Fail   Pass   Fail

Within this subgroup of 7, we have 5 Fails

For the U chart we count the total number of defects within the subgroup and report that against the subgroup size

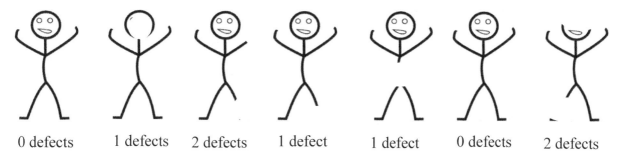

| 0 defects | 1 defects | 2 defects | 1 defect | 1 defect | 0 defects | 2 defects |

If we were using a U chart with multiple categories of defects we would report 7 defects against a subgroup size of 7.

P & U Charts for Attribute Data using the Assistant	
Function	Tests whether the defect count within a sample is stable (in control).
Sample Size	The Assistant gives the choice of whether existing control limits are applied to data or whether control limits are estimated from the data. The subgroup size can be unequal. Average proportion of defective items (denoted by Pbar on the P chart) multiplied by the subgroup size must be 0.5 for each subgroup when estimating control limits from the data. Otherwise, the control limits may not be estimated correctly.
Data type & Format	Both charts use counts of defects within a sample that can either have a set or variable size. The difference is that items counted on the P chart can only be given a single defect classification or a pass. A single item on the U chart can have multiple defects.
Considerations	There are well known issues with P & U charts which led David B. Laney to develop the Laney P' & U' charts. If Minitab suggests using the Laney charts then say yes and trust that Minitab knows best. The issues occur when there is more variation across the data than random sampling would suggest. This results in narrower control limits leading to more false alarms. This is called overdispersion. There is also a reverse of this condition called underdispersion. P & U charts only use tests 1 & 2 within the Assistant.

Example 9.11.1 Party Balloons

Party Balloons Ltd want to know if their balloon manufacturing process is stable. They ask you to produce a control chart of their data using their existing control limits. Naturally, you ask what kind of data do they have and they reply that they test 200 balloons every day and each balloon is rated as a pass or a fail. Their historical lower control limit is 0.01 and the upper is 0.13. The usual mean defect rate is 0.07. The data for this example is in the worksheet called 'Balloons'.

1.   the data into Minitab. There is a single column of data that has 150 rows.
2.   Click ***Assistant<<Control Charts***

3.   Click on the ***P Chart*** box which is used for attribute data where one item can only contribute to 1 defect in the count of defects.

4.   The test menu opens. Our count of defective items within the subgroup is in the column called Defects so select that column.

5.   The subgroup size is always constant so all we need to do is select the appropriate radio button and tell Minitab that the subgroup size is 200.

6.   We will be entering the historical control limits so tell Minitab that we will 'Use known values'. Enter the values as stated.

Click OK to execute the procedure.

Please navigate to the Summary Report.

On the top left of the Summary Report we are told that we have 1.3% out-of-control subgroups. In the adjacent Comments box we are told that the proportion of defectives may not be stable as this exceeds the expected level of 0.7%. Hence, we are in an intermediate area of being possibly unstable.

Still on the Summary Report, we see the P chart that has been produced. Reading this in conjunction with the Stability Report we find out that points 23 & 39 have failed Test 1. The P Chart has some useful summary information at the bottom. We find that 2166 of the 30,000 balloons tested were defective, which makes 7.22%.

It is interesting to note how many tests that it takes to produce a control chart with attribute data rather than continuous data. I would advise that if given attribute data you should be looking for a way to convert it into continuous data. The report card gives us a warning that the process may not be stable as 1.3% of the subgroups are out of control.

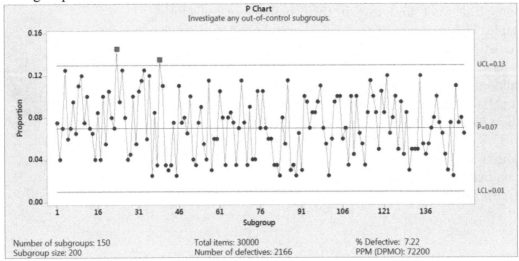

Example 9.11.2   Crazy Coffee

Coffee is big business when it can be sold as a high quality niche product. However, the higher the cost the fussier the customer. Crazy coffee treat their customer complaints as defects and they have categorized the complaints into several types. You have been asked to analyse their data and assess whether the complaints for the store are in control. The data for this example is in the worksheet called 'Coffee'.

1.   Transfer the data into Minitab. There are two columns of data that have 100 rows.

2.   Click *Assistant<<Control Charts*

3.   Click on the *U Chart* box which is used for attribute data where one item can contribute multiple defects to the count of defects.

4.   The test menu opens. Our count of defective items within the subgroup is in the column called Complaints so select that column.

5.   The subgroup size is not constant so we need to tell Minitab that the subgroup count is in the column called Sales. Do this by selecting the appropriate radio button and selecting the Sales column.

6.   We want Minitab to Estimate control limits from the data so select that from the drop down menu when prompted. As soon as you do that Minitab will list the out-of-control points and give you the option to omit the out-of-control points.

7.   Click OK to execute the procedure.

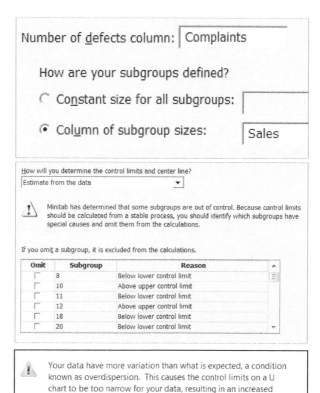

8.   Minitab detected overdispersion in the data and suggests you use the Laney U' chart instead. Click the 'Yes' button to use the Laney U' chart.

Please navigate to the Summary Report. On the top left of the Summary Report we are told that we have 0% out-of-control subgroups. This means that although there are complaints the process of producing complaints is stable.

Still on the Summary Report we see the Laney U' chart that has been produced. Notice that none of the points are out of control and that due to the varying subgroups size the upper control limit is also varying. The Laney U' Chart has some useful summary information at the bottom. We find that there were 2395 complaints in 20,919 Sales. A single sale may have generated more than one complaint.

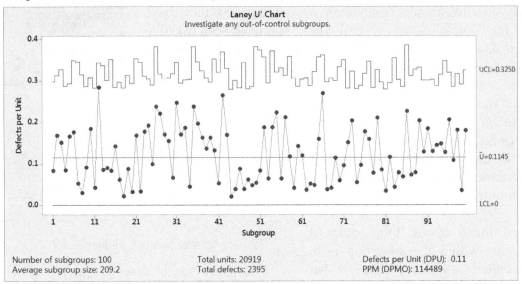

The Diagnostic Report gives us a chart showing the level of variation that is acceptable for the standard P & U charts and the equivalent Laney chart.

Also on the Diagnostic Report we are shown the U chart we would have had against the Laney U' chart. We can see that we would have had many out-of-control points on the U chart which would have led us to a very different conclusion about the stability of the process. The Summary Report gives us the all clear.

9.12 Control Chart Exercise

Exercise 9.12.1 Control Charts

Data is taken from a process in time order. Check for stability using the appropriate control chart. First use the Assistant and estimate control limits from the data. Once you have done that use the classic menu and test the data for all the available tests for special causes.

Analyse the data in File 09 Control Charts.xlsx worksheet Ex 9.12.1 and answer the questions shown below.

1) Is the process stable?
2) When using the Assistant on which chart are the stability issues?
3) When you use the classic menus and use all the tests for special causes are any additional test activated?

10 PROCESS CAPABILITY

10.1   Simple Process Yield Metrics

Process Capability tells you how well your process meets the customer requirements, it's that simple. In the Measure phase you would carry out an initial process capability study and then after you have gone through the Improve phase you could show your achievements and do a final process capability and compare.

Process Capability is a specific methodology for measuring your process defects in Six Sigma. You may also be aware of other measures such as process yield or Defects per Million Opportunities (DPMO).

10.1.1. Yield and DPMO example

Please calculate the yield and DPMO of a process where you have made a total of 625 parts of which 49 are defective.

$$\text{The Process Yield} = \frac{Good\ parts\ produced}{Total\ parts\ produced} \times 100\% = \frac{625-49}{625} \times 100\% = 92.16\%$$

$$\text{DPMO} = Defect\ Rate \times 1,000,000 = \frac{Defective\ parts\ produced}{Total\ parts\ produced} \times 1,000,000$$

$$= \frac{49}{625} \times 1,000,000 = 78,400\text{ppm}$$

92.16% may sound okay as a yield but it means that if you produce 1 million parts with that yield 78,400 parts will be defective out of that million.

Another term that you might hear is Rolling Yield. This is where the yield of a number of sub processes is combined by multiplying the individual yields together. For example, a process has three sub processes with yields Y_A, Y_B & Y_C, the rolling yield would be $Y_A \times Y_B \times Y_C$.

10.2 Introduction to Process Capability

We are now going to focus on Process Capability and try to understand what the calculations actually mean in practical terms. Six Sigma is all about the customer and we call our customer requirements the Voice of the Customer (VOC). We call our process output the Voice of the Process (VOP). We should have in the Define phase determined which parameter we would be monitoring to establish our VOP. And also during the Define phase we would have looked at the needs of our customer and established the VOC. We select VOC and VOP to have the same units so that Process capability, P_p, is a dimensionless number.

$$\text{Process capability} = P_p = \frac{VOC}{VOP}$$

We are going to call process capability, P_p. You may have seen it called C_p in other texts but I believe that leads to an incorrect understanding of process capability so I am going to teach it correctly from the start. Let's go through a worked example and see how we calculate process capability. To help our understanding we are going to limit ourselves to normally distributed data or distributions where the underlying data is normally distributed in the Green Belt Edition. We will have a more detailed discussion about that statement later in the module.

I am going to develop the explanation of process capability calculations using an example of filling a bag with peanuts. This example will continue through the next couple of sections.
When you buy a 200g packet of peanuts the machine that filled the bag of peanuts works to a specification. The lower specification limit (LSL) is 200g, you should never have less than 200g nett weight of peanuts in your bag. But to save on cost the machine also has an upper specification limit (USL) of 220g. VOC is described as 220-200=20g or USL-LSL. This is also called the tolerance width or just tolerance. It is the difference/distance between the USL and LSL.

10.3 Basic Process Capability

The VOP is the width of the distribution delivered by the filling machine. Let's say that we have measured the net weight from 200 samples. This is useful as bag weight also has the same units, grams, as the spec limits meaning that the units will cancel each other out when we calculate the P_p.

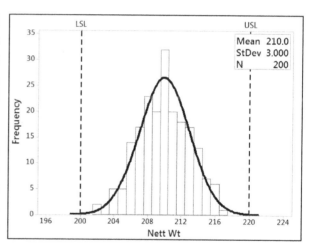

Here is a histogram of our 200 data points. The curve of best fit for its normal distribution is also shown. If you remember back to the core statistics section we said that one of the characteristics of a normal distribution is that 99.73% of the data is within 3 StDevs of the mean.

Or we could say that our process delivers 99.73% of its's population in 6 Stdevs (3 from each side of the mean). This means that VOP is the StDev delivered by the process multiplied by 6. When the distribution is not normally distributed it gets much harder to calculate the VOP. The Green Belt edition of this book only considers normally distributed processes. If you are told that your process is not normally distributed then please consult a knowledgeable Black Belt.
Let's have a look at our process capability equation and substitute our data from the peanut filling machine.

$$\text{Process capability} = P_p = \frac{VOC}{VOP} = \frac{USL-LSL}{6StDevs} = \frac{USL-LSL}{6\sigma} = \frac{220-200}{6\,x\,3} = \frac{20}{18} = 1.111$$

10.4 Z scores

I like to think of process capability as a ratio of widths, it is the width of the spec limits divided by the width of the process delivery.

$$\text{Process capability} = P_p = \frac{VOC}{VOP}$$

A higher value of process capability is better as this means that the process width is small and easily fits within the specification limits. It's good to have a safety margin. If VOC and VOP are equal , then P_p =1, then your process fits exactly within your spec limits and you have no room for error. But if we are hyper technical that is not true because if VOC=VOP=6σ, then only 99.73% of the process is within the specification limits and 0.27% will still be rejects.

While we are thinking of widths, we can also determine the distance from our mean to the USL (or LSL). If we think of this distance in units of StDev we can also get a measure of the capability of our process. This number is expressed in units of StDevs and is called the Z score.

$$Z = \frac{USL - Xbar}{\sigma} = \frac{220 - 210}{3} = 3.333$$

Again, the higher the Z score the more capable the process. There is also another metric called the Z Bench score. This is the distance in units of StDev from the mean to a line that marks all process defects as drawn under the normal curve. All process defects means collecting the defects under both tails and then adding them together.

Let's say that we have done an improvement project on the peanut filling machine and we have reduced the fill weight StDev from 3 to 1.667, a good improvement. What's our process capability now?

$$\text{Process capability} = P_p = \frac{VOC}{VOP} = \frac{220 - 200}{6 \times 1.667} = \frac{20}{10} = 2$$

Our Z score would be 6 as the mean is six StDev's away from either spec limit. This is actually now a Six Sigma process and this is where the name for Six Sigma originates. It's the aspirational target of having a process where the mean is 6 sigma's away

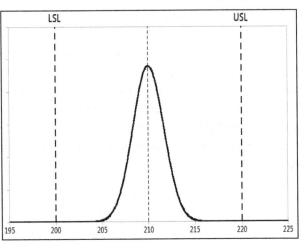

from the nearest specification limit. You may have heard that a Six Sigma process only produces 3.4 defects per million opportunity and has a Yield of 99.99966%.

Process Capability	Z score or Sigma Level	DPMO	Yield%
0.333	1	691462	31
0.667	2	308538	69
1	3	66807	93.3
1.333	4	6210	99.38
1.667	5	233	99.977
2	6	3.4	99.99966

There are tables available that will tell you what your DPMO or Yield% will be for a particular process capability or Z score.

10.5 Sigma Shift

If you look at the table shown above again and look at the Yield% for a Z score of 3 you might get a little confused. The Yield% stated in the table is 93.3% but I have previously said that 99.73% of all data under a normal curve lies within 3 StDev's of the mean. Is 93.3% a mistake in the table? Personally, I don't like the Sigma shift concept but it is not a mistake. What is happening is that a 1.5σ shift is applied to the defects to account for the long term deterioration of process capability. If you see the DPMO of a 6σ process reported as 3.4 you will now know that a 1.5σ shift has been applied to that data. The actual number of defects generated by a 6σ process, in the short term, is actually only 0.002 DPMO.

Like it or not, this reporting convention exists and it does install a safety margin that becomes more important at lower Z scores.

10.6 Off-Centre Distributions

It may feel like a long time ago but I am going to go back to the peanuts where we had a 200 sample distribution and spec limits of 200 to 220g for the fill weight. When we calculated our original P_p it came out at 1.111. What if a clumsy person accidentally knocked into the controls of the filling machine and it started to put more peanuts into each bag. Let's say that the mean increased to 215g. If the mean has moved then the whole distribution will also move but in my story the width of the distribution stays the same. Looking at the plot we can see that many of the bags would be out of specification. Let's work out the process capability for this distribution.

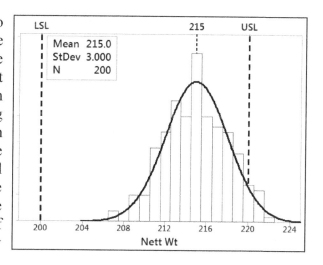

$$\text{Process capability} = P_p = \frac{USL - LSL}{6\sigma} = \frac{220 - 200}{6 \times 3} = \frac{20}{18} = 1.111$$

As this is the same capability value as before we can conclude that an off-centre mean does not affect this type of process capability calculation. We need a modified calculation that can cope with means that are not centred. The calculation that we need to use is based on the distance from the mean, Xbar, to the nearest specification limit divided by half the process width. It looks like

$$\text{Process capability} = P_{pk} = \frac{Xbar - LSL}{3\sigma} \text{ or } \frac{USL - Xbar}{3\sigma}, \text{ whichever is lower.}$$

Notice that the new symbol is P_{pk}. Our new process capability becomes

$$\text{Process capability} = P_{pk} = \frac{USL - Xbar}{3\sigma} = \frac{220 - 215}{3 \times 3} = 0.556.$$

If you see both P_{pk} and P_p in a capability report and their values are similar you will know that the distribution is at the centre of the spec limits. Otherwise, P_{pk} will always be lower than P_p.

10.7 Overall and Within Capability.

In section 9.4 we said a subgroup was a group of items that are made under similar conditions and that the subgroup was captured in a short space of time. We subgroup in order to reduce the amount of analysis we have to do and it can protect us from non-normal distributions. We also said that our subgroup should only contain short term random variation and not special cause variation. We saw that an IMR chart was used when subgrouping was not possible and Xbar R & S were used when it was possible. Process capability also uses subgroups when possible but rather than employ different tools it gives you different metrics.

Overall process capability is P_{pk}, but we are given another measure of capability for just the short term random variation seen within subgroups. This is Within Process Capability or C_{pk}.

If you remember we said that the Voice of the Process, VOP, was 6σ. The VOP for C_{pk} is calculated using six times the StDev within the subgroups, $6\sigma_{within}$. As $6\sigma_{within}$ will be less than $6\sigma_{Overall}$ this means that C_{pk} will be greater than P_{pk}. This is even true when there isn't any special cause variation due to the way within StDev is calculated.

All I need is a good C_{pk}.

The key point is that if special cause variation is present C_{pk} will be greater than P_{pk}. But the C_{pk} value is aspirational as it can only be achieved if you work hard to remove all the special cause variation. Now you know the secret that a good C_{pk} value does not always indicate a capable process. Therefore, if you have a supplier telling you that there C_{pk} is 2.0 always ask what is the value of the overall capability as it may be much worse.

10.8 Normality.

Earlier in this module I said that 'we are going to limit ourselves to normally distributed data or distributions where the underlying data is normally distributed'. You might have thought that was an odd way to phrase the sentence and that there might be something more to that statement. If you did you would be right. Give yourself a pat on the back ! When conducting a process capability study you can expect to conduct or see the results of a normality test. If the results show that the data is normally distributed you can proceed without any issues. However, if the results show the distribution is not normal then things get a bit sticky.

Take a look at Distribution1 which is made up from 200 data points. We see that the fitted normal curve matches the data pretty well. And when it is tested for normality a P value of 0.68 is returned with the Anderson-Darling test which indicates that the data probably came from a normally distributed population. We would not have a problem using the capability tools for normal data described within this module for this data.

Now take a look at Distribution2 which is also made up from 200 data points. The fitted normal curve does not match the data. The data returns a P-value of less than 0.005 indicating that the data probably does not come from a normally distributed population. With a bit more experience or with help from a Black Belt you could try transforming the data or applying a different distribution to the data. If I ever get round to writing it that will be covered in the Black Belt edition of this book. It is covered in my last book, Problem Solving and Data Analysis using Minitab.

Distribution2 can be fitted with a Gamma distribution and the VOP part of the capability calculation can be modified to cope with a Gamma distribution. The point for Green Belts is that the shape of the histogram is clearly not meant to be aligned with a normal distribution.

Finally we get to the sticky bit I mentioned earlier. Distribution3 is made up from 200 data points again. It is fitted with a normal curve which matches the data pretty well. The Anderson-Darling test for normality returns a P-value of 0.02 and as you know this indicates that the data probably does not come from a normally distributed population.

This bit is sticky as it relies on guess work, however, the risk of making a mistake is reduced by experience and combining our knowledge of SPC. The guess that must be made is whether the underlying distribution is normal and is being affected by special cause variation or whether the underlying distribution is of a different type. If your judgement and SPC indicate the problem is due to special cause variation then you can use the tools described in this chapter in order to calculate capability metrics. But remember, due to the random nature of special cause variation any metrics calculated when special cause variation is present should not be used for predicting future trends. They should only be used to describe the sample data set.

However, if you feel it is another distribution or the data requires transforming please wait for the Black Belt edition or ask a suitably experienced and qualified Black Belt for help.

10.9 Summary of Process Capability

1. Process capability is described as the Voice of the Customer, VOC, divided by the Voice of the Process, VOP.

$$\text{Process capability} = P_p = \frac{VOC}{VOP} = \frac{USL - LSL}{6 StDevs}$$

VOP is taken to be six StDevs. VOC is the tolerance.

2. An overall capability of 2 describes a six sigma process. The specification limits will be six StDevs away from the mean.

3. We can use look up tables to find the Yield% or DPMO for some capability levels. However, we need to be aware of the 1.5 sigma shift that is applied to represent the deterioration of capability over time.

4. P_p is helpful as a learning tool but it is not very good when the process is not centered. We therefore start to use P_{pk} which looks at the distance of the mean to the nearest specification limit.

5. P_{pk} is used to represent overall capability. C_{pk} represents within capability, the calculation is based on the within subgroup StDev. If special cause variation is present C_{pk} is aspirational.

6. The methods and examples shown in the Green Belt Edition are for continuous data related to situations where the underlying distribution is normally distributed.

10.10 Process Capability for Continuous Data

Process Capability for Continuous Data within the Assistant	
Function	Reports the capability of a process which uses continuous data. Process capability is used to understand how well the process can meet the customer requirements. Minitab offers the Complete analysis or the Snapshot analysis within the Assistant.
Sample Size	The recommendation is to have at least 100 data points in order to ensure all sources of variation are captured.
Data type & Format	Time ordered continuous data captured in sub groups is preferred. However, if that is not possible individual data captured over a long period is also suitable. If only individual data over a short period is available use the Snapshot analysis. Also use this if the data is not in time order.
Considerations	The data should be normally distributed or close to being normal. The Assistant may offer to transform your data under certain conditions but that is not covered in this edition.

Example 10.10.1 Yellow Dot Squash Ball

The World Squash Federation has strict specifications for the equipment used in the game of squash. The single yellow dot ball must have a diameter between 39.5mm and 40.5mm. Brauer Squash Balls Ltd empties one of its boxes and checks the diameter of 100 squash balls. Use their data on diameter to conduct a capability assessment of their manufacturing process.

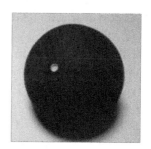

All data for this chapter is in '10 Process Capability.xlsx' and the data for this example is in the worksheet called 'Ball Diameter'.

As a box of squash balls has been emptied and then measured we have no way of knowing if they were made in time order. Additionally, because we don't know anything about the time they were made we cannot produce sub-groups. It is for these reasons that we must use the Snapshot Analysis for Process Capability.

1.   Transfer the data from the spreadsheet into Minitab.

2.   Click ***Assistant<<Capability Analysis***

3.   Click on the ***Capability Analysis*** box which is used for continuous data.

4.   The test menu opens. To start with we need to select whether we want to do the Complete or Snapshot analysis using the radio buttons. Select 'Snapshot'. When Snapshot is selected any menu options used for the input of subgroups disappear.

5.   Under Process Data, use the drop-down selector to tell Minitab that 'Data are in one column'. Select Diameter as the single column of data.

6.   Enter the specification limits of '39.5' and '40.5'. As it is sensible to have the process in the centre of the specification limits we can check whether our process has a mean of 40. Enter the target for the mean as '40'.

7.   Click OK to execute the procedure and generate the Report Card and Summary Report.

In the top left corner of the Summary Report we are shown the histogram of our process data with fitted Normal curve, the specification limits and target for the process mean. We can see that our squash ball distribution is closer to the USL than the LSL. None of the balls that were checked are out of specification.

Below the Capability Plot we have the Normality plot for our process data. With a P-Value of 0.856 we can say that our sample data probably did come from a normally distributed population. This is a very important step in the analysis as it is the fitted curve that lets us predict the shape of the population.

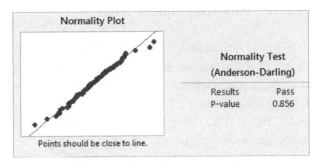

Normality Plot	Normality Test (Anderson-Darling)	
	Results	Pass
	P-value	0.856

Points should be close to line.

On the right, underneath the Customer Requirements section we have the Process Characterization which delivers our capability data. As we used the Snapshot analysis, with no option for subgrouping, all the capability metrics are for Overall Capability.

We are told that the sample mean is 40.199 and that the mean is off-target. If you think back to the 1 sample t Test this means that the population of ball diameters is not likely to have a mean diameter of 40.

Process Characterization	
Total N	100
Mean	40.199
Mean off target	Yes
P-value	0.000
Standard deviation	0.069176
Capability statistics	
Pp	2.41
Ppk	1.45
Z.Bench	4.35
% Out of spec (observed)	0.00
% Out of spec (expected)	0.00
PPM (DPMO) (observed)	0
PPM (DPMO) (expected)	7

Our process has a simple capability , P_P, of 2.41. As this value is above 1 we know that the process width fits within the spec limits. As the overall capability, P_{pk}, is significantly less than P_p we can establish that the process is not centered. Also, as P_{pk} is greater than 1 we know that the process is not breaching the closest spec limit.

We are then given data on %defects and PPM (parts-per-million) or DPMO defects. Expected and observed relates to the fitted curve and the actual sample, respectively.

The conclusions from this analysis would be that the process is performing well against the spec limits. However, if it were centered it would be quoted as being a Six Sigma process.

Process Characterization	
Total N	100
Mean	40.199
Mean off target	Yes
P-value	0.000
Standard deviation	0.069176
Capability statistics	
Pp	2.41
Ppk	1.45
Z.Bench	4.35
% Out of spec (observed)	0.00
% Out of spec (expected)	0.00
PPM (DPMO) (observed)	0
PPM (DPMO) (expected)	7

The report card tells us that our data was normally distributed, therefore, this analysis was appropriate. The amount of data we had was sufficient for establishing normality and giving accurate results. Finally we are given information on the selection of the Snapshot analysis.

Check	Status
Normality	✓
Amount of Data	✓
Complete Analysis vs Snapshot	ⓘ

Example 10.10.2 More Squash Balls

Brauer Squash Balls Ltd want to qualify a secondary supplier , Parky Squash Balls limited. Parky Squash Balls claim that none of their squash balls will be out-of-spec on weight. The weight specification on squash balls for the WSF is 23g to 25g. Parky Squash balls send data from their production line on ball weights using a subgroup size of 3. Use their data on ball weight to conduct a capability assessment of their manufacturing process.

All data for this chapter is in '10 Process Capability.xlsx' and the data for this example is in the worksheet called 'Ball Weight'.

1.   Transfer the data from the spreadsheet into Minitab. There are two columns of data. The 'Weight' column contains the continuous data of ball weight and the 'Group' column is an index of the subgroup number.

2.   Click *Assistant<<Capability Analysis*

3.   Click on the *Capability Analysis* box which is used for continuous data.

4.   The test menu opens. As we have data in subgroups we can use the Complete Analysis. Select the radio button for the 'Complete' analysis.

5.   Under Process Data, use the drop-down selector to tell Minitab that 'Data are in one column'. Select Weight as the single column of data. We could use the radio button for a subgroup with a constant size or we can tell Minitab which column the subgroup IDs are in. I have opted for the latter.

6.   Enter the specification limits of '23' and '25'. As it is sensible to have the process in the centre of the specification limits we can check whether our process has a mean of '24'.

7.   Click OK to execute the procedure.

Let's start with the Summary Report which is mainly based on the overall capability. The only exception is the bar display which tells us how capable the process is in terms of Z Bench score. Here we get the Z actual (overall score) and the Z potential score. Although, there should be no out-of-spec ball weights the score is less than 3. We are also told that the process mean is different to 24.

Process data

How are your data arranged in the worksheet?

Data are in one column

Column: Weight

How are your subgroups defined?

○ Constant size for all subgroups:

● Column of subgroup IDs: Group

Specification limits (at least 1 required)

Lower spec: 23

Upper spec: 25

Mean test (optional)

Enter the target value for the process mean.

Target: 24

On the bottom left of the Summary Report we have the Overall Capability Plot. We see the sample data as a histogram together with the fitted Normal curve using the Overall StDev. It is clear that the mean is to the right of the target and is closer to the USL than the LSL.

On the right, underneath the Customer Requirements section we have the Process Characterization which delivers our capability data.

We have a simple capability , P_P, of 0.99. This value is very close to 1 which means that the process width is just shy of fitting within the specification limits. As the overall capability, P_{pk}, is 0.68 we can establish that the process is not centered and should be making defective parts.

When we are given data on %defects we are told that there should be 2.01% defective parts. This should be setting off alarm bells. The capability study states that there should be 2.01% defects but Parky Squash balls state that none of their balls will be out-of-spec. Let's look at the rest of the data before we make any conclusions.

Process Characterization

Mean	24.306
Standard deviation (overall)	0.33812
Actual (overall) capability	
Pp	0.99
Ppk	0.68
Z.Bench	2.05
% Out of spec	2.01
PPM (DPMO)	20097

Let's have a look at the SPC charts on the Diagnostic Report. We are presented with an Xbar R chart. From the chapter on control charts we already know that that is the appropriate chart when you have a subgroup size of 3. We see that two points are out of control on the Xbar half of the chart. It does not tell me anywhere why these points are out of control but I deduce that it is because of Test 2 (9 points all in a row on either side of the centre line).

Below the Xbar R chart we have the Normality plot for our process data. With a P-Value of 0.011 we can say that our data probably did not come from a normally distributed population. However, the fitted curve fits our sample data rather well, it's only the right hand side of our sample data that is missing. We discussed Normality of our data in section 10.8. This is the occasion that we have to think about whether the underlying distribution is

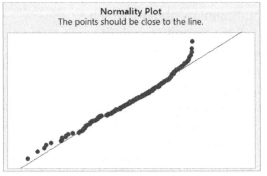

Normality Plot
The points should be close to the line.

normal and is being affected by special cause variation or whether the underlying distribution is of a different type. We can only use the metrics in this study if we can conclude that the low P-Value for normality is due to special cause variation.

Again just keep this in mind until we review all the data.

We then get to the Process Performance Report. This adds Within (or Potential) capability data to the information we have seen in the Summary Report already. Rather than go over the differences between the Actual and the Potential data let's have a look at the Observed and Expected data. The Observed % Out of spec is 0%. As stated by the manufacturer you won't get a ball that is out-of-spec on weight. But the Expected % Out of spec is 2.01%. What this probably means is that the manufacturer is checking all the weights and removing those that are out-of-spec. Hence, the really nice distribution with the right hand side chopped off. This is also why the P -value for the Anderson Darling test was so low. This removal of the out-of-spec balls is a form of special cause variation.

The conclusion is that if you are buying from this manufacturer you want them to continue with the 100% inspection. On the downside it is probably their customers that are paying for the 2% of defects and the 100% inspection. I would steer well clear of this company.

What this example does show is a really positive facet of capability studies. And that is you don't have to have all the analysis of a parameter to make an assessment of a process. You only have to have enough samples to be able to fit a distribution and check SPC charts.

Normality Test (Anderson-Darling)	
Results	Fail
P-value	0.011

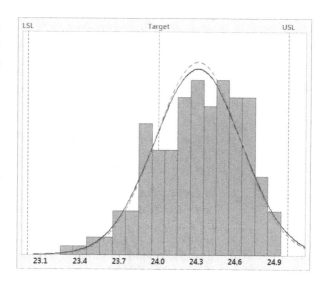

Capability Statistics	
Actual (overall)	
Pp	0.99
Ppk	0.68
Z.Bench	2.05
% Out of spec (observed)	0.00
% Out of spec (expected)	2.01
PPM (DPMO) (observed)	0
PPM (DPMO) (expected)	20097
Potential (within)	
Cp	1.02
Cpk	0.71
Z.Bench	2.13
% Out of spec (expected)	1.67
PPM (DPMO) (expected)	16672

10.11 Process Capability for Attribute Data

Process Capability for Attribute Data using the Assistant	
Function	Reports the capability of a process which uses attribute data to describe defective items. Unlike continuous data this capability is reported in defects per unit and % yield for Poisson Capability. And %Defects and DPMO for Binomial Capability. Much like the attribute data selection for control charts there are two types of capability to choose. Where the items being checked are only designated as pass or fail, no matter the defect, we use Binomial Capability. When an item can have more than 1 defect and we are counting the total defects of a subgroup we use Poisson Capability.
Sample Size	The recommendation is to have at least 100 data points in order to ensure all sources of variation are captured.
Data type & Format	Both capabilities use counts of defects within a sample that can either have a set or variable size. The difference is that items counted on the Binomial Capability can only be given a single defect classification or a pass. A single item on the Poisson Capability can have multiple defects.
Considerations	In order to establish whether the process is stable Binomial Capability will use the P chart and Poisson will use the U chart. If the charts are suffering from over or under dispersion Minitab will offer to convert them to the equivalent Laney chart. If this happens use the Laney chart. Usually, around 25 subgroups of data is sufficient to deliver accurate results. If required, Minitab will report the subgroup size that is required to deliver accurate results.

Example 10.11.1 Late Deliveries.

An online retailer wants to check the capability of its on-time delivery service. They collect data over 40 days on the number of dispatches that they make and whether the dispatch was late or not. They have an internal target of only having 3% of orders as late. Can you establish their capability and state whether the process is stable so that the actual figure can be used to make future predictions?

All data for this chapter is in '10 Process Capability.xlsx' and the data for this example is in the worksheet called 'Late Deliveries'.

1.   Transfer the data from the spreadsheet into Minitab. There are two columns of data. The 'Total Orders' column contains the number of orders shipped that day and the 'Late Order' contains the number of those orders that were late. In this example 'Late' is defective.

2.   Click *Assistant<<Capability Analysis*

3. Click on the **_Binomial Capability Analysis_** box. We are using Binomial as the order only has two states; On-time or Late, with Late being considered defective.

4. The test menu opens. Enter Late Orders as the column that contains the count of defective items. Select the Radio button for 'Column of subgroup sizes' then select Total Orders as shown.

5. In this analysis we don't compare the ratio of the VOP to the VOC. We actually conduct a test to check if the defect rate of the population is at a particular maximum level. We will enter 3%.

6. Click OK to execute the procedure.

Starting with the Summary Report we see that on the top left we have the results of the Hypothesis Test which asks is %defective at or below 3%. The answer is No so we must be above 3%.

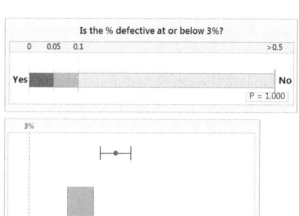

The histogram on the bottom left shows our data against the 3% target and it also shows the 95%CI of the defects. Therefore, we can say that the mean defect rate of the population is likely to be above 3%, in fact we are later told that it is between 4.38 and 4.98.

On the top right of the Summary Report we are given the Process Characterization data. We are told that 19,609 items were tested. You can see the immense amount of data collection that is required to drive Attribute Analysis and why you should always try and convert to continuous data collection systems wherever possible.

Process Characterization	
Number of subgroups	40
Average subgroup size	490.225
Total items tested	19609
Number of defectives	916

We are then given the Overall Capability data and there isn't a great deal of it. We have a %defective of 4.57 which gives us a DPMO of 46,713. This is equivalent to a Z score of 1.68.

Process Capability (Overall)	
% Defective	4.67
95% CI	(4.38, 4.98)
PPM (DPMO)	46713
Process Z	1.68

On the Diagnostic Report we have the P Chart. You will remember that the P Chart is the appropriate chart for attribute data that considers only the ratio of defective items to parts tested. Where a part can only have two designations, either as a defective or good part.

As we have a stable process we can use the capability data in the summary report to predict future performance.

The Cumulative % Defective chart shows how accuracy of the estimate is improved by having more subgroups of data.

The Report Card, not shown here, confirms that we had a stable process and that we have a sufficient number of subgroups. The report card also makes the comment that if the 95% CI for the estimate of mean defects was too wide we could reduce the size of the CI by obtaining more data.

Example 10.11.2 Fish Distribution.

The EU Council Regulations fix the quotas that EU countries are allowed to fish in certain areas. They limit fish types, size and quota for a particular country. A number of boats had their catches inspected within the IVb region over the last year. The total number of fish within the catch and the number of violations were recorded. Note, each fish could be subject to a number of violations. EU law states that the total number of violations for 100 fish should be no more than 4, which works out as 0.04 Defects per Unit (DPU). Please establish the capability of the fishing data collected and establish if it is stable.

Gadus morhua

All data for this chapter is in '10 Process Capability.xlsx' and the data for this example is in the worksheet called 'Poisson'.

1.   Transfer the data from the spreadsheet into Minitab. There are two columns of data. The 'Total catch' column contains the total number of fish within the catch and the 'Violations' column contains the total number EU rules that were breached.
2.   Click *Assistant<<Capability Analysis*
3.   Click on the ***Poisson Capability Analysis*** box. We are using this as a single fish can have more than one violation.

4. The test menu opens. Enter **Violations** as the column that contains the count of defects. Select the Radio button for 'Column of subgroup sizes' then enter Total Catch as shown.

5. This analysis conducts a test to check if the defect rate of the population is at a particular maximum level. We will enter 0.04 defects per unit.

6. Click OK to execute the procedure.

7. Minitab detects Over-dispersion in our data which could result in the control limits of the U chart being too narrow. It is suggested that we use the Laney U chart instead. Click Yes to use the Laney U Chart.

Starting with the Summary Report we see that on the top left we have the results of the Hypothesis Test which asks is the DPU at or below 0.04. The answer is Yes.

The histogram on the bottom left shows our data against the 0.04 DPU target and it also shows the 95%CI of the violations. We can see that the mean violation rate of the population is likely to be below 0.04 DPU, in fact we are later told that it is between 0.0234 and 0.0307.

On the top right of the Summary Report we are given the Process Characterization data. We are told that 8112 items were tested.

Below the Process Characterization data we are given the Overall Capability data. The average DPU from the sample is 0.0269 and the Yield is 97.3%, where Yield is defined as the chance of producing a unit with no defects.

Process Characterization	
Number of subgroups	32
Average subgroup size	253.5
Total units tested	8112
Total defects	218

Process Capability (Overall)	
Defects per unit (DPU)	0.0269
95% CI	(0.0234, 0.0307)
Yield	97.3%
Yield is the chance of producing a unit with no defects.	

On the Diagnostic Report we have the Laney U Chart. We have a stable process so we can use the capability data in the summary report to predict future performance.

The Cumulative % Defective chart shows how accuracy of the estimate is improved by having more subgroups of data, not shown here.

The Report Card, not shown here, confirms that we had a stable process and that we have a sufficient number of subgroups.

10.12 Process Capability Exercise

Exercise 10.12.1 Process Capability

Data is taken from a process in time order with a subgroup size of 7. Use the Assistant to calculate capability metrics using the Complete Analysis for continuous data. The LSL is 87, the USL is 97 and the target for the process mean is 92.

Analyse the data in File 10 Process Capability.xlsx worksheet Ex 10.12.1 and answer the questions shown below.
1) Is the process stable and is it normally distributed?
2) How capable is the process?
3) Is the process breaching either spec limit?
4) Is the process aligned between the spec limits?

11 Evaluation of Measurement Systems

11.1   What is Measurement System Analysis (MSA)

The first thing to keep in mind is that Measure has a stage dedicated to it in DMAIC. Everything else you have been doing is a study within one of the DMAIC stages. The objective of the measure phase is to measure your current state and understand the gap to the required state. In order to start measuring you must have a reliable measurement system. Understanding your measurement system is extremely important and yet it takes an experienced practitioner to give it the respect it deserves. On this occasion experienced means someone who has not done the Measure step properly in a past project and then regretted it.

Variance due to measurement

Variance due to Process

Total observed Variance = $\text{Var}_{\text{weigh scale}} + \text{Var}_{\text{process}}$

Maximum acceptable level of Variance.

Let's say that we had a process where we were filling bags of sand to sell. The process filled the bags and we weighed them on a cheap set of scales. The bag filling process will have variation and I have tried to show a bar whose length represents the variance. The weigh-scale also has variation. This might appear harder to appreciate but if you weighed the same weight on it over and over again it would give slightly differing values, it is a cheap weigh-scale after all. We have drawn the bar representing the variance of the weigh-scale underneath it. As we have used variances and not StDevs we can add the variances together to show the total observed variance.

We can then compare our Total Observed variance with what we deem is acceptable.

Variance due to measurement

Variance due to Process

Total observed Variance $=\mathrm{Var}_{weigh\ scale} + \mathrm{Var}_{process}$

Maximum acceptable level of Variance.

Okay, now our process is not filling bags with sand anymore. We are filling them with small diamonds. Suddenly our maximum acceptable level of variance changes. It's obvious we don't want to give away more than we have to and our customers are very sensitive to being short changed.

We need to change our total observed variance. Do we tackle the measurement system or the process? Well if we don't try and understand the error generated by our measurement system we won't make and informed choice.

In simplistic terms, the MSA technique we are going to concentrate on looks at our measurement error and either compares it to our process variation or our customer tolerance. Depending on the value of the ratio our measurement system will be graded as acceptable, marginal or unacceptable.

Although not covered here, if the measurement system must be improved we need to understand the type of measurement error that caused the problem and then figure out how to eliminate it or reduce it.

11.2 Why MSA is fundamental to DMAIC

This section is here purely to say 1) Take MSA seriously, 2) Don't try and leave this step out and 3) Don't give in if you are being leveraged to ignore this step.

If the fact that the observable reading always contains measurement error has not been enough to satisfy doubters of MSA you could still face the arguments shown below for not doing the MSA.

1) MSA can be time consuming, both in the initial study and especially if improvements to the measurement system are required. Replacing a measurement system is going to be hugely time consuming.

2) The measurement system you are assessing has been in use for some time without any issues being reported.

3) There does not appear to be any added value by conducting an MSA only a delay from the time it takes.

The response to these arguments are

1)   Yes, it can be time consuming but in the long run it will save time and improve the process.

2)   There has been error in every measurement system ever built. Even established measurement systems will add error to the observed measurement. You will never really find out how much until you assess the measurement system.

3)   The value of this step is added through successful completion of the project. Most legacy measurement systems will probably not be rated as adequate. Missing out the measurement step altogether usually leads to the project team back tracking to complete the measure phase later on.

11.3 When to Apply MSA

As soon as we have finished the Define phase on the DMAIC roadmap we should know what is our key output variable. The first thing we do in the Measure phase is set up the MSA exercise on the systems that measure that key output variable. Once we have a reliable measurement system we can then start to measure the process and assess where the gaps are and conduct SPC and Process Capability studies.

What about when we have completed the Analyse phase and we understand which key input variables affect the key output variable? Is it as important to have robust measurement systems in place for the key input variables? The answer is yes, we should check that our key input variables are being reliably measured as well.

11.4 What We Cover

MSA is covered within the Assistant and within the traditional menu's and there are a number of tools that can be used. We are going to be covering essential tools for Six Sigma Green Belts. These are the Gage R&R Study (Crossed) and the Attribute Agreement Analysis. To support the Gage R&R Crossed study we will also look at the Gage run Chart in the classic menu's. I don't cover how to produce the Gage R&R worksheets as this is simple.

It is my intention to cover Gage R&R nested, Type 1 Gage study and Linearity and Bias Studies in the Black Belt edition. But if you cannot wait you can find them covered in my first book 'Problem Solving and Data Analysis using Minitab'.

There are other types of project where the Key Output Variable may also depend on transactional systems where the tools mentioned above are not required. For instance on a Stock Accuracy Project where the final metric depends on transactions as well as measurement systems. In this case, Process Mapping and Failure Modes and Effects Analysis (FMEA) can be used to reduce the measurement risk. As this is a Minitab book this methodology won't be covered here but I wanted to make you aware there were still options outside of Minitab to improve transactional measurement systems.

11.5 Types of Measurement Error.

Two of the most important terms in MSA are Precision and Accuracy. I have always seen precision and accuracy taught by firing arrows at targets so I thought I would try something different. Precision relates to the spread of the measurements and accuracy relates to how well the mean of the measurements aligns to the real value.

In order to provide an example based definition of Precision and Accuracy I am going to take the opportunity of putting a picture of my kids into the book. It was taken around 2010. My youngest daughter, Raeesa is at the front, then my son Humzah in the middle and then my oldest daughter Iqra at the back. Let's pretend that I give them each the task of measuring Iqras height, they have to take 100 separate measurements. As fathers are very knowledgeable I know that Iqras real height is 165cm. Using the measurements provided by Iqra, Humzah and Raeesa I form the Normal distributions of their measurements and display them on the chart shown against the real height of 165cm.

Raeesa had a few problems measuring Iqras height as she was a bit shorter and suffered a parallax error which made the mean of her measurements different to the real value. But her measurements did not have much variation. We can say that her measurements are not accurate but they are precise as accuracy relates to alignment with the mean and precision the spread of measurements.

Next we will look at Humzahs measurements. The mean of his measurements aligns to the real value and his measurements did not have much variation. We can say that Humzahs measurements are accurate and precise.

Finally, we will look at Iqras measurements. The mean of her measurements aligns to the real value. However, as she had to measure her own height her measurements did have a lot of variation. We can say that Iqras measurements are accurate but not precise.

There is another error type that usually does not get a significant mention and this is Resolution. Resolution for measurement systems is the smallest degree as to which a change can be detected. An example of a system with poor resolution would be measuring a 100m sprint race with a sundial. We usually eliminate resolution error when we design/purchase a measurement system. A good rule of thumb is that the measurement system should be able to resolve to 1/10th of the tolerance width.

11.6 Accuracy Errors

Accuracy errors can be broken down into Bias, Linearity and Stability errors. Let's say that I have an ordinary pan weigh-scale and 10, 20, 30, 40 & 50 gram weights.

I put the weights one at a time and record real load versus the observed measurement from the weigh scale. If I had a bias error I would find that difference between the real load and the observed measurement was constant across the range of weights. The error that is the difference between the real and observed measurement is called the offset. For this weigh scale we have a positive offset of 4 grams. Even when there is no load on the weigh scale it is still reading 4 grams. A bias error can have a positive or negative offset. Minitab can tell us if the bias error is statistically significant using the right analysis.

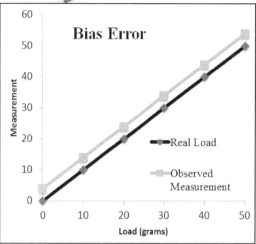

If my weigh scale had an offset that changed across the range of measurements that would be called a Linearity Error. Minitab can tell us if the linearity error is statistically significant using the right analysis.

In the previous two cases the x-axis on the graph was the range of the weights used. Stability Errors are different in that they manifest themselves over time. So let's say that I placed only the 30 gram weight on the weigh scale and took scale readings every 10 hours. A stability error would show itself as an increasing offset over time.
It is possible to have a measurement system that has all three types of accuracy errors.

11.7 Precision Errors

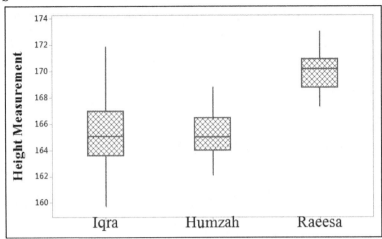

If you remember back to when we started this section we used the narrative of my kids measuring Iqras height. Let's go back to that example for the next section and have a look at what the boxplot of the data might have looked like.

Precision Errors break down into two components and these are called Repeatability and Reproducibility. Repeatability is the measurement error produced when one person repeatedly measures the same thing. We can see that all three kids contribute to the total repeatability error. We can also see that Iqra has the highest repeatability error of the three. Reproducibility is the measurement error that is obtained due to different people measuring the same thing. We have a reproducibility error because Raeesa is measuring differently to Iqra and Humzah.

Reproducibility can be further broken down into an Operator*Part error if the interaction is present, otherwise it is all down to the difference in Operators/measurers. The Operator*Part interaction occurs when an operator is having trouble measuring a particular part.

11.8 A Breakdown of Measurement Errors

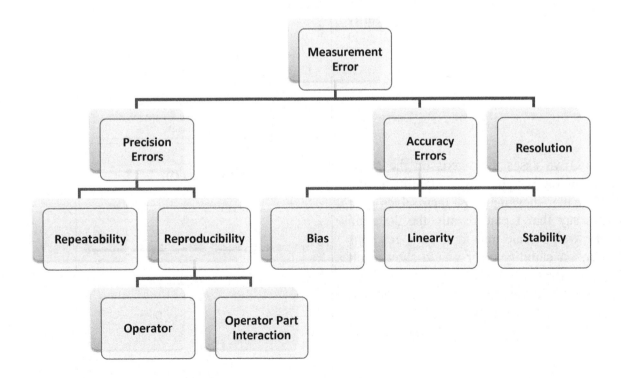

11.9 The Tool Table

Type of Error	Diagnosed using this tool.	Covered in this book.	Covered in 'Problem Solving & Data Analysis using Minitab'	To be covered in Black Belt Addition
Bias and Repeatability	Type 1 Gage Study	No	Yes	Planned
Linearity and Bias	Linearity and Bias Study	No	Yes	Planned
Stability	Run Chart	No	No	No
Repeatability & Reproducibility (R&R)	Gage R&R, Crossed or Nested.	Crossed only.	Crossed & Nested	No
R&R, within additional optional factors.	Gage R&R Expanded	No	No	Planned
Agreement between apraisers for an Attribute Measurement System	Attribute Agreement Analysis	Yes	No	No
Bias and Repeatability for an Attribute Measurement System	Attribute Gage Study	No	No	Planned

From the table it might look as if we are not covering a lot of material in this book. However, the crucial tool for Green Belts is the Gage R&R Crossed. We are now going to start to concentrate on the Gage R&R and learn a bit more terminology that is even more focussed on Gage R&R. You will finally get to know what is the difference between a Crossed and Nested study.

11.10 Gage R&R Introduction

A Gage R&R study will establish the Repeatability and Reproducibility of a measurement system. Repeatability is the measurement error when the same person measures the same thing repeatedly. Reproducibility is the measurement error when different people measure the same thing. Let's call the 'same thing' the part and the measurer an operator (an operator does not actually have to be a person it can be a machine). Whether it's the same operator or different operators you can appreciate that Gage R&R involves a lot of measuring the same part over and over.

Therefore, if your measurement system is measuring parts that are transient you cannot perform a Gage R&R. This may not apply to everyone but I work in the Chemical Process Industry and we have lots of instrumentation measuring the process. We have a lot of instruments measuring parameters like flow, pressure and temperature of the continuous process. However, you would not be able to conduct a Gage R&R because the part is transient and you cannot perform repeat measurements. For example, if you had a process flowmeter which was measuring water delivery through a pump you could ask an operator to take one measurement. However, you would not have a part where you could ask different operators to measure it or the same operator to take repeat measurements. The best approach for these types of measurement system is sending them back to the manufacturer for calibration or to try and check one instrument against another.

Also, if you are measuring something that will change in a short time scale you also need to take care that your operators are not measuring a part that is changing.

As a minimum you need three columns of data to make your Gage R&R study work. You need a column identifying the Operators and Parts and the continuous data for the Measurement.

Formed in 1982, the Automotive Industry Action Group (AIAG) was a non-profit organisation that was originally created to form a framework for quality improvement in the automotive industry. It's membership and scope has increased considerably since then but in the early years they suggested the framework for a Gage R&R Crossed should be as a minimum 3 operators, 2 repeats and 10 parts, which made 60 measurements in total. At that time it was thought that 10 parts were sufficient to give an accurate measure of the part to part variation. However, in the development of the Assistant the research conducted by Minitab has found that 10 parts may not be sufficient to provide an accurate measure of the part to part variation. Minitab now recommends that the historic standard deviation is entered as a separate parameter. If that is done then 10 parts will be sufficient for the study. If a historical standard deviation is not available then you need to have more than 10 parts. The more the better, typically 15 to 35.

The parts used must be selected randomly and must be normal good parts produced by the process. The reason for this is that the amount of measurement error will be compared to the process variation. If we artificially increase the part to part variation by selecting out-of-specification parts then that will make our measurement system better than it really is. However, this does not apply if we enter a historic standard deviation which is only taken from good parts.

Operator selection is also important. Operators should be randomly selected out of the group that actually conducts the measurements as a part of their role. Don't make yourself an operator if you are short of volunteers, unless the measurement is within your normal duties.

At the heart of the Gage R&R is a 2 way ANOVA where Parts and Operators are Random Factors. If we start to deliberately select them it will cause a problem with the mechanics of the ANOVA study.

Also, when asking the operators to measure the parts keep the part numbers hidden from the operators, this is called a blind study. And randomise the order the operators are measuring the parts. If this is not done operators tend to remember their previous measurements, especially if they had a problem with a particular part.

When using the Assistant for Gage R&R you will be presented with one decision bar in the Summary Report that will tell you whether your measurement system is Acceptable, Marginal or Unacceptable. This decision is based on whether the ratio of measurement system variation to process variation is <10%, between 10% and 30% or >30%. This is called the %Study Variation. If, as recommended, a historical process variation value is entered then %Study Variation will be called %Process Variation.

If the measurement system is associated with a tolerance (specification limit) you should also enter it into the procedural menu's. This will generate another decision bar which will ask whether you can differentiate good parts from bad. This decision is based on whether the ratio of measurement system variation to tolerance is <10%, between 10% and 30% or >30%. It's the same numbers again so it is easy to remember. This metric is called the %Tolerance.

With two decision bars it is possible to get conflicts and then things get interesting. For example if your %Study Variation is marginal but your % Tolerance is unacceptable at 31% what do you do? Would you improve the measurement system or would you try and change the process specifications to get a larger tolerance. Or what if the %Tolerance was <10% but the %Study Variation was unacceptable?

The key to the dilemma is to consider whether the MSA is being conducted to improve the process performance or whether it is to improve the recognition of defective parts. For process improvement %Study Variation becomes the primary metric and for recognition of defective parts it is %Tolerance.

The standard gage structure is the crossed structure as shown in the upper diagram. Each operator will measure each part more than once. This is because repeat measurements are required to calculate the repeatability term. Notice how the arrows cross each other, I like to think that is how this type of Gage R&R got its name.

It is possible to have measurement systems that are destructive. For example, fire resistance testing of safety devices, bursting disc failure or strength testing. In order to conduct repeat measurements for this type of testing we need to be able to make a batch of parts that have identical properties. If we can make enough identical parts so that all the operators can measure every part the required number of times then we can still use the Gage R&R Crossed.

However, if we can't make enough identical parts that every operator can measure them with the required repeats then we can use the nested structure. Using this method parts are nested with a single operator. If identical parts cannot be manufactured then a Gage R&R study cannot be conducted.

We should now know enough Gage R&R terminology to go into the examples and exercises.

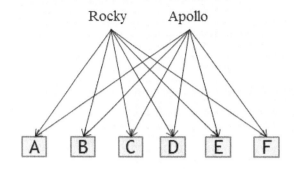

Crossed Structure without shown repeat measurements

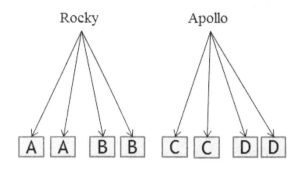

Nested Structure, shown with repeat measurements

11.11 Gage R&R Crossed

Gage R&R Crossed	
Function	Determines whether a measurements system is suitable in terms of precision errors, reproducibility and repeatability.
Sample Size	The sample size is driven by the need to have as a minimum 3 operators checking 10 parts with a repeat reading. The minimum data requirements are dependant upon having a value for the historical process deviation which is entered into the procedural menu.
Data type & Format	Continuous measurement data is required.
Considerations	Gage R&R assumes that the gage is calibrated and ready to use. Try to employ a blind study with the order of the parts randomised. The parts should be randomly selected from a stable process and should be normal good parts. Parts should not be taken at the extremes of the process. Operators for the study should be randomly selected, the number of operators used affects the accuracy of the reproducibility value.

Example 11.11.1 Lithium Concentration in Drinking Water

Khan Smart Water claims to contain lithium in ionic form which boosts intelligence. The team in the lab uses X-ray Fluorescence Spectrometry to verify the lithium concentration. In order to ensure they were

working consistently a Gage R&R crossed data collection exercise was conducted. The data collection involved 4 lab operators, 4 repeat measurements and 8 parts. By checking previous analytical data it was found that the process StDev was 0.14 µg/ltr. Analyse the result of the Gage R&R and establish if the measurement system is acceptable. If it is not acceptable make recommendations for improvement.
All data for this chapter is in '11 MSA.xlsx' and the data for this example is in the worksheet called 'Water'.

The first thing we are going to do is look at all the data and get a feel for what the results are going to show. The Assistant is very visual when it presents results anyway but I find the Gage Run Chart an excellent first tool for looking at the results of a Gage R&R Crossed study. It is accessed via the classic menu's.

1. Transfer the data in to Minitab. There are 3 columns of data.

2. Click **Stat<<Quality Tools<<Gage Study<<Gage Run Chart**

3. Enter the column headings as shown into the main menu.

4. It is always useful to log some information about your study especially when different iterations are used and then it becomes difficult to distinguish the charts from the different studies. Click on the **Gage Info** button. Enter the appropriate details.

5. Click OK & OK again to create the chart.

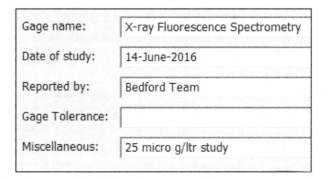

Part numbers:	Part
Operators:	Operator
Measurement data:	Measurement

Gage name:	X-ray Fluorescence Spectrometry
Date of study:	14-June-2016
Reported by:	Bedford Team
Gage Tolerance:	
Miscellaneous:	25 micro g/ltr study

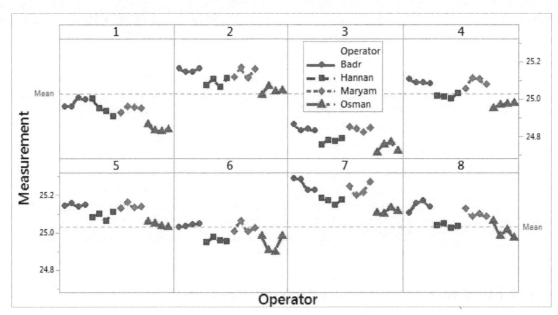

Navigate to the Gage Run Chart. The number above each of the sub-charts indicates the part that was measured. Within each sub-chart are the 4 repeat measurements made by the 4 operators. To look for the range of the parts look to the highest average measurements compared to the lowest. I estimate the part 7 has the highest concentration and part 3 has the lowest concentration. To look for repeatability issues check how well the operators agree with themselves within the subplots. To check for reproducibility issues check how well the operators agree with each other across the subplots. I estimate that I see more reproducibility than repeatability.

Having got a feel for what we expect the results will show we can now produce the results of the full study and examine them.

6. Click **Assistant<<Measurement System Analysis**

7. Click on the **Gage R&R Study (Crossed)** box which is used for continuous data.

8. The test menu opens. Enter the data columns into the menu as shown. Using the appropriate column headings makes life much easier.

9. In the Process Variation section you can see that using the historical StDev is the default option. Enter 0.14 as the historical value of StDev. As we only had 8 parts we were in danger of not getting a good estimate of process variation had we not entered a historical value.

10. Click OK to execute the procedure.

In the top left corner of the Summary Report we have the decision bar which tells us that we cannot adequately assess process performance with this measurement system. Our total %Process Variation is 42.4% and we need to be less than 10% for our measurement system to be acceptable, between 10% and 30% for marginal.

Below the decision bar we have the Variation by Source plot which shows how the Total Gage Variation can be broken down. If you click on the bars you can get the exact percentages. But hang on a minute! 38+17 does not equal 42! Unfortunately, that's how these metrics work as they are based on percentages of StDevs. As they are based on StDevs they no longer make sense when added together. What we can say is that Reproducibility is greater than Repeatability.

On the top left of the Variation Report we have the Operator by Part plot. This plot can show reproducibility issues and

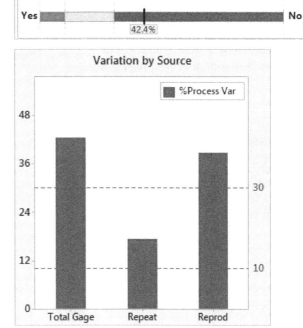

Operator Part interactions. In this chart we have 4 series, one for each Operator, they show the average of the measurements by the Operator for each part. In the diagram the profiles for each operator are almost parallel with almost a constant bias between some of the operators. This indicates the operators are consistently getting different results.

If there were an operator part interaction the lines would not be parallel and would probably cross. As our lines are parallel and not on top of each other we have reproducibility errors. Incidentally, as we don't know the real measurement for any of the parts we cannot say which operator is reading high or low compared to the real value.

On the bottom left of the Variation Report we have the Operator Main Effects plot. This shows the measurements taken by the operators for all parts in the form of a box plot. Badr and Maryam are taking measurements which are higher than those of Hannan and Osman. Again we don't know whose measurements are correct.

On the top right of the Variation Report we have the Test-Retest Ranges, which can highlight repeatability issues. The chart on the left shows the Operator Ranges by Part. On average Badr had the lowest repeatability error and Osman had the highest. We also see that Hannan measured most of the parts reasonably well apart from one which he had trouble. We can hover the mouse pointer over that part to find out that he had issues with part 1.

The chart on the right shows the Part measurement ranges by Operator. The part which had the greatest measurement range was part 8.

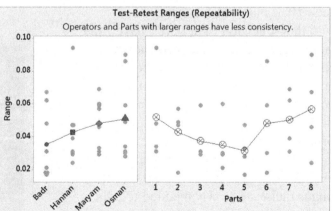

On the bottom right we are given the breakdown of %Study Variation and %Process Variation. The list of numbers match pretty well. This indicates that the StDev calculated from the parts in the study matched the historical StDev value.

Source	StDev	%Study Variation	%Process Variation
Total Gage	0.059	43.42	42.39
Repeatability	0.024	17.58	17.16
Reproducibility	0.054	39.71	38.76
Operator	0.054	39.71	38.76
Part-to-Part	0.123	90.08	87.94
Study Variation	0.137	100.00	97.62
Process Variation	0.140	102.44	100.00

Finally, we reach the Report Card which gives information on the number of parts that should be used for the study and the process standard deviation. The Report Card is not shown here.

In conclusion, this measurement system would be rated unacceptable. It suffered from both repeatability and reproducibility issues, but the reproducibility was by far the bigger issue. There is a almost constant bias between the operators indicating that they are doing something consistently different in the measurement procedure.

Example 11.11.2 Improved Procedure for analysis of Lithium Concentration in Drinking Water

Following the poor results from the previous gage study the lab team have reviewed their procedures and implemented standard working with visual standard operating procedures. The team has now conducted a data collection exercise for a Gage R&R Crossed using the improved procedures.

The number for process StDev remains at 0.14 µg/ltr. The team now also want to introduce specification limits for lithium ion concentration which are 24 to 26 µg/ltr . Analyse the result of the Gage R&R and establish if the measurement system is acceptable. If it is not acceptable make recommendations for further improvement.

All data for this chapter is in '11 MSA.xlsx' and the data for this example is in the worksheet called 'More Water'.

Let's start by looking at the Gage Run Chart again.

1. Transfer the data in to Minitab. There are 3 columns of data.

Part numbers:	Part
Operators:	Operator
Measurement data:	Measurement

2. Click **Stat<<Quality Tools<<Gage Study<<Gage Run Chart**
3. Enter the column headings as shown into the main menu.

4. Click on the **Gage Info** button and enter some useful information regarding the study.
5. Click OK & OK again to create the chart.

Navigate to the Gage Run Chart. The same parts were used for this study so part 3 and 7 still represent the range of the parts. By looking at the chart I would conclude that there appears to be better agreement between the operators than in the previous study, which means Reproducibility should have improved. I don't think the repeatability of the operators has improved.

Let's run the full Gage R&R study and see if the Reproducibility has improved.

6. Click *Assistant << Measurement System Analysis*

7. Click on the *Gage R&R Study (Crossed)* box which is used for continuous data.

8. The test menu opens. Enter the data columns into the menu as shown.

9. Enter 0.14 as the historical value of StDev.

10. On this occasion we have the tolerance values for the process so we can check whether the measurement system can distinguish good parts from bad. Enter the tolerance as shown or enter a tolerance width of 2.

11. Click OK to execute the procedure.

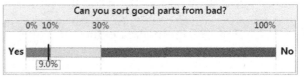

In the top left corner of the Summary Report we now have two decision bars. The first is the same as before and asks us if we can adequately assess process performance with this measurement system. Our total %Process Variation is 21.3% which is a great improvement on the time before but still only grades our measurement system as marginal.

The other decision bar asks whether we can sort good parts from bad based on our tolerance/specification limits. As this value is 9% our measurement system is actually graded as acceptable for sorting defective parts.

Below the decision bar we have the Variation by Source plot which shows how the Total Gage Variation can be broken down in terms of both %Process Variation and %Tolerance. Remember both of these metrics are totally different and have different meanings. This chart tells us that reproducibility is now less than repeatability, which indicates that those improvements the team made really worked. The repeatability component of %Process Variation is now 15.88% which is a very small reduction on the previous study.

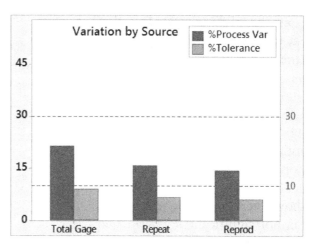

On the top left of the Variation Report the Operator by Part plot shows that we still have a very slight bias between the operators. We also see that again the tie lines are mostly parallel indicating that an operator part interaction is not present. An operator part interaction really means that a particular operator is having problems with a particular part.

On the bottom left of the Variation Report the Operator Main Effects shows that Badr and Maryam are still taking measurements which are higher than those of Hannan and Osman. The improvements made between the studies have made things better but perhaps there is still work to be done. Further improvements might make the %Process Variation acceptable as well.

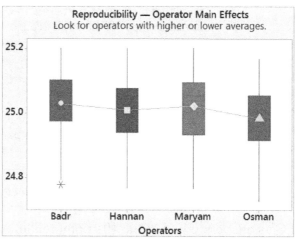

Let's go to the top right of the Variation Report where we have the Test-Retest Ranges. From having the lowest repeatability error Badr has now gone to having the highest. Previously, Hannan had issues measuring part 1, these problems have now disappeared.

The chart on the right shows the Part measurement ranges by Operator. The part which had the greatest measurement range is still part 8.

On the bottom right we are given the breakdown of %Study Variation, %Process Variation and %Tolerance. One thing that I did not mention previously is that if there were an operator part interaction its contribution to Total Gage variability would be shown here. As the operator part interaction is not significant it is removed from the calculation.

Finally, we reach the Report Card which gives information on the number of parts that should be used for the study and the process standard deviation. The Report Card is not shown here.

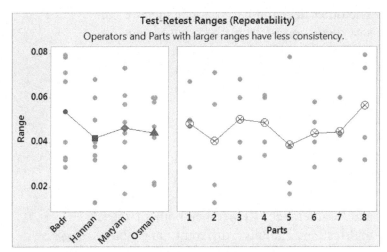

Source	StDev	%Study Variation	%Process Variation	%Tolerance
Total Gage	0.030	23.87	21.46	9.01
Repeatability	0.022	17.67	15.88	6.67
Reproducibility	0.020	16.05	14.43	6.06
Operator	0.020	16.05	14.43	6.06
Part-to-Part	0.122	97.11	87.29	36.66
Study Variation	0.126	100.00	89.89	37.75
Process Variation	0.140	111.25	100.00	42.00

Tolerance (upper spec – lower spec): 2

11.12 Attribute Agreement Analysis within the Assistant

Attribute Agreement Analysis in the Assistant	
Function	This analysis checks for consistency and accuracy across appraisers. The keyword is 'appraisal' and not measurement. This procedure rates systems of inspection for subjective ratings provided by appraisers.
Sample Size	The recommendation is to have at least 3 appraisers and have 2 repeats. The minimum number of parts required is not specified. However, to generate useful confidence intervals around 15-20 parts should be the starting point.
Data type & Format	The consistency of checks against a binary 'pass' or 'fail' is assessed in the method used by the assistant. The method used within the classic menu's can assess for classifications with more than two levels.
Considerations	Each appraiser should check the same number of items. Each part must be correctly appraised by a master appraiser. This appraisal is known as the 'Standard' for the part. Parts should be presented to the appraiser in a randomised order with part number not visible to the appraisers.

Example 11.12.1 Used Car 101 Point Reliability Check

Hurts Used Cars are very proud of the 101 point reliability check they carry out on their used cars prior to sale. They take it so seriously that they regularly test their engineers using Appraiser Agreement Analysis. They take 20 cars and have them assessed by their Chief Engineer. If they pass all 101 checks they get a Pass designation but if they fail any check they get an overall fail designation. Four engineers have conducted the checks on the 20 cars and the data has been recorded. Analyse the data to check how well the four engineers agree with the Chief Engineer.

All data for this chapter is in '10 MSA.xlsx' and the data for this example is in the worksheet called 'Cars'.

1. Transfer the data in to Minitab. There are 4 columns of data.
2. Click **Assistant<<Measurement System Analysis**
3. Click on the **Attribute Agreement Analysis** box which is used to assess appraisers.
4. The test menu opens. The Engineer column gives the name of our appraisers so enter that against Appraisers. Our part descriptions, listed as numbers between 1 & 20, are listed in the Vehicle column, enter that against Test Items. The Eng Result column is the decision the engineers/appraisers made so that goes against Appraisal Results. Our known standard is in the column called Chief Engineer.
5. As we can use any words to express a 'good part' we have to tell Minitab what we are calling acceptable items, enter 'PASS' using the drop down selector.
6. Click OK to execute the procedure.

The Assistant generates 4 pages in the report and packs a lot of information into the report. We will cover some of the highlights for this analysis.

At the top left of the Summary Report we have our decision bar which asks is the overall% accuracy acceptable. There can be no guidance on what the right score might be as it is specific to the appraisal system you are checking. For this appraisal I would say that 58.1% agreement is not acceptable.

Below the decision bar we can see the scores for the appraisers. We see that they all scored into the sixties with the exception of Miro who scored a very poor 42.5% agreement.

Enter the columns containing the following:

Appraisers:	Engineer
Trials:	(optional)
Test items:	Vehicle
Appraisal results:	'Eng Result'
Known standards:	'Chief Engineer'
Value of good or acceptable items:	PASS ▼

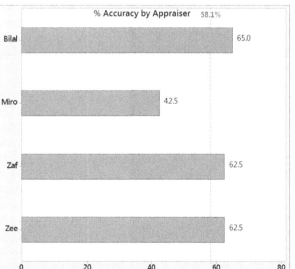

On the top right of the Summary Report we are given the Misclassification Rates. We can see the breakdown and see that 38.6% of the Passes were graded incorrectly as Fails, with 45.8% the other way. On 28.7% of occasions the appraisers rated the same vehicle differently between their own repeat measurements. At least this indicates the parts were kept blind and the study was probably randomised.

Misclassification Rates	
Overall error rate	41.9%
PASS rated FAIL	38.6%
FAIL rated PASS	45.8%
Mixed ratings (same item rated both ways)	28.7%

Let's move on to the Accuracy Report to see if we can establish what is happening. On the top left we see 95% confidence intervals for appraiser agreement with standard. As Miro's 95%CI overlaps with the other engineers we cannot say that he is appraising differently. This is a shame even though we had 20 parts the 95%CIs are still fairly wide.

The other graph of interest, which is shown on the top left of the Accuracy Report, shows how well the Appraisers agreed when the Standard was a Pass. We see that on this occasion that Miro is grading more cars as Fails when they are actually Passes. In terms of agreement this is actually a bad thing but for the customer it might not be a bad thing as Miro is risk averse. However, he will be sending more cars for repair than required by the Chief Engineer.

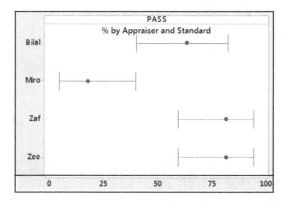

The other part of this graph looks at how well appraisers agreed when the standard was a fail. On that graph, which is not shown here, all 95%CIs overlap. Again, reducing the CIs with more samples might show something different.

Let's move onto the Misclassification Report and see what part of the story this reveals. On the top left and right we can establish which parts were most often misclassified. I have shown the chart for Passes rated as Fails and we see that part 6 was most often misclassified. If one part stood out it might be worth investigating the part and finding out if there was something obscure about the part.

At the bottom of the Misclassification Report we have three charts detailing appraiser misclassification rates. On the %Pass rated Fail chart we see that Miro rated over 80% of the Passes as Fails. Miro definitely needs training to align his checks with the Chief Engineer.

The %Rated both Ways chart is interesting. Bilal did not rate any of the vehicles differently between the repeat runs. This might mean that he is very consistent or he had a system of recording how he rated the parts and they were not blind. That's another conversation the Chief Engineer needs to have.

11.13 MSA Exercises

Exercise 11.13.1 Form a Gage Run Chart and then Conduct Gage R&R Crossed Study

A Gage R&R study has been conducted with 3 operators, 3 repeats and 14 parts. The study does not have a historical StDev or Tolerance. Form a Gage run chart and then conduct the analysis of the Gage R&R Study and then answer the questions shown below.

The data in File 11 MSA.xlsx worksheet Exercise1.

    1)   Does the Gage Run Chart indicate any particular types of problem?

    2)   How is the measurement system rated?

    3)   What is the biggest issue for the study, is it repeatability or reproducibility?

    4)   If there are repeatability issues who is causing them?

    5)   Are there any other issues?

Exercise 11.13.2 Conduct an Attribute Agreement Analysis

Data collection for an Attribute Agreement Analysis has been conducted with 3 operators, 2 repeats and 40 parts. Conduct the analysis and answer the questions shown below and then answer the questions shown below.

The data in File 11 MSA.xlsx worksheet Exercise2.

    1)   How is a good appraisal system?

    2)   Are any of the Appraisers different from the other Appraisers?

    3)   Are any of the part difficult to appraise?

    4)   Are the appraisers failing more good parts or passing bad parts?

12 Regression

12.1   What is Regression?

Regression is the name for a number of techniques that we use to build a mathematical model of our process. Along with regression you will probably hear the term correlation. Correlation is about defining the strength of a linear relationship between a predictor and a response.

Let's say that I have been doing a project on an all-you-can-eat buffet and we have data on the buffet budget against our key output variable for the project, which is customer satisfaction score. Wouldn't it be great if I could mathematically predict what the customer satisfaction score would be for a 50 Buffet Budget. If I use regression it will fit the line that best describes the data and give me the equation for that line using a procedure called Least Squares. I am also told the amount of variation in the data that the equation describes, that's the R-Sq (adj). And because I asked for them I have 95% confidence and prediction intervals on the graph.

For a budget of 50 I can use the regression equation to predict my customer score.
Customer Score= -4.092+ 0.3561*Budget
Customer Score= -4.092+ 0.3561*50
Customer Score= 13.7

If there were no error in the regression equation I would get a customer satisfaction score of 13.7 for a budget of 50. The 95% Confidence Interval (CI) tells me where the mean of repeated measurements of a Buffet budget of 50 would be. The Prediction Interval (PI) tells me with 95% confidence that a single point would be within the upper and lower limits of the PI.

Simple Regression limits itself to systems with one predictor and one response. However, the main regression procedures can model systems with a greater number of predictors. When we have two predictors and one response we get to the limits of 3D space and our graphing capability as shown in the 3D scatterplot. When we start adding more predictors we are limited with graphics but can still form the equations using Regression. We can still form graphs but we have to select the predictors we wish to vary in the graph and just hold the others.

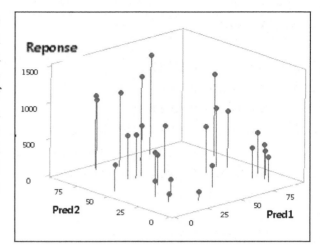

Just for a bit of revision on how we form equations, if we have
$Y = 3X_1^3 + 5X_2^2 + X_1*X_2 + 5.3$

It is normal convention in equations and graphs that Y represents the response and X the predictors. We have 4 terms in this equation

Term $1 = 3X_1^3$, Term$2 = 5X_2^2$, Term $3 = X_1*X_2$, Term $4 = 5.3$
Term 1 is a cubic term as X_1 is raised to the power of three, meaning it's $X_1 * X_1 * X_1$. The coefficient of Term 1 is 3.
Term 2 is a quadratic term as X_2 is raised to the power of two. The coefficient of Term 2 is 5
Term 3 is an interaction of X_1 times X_2. Both X_1 & X_2 are linear in this term as they are raised to the power of one.
Term 4 is called the constant. It is a number.

There are two predictors in the equation X_1 & X_2. We could use a 3D scatterplot to plot the 3D representation of this equation.

12.2 What are we Covering?

We would have stuck to the Assistant for this chapter but Minitab17 has dropped the cubic relationship from the Simple Regression routine. In order to cover cubic relationships in the 'Simple' routine we will use the classic menus.
Then we are going to move onto Multiple Regression and Optimisation using the Assistant. The Optimisation part is just an add-on to the Multiple Regression Procedure.
You can see that building mathematical models using regression can be very useful within the Analyse step of DMAIC. In the real world the prediction capabilities of regression are used in design, modelling, pattern recognition, artificial intelligence etc.

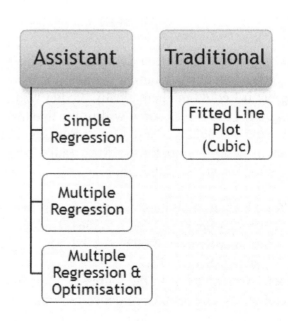

12.3 Simple Regression

Simple Regression	
Function	Produces a regression model for simple systems where there is one predictor and one response.
Sample Size	One of the assumptions for Simple Regression is having normally distributed residuals. For this not to be an issue a sample size greater than 15 is required. If a precise estimate of model error is required then a sample size greater than 40 is recommended.
Data type & Format	Numeric data is required for the predictor and the response
Considerations	Data for the study should be randomly selected to provide a cross section of the range of the predictor. Data should be recorded in the worksheet in time order. This allows for the detection of time related patterns within the data. Just because a predictor and response can be modelled together it does not mean they have a real world relationship. Minitab cannot check a real world link exists so this is up to you. A model equation of the form Y=3.14+6X may indicate that any value of X can be entered to predict the value of Y but you should only enter values of X within the range of the data used to form the equation. In other words, do not extrapolate.

Example 12.3.1 House Prices and Owner Ages

As part of her Geography project Iqra collects data on the average age of house owners and the value of their properties in Ellesmere Port, Cheshire. Iqra feels that as a person becomes more established they can afford a more valuable house. Iqra has two columns of data, one is the predictor called Age. The other is the response called House Price (unit of 1000£). The data is not recorded in time order.

Use the Simple Regression procedure to establish if a mathematical relationship can be found between Age of owners and House Prices.

All data for this chapter is in '12 Regression.xlsx' and the data for this example is in the worksheet called 'Houses'.

As we are happy that there is probably a link between average age of house owners and house prices we can continue and form the model.

1. Transfer the data in to Minitab. There are 2 columns of data.
2. Click *Assistant<<Regression.*
3. Click on the *Simple Regression* box which is used when there is only one predictor.

4. Enter the column headings. House Price is the response and Age is the predictor for House price.

5. We can then ask Minitab to find the best model for us or we can choose between Linear and Quadratic. The Cubic model no longer appears in the Assistant. Leave 'Choose for me' as the selected option.

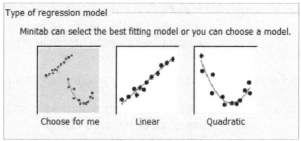

6. Click OK to produce the five page report.

In the top left corner of the Summary Report we have three decision bars. The first confirms that there is a relationship between the Predictor and the Response.
The second tells us that 85.96% of the changes in the response can be explained by changes in the predictor.

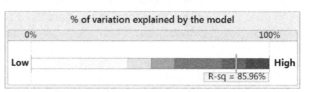

The final decision bar, which makes an appearance when the fitted model is linear, confirms whether there is a correlation between Y and X. 0.93 is the value of the correlation coefficient, the closer the value is to 1 or -1 the more strongly linear the relationship. A positive value for the correlation coefficient indicates a positive gradient of the line of best fit.

The top right of the Summary Report gives us the fitted line plot. As this is repeated later in the report I have not shown it hear. However, it is worth looking at the model equation. An equation like this indicates that the model is not limited in terms of the X values but we should not extrapolate outside the area of the study. The main reason for this is that the model may change or in this case certain values could give you ridiculous answers. For example, an X-value of 19 years old is outside the range of the study but if you used the prediction equation your house would have a negative value!

$$Y = -61.69 + 3.308 X$$

The top of the Model Selection Report shows the fitted line plot but again as it is repeated in a slightly different format I have not shown it here. Below that we see the data for model selection. The alternative model, which is the Quadratic, was tested as well but it was found that the Quadratic term was not significant with a P-value of only 0.655. Therefore, the quadratic term was removed. For the selection of the linear model we see that the linear term was significant.

Statistics	Selected Model Linear	Alternative Model Quadratic
R-squared (adjusted)	85.71%	85.52%
P-value, model	<0.005*	<0.005*
P-value, linear term	<0.005*	0.002*
P-value, quadratic term	—	0.655
Residual standard deviation	19.218	19.352

The Diagnostic Report shows us the value of our Residuals against the fitted values. Minitab will identify any unusual points for which we should examine the experimental data and set-up. It is unusual that we don't have any unusual points to check. If you want to review information on Residuals look back to section 8.6.1 ANOVA GLM. On the right hand side of the diagnostic report Minitab suggest the patterns that we should look out for. One of the common ones is strong curvature in the residuals. This indicates that a higher order term has been missed. If you see this pattern in the residuals then perhaps Simple Regression is not the tool to use.

On the Prediction Report we have the Prediction Plot, which is why I didn't show you the plotted data on two previous occasions. The prediction plot has the 95%PI. These show graphically where new data points could fall. The Prediction Report gives a list of selected X values and gives the Y value predicted by the model equation but also gives the 95%PI. For example, for an X of 27 years the model equation predicts a value of 27.638 k£. However, due to the error a single Y value might fall anywhere between -12.004 and 67.280 95% of the time.

Unfortunately, the prediction report does extrapolate predictor values outside of the range of the study.

The Report Card, not shown here, gives us the all clear on our analysis.

X	Predicted Y	95% PI
18	-2.1371	(-42.551, 38.277)
21	7.7879	(-32.343, 47.919)
24	17.713	(-22.161, 57.586)
27	27.638	(-12.004, 67.280)
30	37.563	(-1.8752, 77.001)
33	47.488	(8.2267, 86.749)
36	57.413	(18.301, 96.525)
39	67.338	(28.347, 106.33)
42	77.263	(38.366, 116.16)
45	87.188	(48.355, 126.02)
48	97.113	(58.316, 135.91)

Example 12.3.2 Pump Curve

Humzah has been asked to study the characteristics of a particular pump in a circuit. He has taken readings of various flowrates that the pump can deliver and then measured the pressure that the pump achieved at these flowrates. This is called the Pump Curve. He has been asked to model the Pump Curve and also whether the high pressure alarm should be set to 80 pressure for a flow of 50. This means that Humzah has been asked to find out if 50 flow, 80 pressure is close to the 95% Prediction Interval but not within it as the alarm should not be sounding frequently. The data is not in time order.

All data for this chapter is in '12 Regression.xlsx' and the data for this example is in the worksheet called 'Pump'.

1. Transfer the data in to Minitab. There are 2 columns of data.
2. Click **Assistant<<Regression.**
3. Click on the **Simple Regression** box.

4. Enter the column headings. Pressure is our response and Flow is the predictor for Pressure.

5. Leave 'Choose for me' as the selected option.
6. Click OK to produce the five page report.

In the top left corner of the Summary Report we have two decision bars. The first confirms that there is a relationship between the Predictor and the Response.

The second tells us that 85.57% of the changes in the response can be explained by changes in the predictor. This indicates a good model.

The top of the Model Selection Report shows the fitted line plot and I have added the Regression Equation. We are shown that we have three unusual data points which can cause the regression line to be pulled away from other points and one point with a large residual which does not fit the equation well.

Below that we see the data for model selection. The Quadratic model was selected as the Quadratic term was significant with a P-value of <0005.

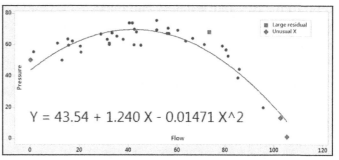

$$Y = 43.54 + 1.240 X - 0.01471 X^2$$

On the Prediction Report we have the Prediction Plot and the prediction data table. I have removed the data related to a flow of 50 and put it on the chart. We see that according to the model a flow of 50 will give a pressure of 68.78, however, individual points could be anywhere between 56.09 and 81.47. This means that our alarm setting of 50 flow and 80 pressure would be within the prediction interval. As it is within the 95%PI it would not be suitable as an alarm value as it could be sounding frequently.

Let's see if we can learn anything by changing to a Cubic model. The cubic model is the next step up from the quadratic as it contains a term raised to the power of 3. Unfortunately, Minitab17 has dropped the cubic model from the Assistant so we need to go to the classic menus.

7. Click **Stat<<Regression<<Fitted Line Plot**

8. Enter the column headings. Pressure is our response and Flow is the predictor for Pressure.

9. Click on the radio button to use the Cubic model.

10. Click on the **Options** button and select the tick box for 'Display prediction interval'. Click OK.

11. Click on the **Graphs** button and select the Four-in-One Residuals Plot. The classic method relies on us to check if there are any issues with the residuals to validate our study rather than check the Report Card.

12. Click OK & OK again.

Statistics	Selected Model Quadratic	Alternative Model Linear
R-squared (adjusted)	84.79%	23.69%
P-value, model	<0.005*	0.001*
P-value, linear term	<0.005*	0.001*
P-value, quadratic term	<0.005*	—
Residual standard deviation	6.121	13.710

| 50 | 68.783 | (56.093, 81.472) |

Response (Y): Pressure

Predictor (X): Flow

Type of Regression Model
◯ Linear   ◯ Quadratic   ⦿ Cubic

Display Options
☐ Display confidence interval
☑ Display prediction interval

Residual Plots
◯ Individual plots
☐ Histogram of residuals
☐ Normal plot of residuals
☐ Residuals versus fits
☐ Residuals versus order
⦿ Four in one

If you go to the Session Window and check the Sequential analysis of Variance you can see that the Cubic term is significant.

Now go to the newly created Fitted Line Plot. At the top of the plot you can see the new regression equation that contains the cubic term. The coefficients for the other terms and the constant have also changed. This model gives a better fit to the data as the R-Sq value has gone from 85.6% to 92.3%.

We now need to check our data point of 50 Flow & 80 Pressure and check if that lies within the Prediction Interval or just outside it.

13. Right click on the graph and select *Add<<Reference Lines.*
14. Enter '80' for the Y value and '50' for the X value. Then click OK.

The intersection of the two reference lines is the proposed alarm setting. With the Cubic model this is just outside of the prediction interval and therefore suitable for an alarm setting. It is now suitable because we have a more accurate model.

We also need to check the Four-in-One Residual Plot, as we did in the ANOVA GLM section.

The Normality plot shows that the Residuals are normally distributed and the Versus Fits shows that the residuals are equally spaced about the zero line. All other sub plots show that the Cubic study was valid.

Sequential Analysis of Variance

Source	DF	SS	F	P
Linear	1	2464.20	13.11	0.001
Quadratic	1	5756.47	153.65	0.000
Cubic	1	648.89	31.68	0.000

Pressure = 53.40 + 0.1422 Flow + 0.01182 Flow^2 - 0.000170 Flow^3

12.4 Introduction to Multiple Regression the Assistant

The Multiple Regression routine in Minitab 17 is a magical black box that gives the user special powers, or so it would seem. In order to use this magic we enter the predictors and the response data into the worksheet and complete a fairly simple menu where we tell Minitab which are the predictors and the response. For the enchantment to work we must have between two and five numerical predictors. We also have the option of adding a categorical predictor, which can have two or more unordered states. When we run the procedure the Assistant will work its magic and produce the report.

The report will tell which of the predictors are significant and how they are linked to the response in terms of Regression Equations. In this routine Minitab will check for interactions between the predictors and can check for quadratic terms. I think this is magic as once you have gathered the data building a regression model is easy to do and is only a few clicks away.

Disclaimer-Minitab 17 does not do magic.

Minitab 17 will employ a Stepwise Regression process to build up the model. It will first add the term that has the most effect on the response. It will then keep adding or subtracting terms as long as that action has the most significant effect on the response. One difference that you will see from ANOVA GLM for term selection is that a Significance value of 0.1 is used rather than 0.05 as in ANOVA GLM. The Stepwise production of the model and P-values can be seen on the Model Building report.

By default the Assistant will check for quadratic terms and interactions. The Assistant won't check for cubic terms unless the user pre-forms the cubic term in the worksheet and enters it as one of the predictors.

Rules of hierarchy apply in model selection. Let's say that we have two predictors, A & B. On the first round A is found to be significant. On the second round A*B, the interaction term, is significant but B is not. Stepwise Regression will automatically add B to the model as it is in the significant interaction.

12.5 Multi-colinearity and Variance Inflation Factors

We briefly discussed Variance Inflation Factors (VIFs) in the ANOVA GLM section but I'm afraid we have to do it here again. Multi-colinearity is when at least two of the predictors in a Regression study are correlated with each other. Weak multi-colinearity is usually not a problem but strong multi-colinearity can cause specific problems. The problem with multi-colinearity are that it can increase the variance of the coefficients of the predicted terms, hence the name Variance Inflation Factor. The issue is that if you run the regression again with slightly different values of input predictors the coefficients of the terms may be different and you may even have terms going from not significant to significant and vice-versa. We call that instability in the model.When using the traditional menu's we would use VIFs to detect and assess the level of multi-colinearity.

However, with reference to Jim Frost's Minitab Blog 'What Are the Effects of Multicollinearity and When Can I Ignore Them?' Multi-colinearity won't affect the overall strength of the model and you should be able to make good predictions.

Even though Multiple Regression in the Assistant is a fantastic tool for Green Belts to use it does not mention the level of multi-colinearity within the predictors and how this effects the estimation of the coefficients of the final model, so what can we do to protect the study.

1)   If we are running an initial data collection study we could choose predictors that are not correlated. However, sometimes we are forced to study historical data and we don't get that luxury.

2)   The Multiple Regression routine only allows 5 numerical predictors so we could check for strong correlation before we start the study. If strong correlation is present then assess whether you need both predictors in the study or can one of them be removed. The other possibility is to substitute both with a new replacement predictor.

3)   Multiple Regression within the Assistant uses something call Standardised Predictors within the calculations. These reduce the VIFs produced by interaction terms and quadratics. If you think about it quadratic and interaction terms will be correlated to their parent predictors.

4)   Seek assistance from a Black Belt and ask them to confirm the VIFs generated by your model using the classic menu's. We cover how to do this as well, by the way.

Also bear in mind that Multi-colinearity won't affect the overall strength of the model and you should be able to make good predictions if that is the requirement of your study.

12.6 Multiple Regression using the Assistant

Multiple Regression using the Assistant	
Function	Produces a regression model for systems with multiple predictors and one response.
Sample Size	One of the assumptions for Multiple Regression is having normally distributed residuals. For this not to be an issue a sample size greater than 15 is required. If a precise estimate of model error is required then a sample size greater than 40 is recommended for up to 3 terms and 45 for up to 6 terms.
Data type & Format	Numeric data is required for the numerical predictors and the response.
Considerations	Data selected for the study should be randomly selected to provide a cross section of the range of the predictors. Data should be recorded in the worksheet in time order. This allows for the detection of time related patterns within the data. Do not extrapolate the model beyond the bounds of the study data. Unusual data points and large residuals can indicate stability issues with the model. These points should be studied for unusual occurrences.

Example 12.6.1 Analysis of liquid effluent from a Paper Mill

Reinhart is leading a Six Sigma DMAIC project within a Paper Mill. The team have been asked to understand the factors leading to the Chemical Oxygen Demand (COD) within the sites liquid effluent. The team are currently in the Analyse Phase and have identified four predictors that might be linked to the COD of the liquid effluent. These predictors are Mixer Speed, Aeration Rate, Ozone Concentration and Ozone Pressure. Help Reinhart carry out a Multiple Regression exercise and confirm which predictors affect the liquid effluent COD. Form the Regression Equation and state how much of the changes in the COD can be explained by changes in the predictors.

All data for this chapter is in '12 Regression.xlsx' and the data for this example is in the worksheet called 'Paper'.

To start off we are going to check if any of the predictors are correlated.

1. Transfer the data in to Minitab. There are 5 columns of data.

2. Click **Stat<<Basic Stats<<Correlation.**

3. Enter the 4 predictors so we can check if they are correlated. These are M_Speed, Aeration, Oz_Conc and Oz_Press. Click OK.

4. Go to the Session Window to check the results.

For each pair wise comparison we get the Correlation Coefficient on top and the P-value on the bottom. The Correlation Coefficient ranges from -1 to +1. A coefficient of magnitude 1 indicates perfect correlation, 0.3 is weak, 0.5 is moderate and 0.7 as a strong correlation. Aeration & Oz_Press have a moderate to strong correlation. Aeration and Oz_Conc have a weak correlation.

We are going to have a look at the predictors and their correlation graphically by producing a Matrix Plot.

5. Click **Graph<<Matrix Plot.**

6. With the Simple Matrix Plot selected as default click OK.

7. Enter the 4 predictors again as the Graph Variables.

8. Click on the **Matrix Options** button and select Lower left. I always opt to look at the lower left of a Matrix Plot as I believe it is easier to analyse than the full plot.

9. Click OK and OK again.

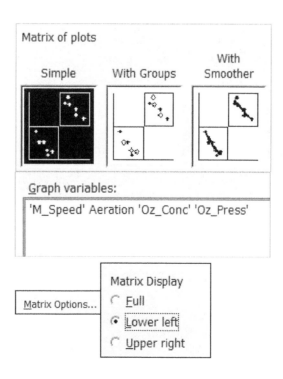

We can see the Correlation of Oz_Press and Aeration as a cluster of points going from the bottom left of the sub-plot to the top right. There are no distinguishable patterns in any of the other plots.

We have seen statistically and graphically that two of our predictors are correlated which may lead to multi-colinearity, which would in turn affect the stability of our model. We might consider removing either Aeration or Oz_Press as a predictor but before we make any decisions regarding taking out a predictor we will go through the Multiple Regression Procedure and see what happens with the results.

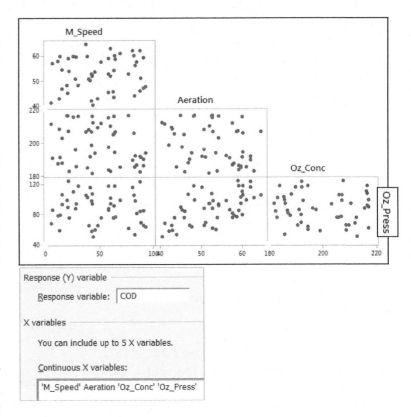

10. Click *Assistant<<Regression.*
11. Click on the *Multiple Regression* box.

12. Enter COD as the response. Then enter all 4 of the predictor variables as the X variables. Note, the tick box to investigate higher order terms is engaged by default.
13. Click OK to make the magic happen and produce the 5 page report.

In the top left corner of the Summary Report we have two decision bars. The first confirms that there is a relationship between the Response and at least one of the Predictors.

The second tells us that 87.43% of the changes in the response can be explained by changes in the predictors. This indicates a good model.

At the bottom of the Summary Report we are given 4 scatter plots. These are for each of the predictors against the Response, COD. M_Speed is greyed out as changes in M_Speed were not affecting COD.

We can see that Oz_Press has a strong positive correlation with the Response.

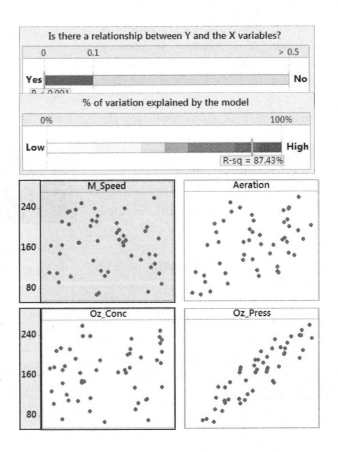

In the Comments section in the top right of the Summary Report we are told that there are four terms in the model. Three predictors and the interaction between Aeration and Oz_Press.

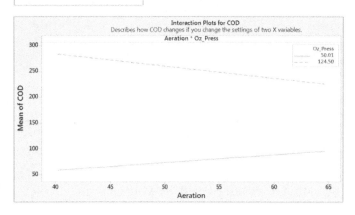

Next we are going to move onto the Effects Report which you only get to see if you have an interaction term in the model. This contains the Interactions Plot and Main Effect plots. We learned how to produce these plots in the Traditional Menu's when we covered ANOVA GLM.

At the top of the Effects Report we have the plot of the Aeration*Oz_Press interaction. This shows that if Oz_Press had a low value (50) increasing Aeration from 40 to 65 will increase the value of COD. However, if Oz_Press has a high value (124.5) then increasing Aeration from 40 to 65 will have the opposite effect and reduce the value of COD.

Below that we have 3 Main Effects plots, one for each predictor. The effect of each predictor is isolated and shown against the effect on the response. The same Y-axis scale is used for each plot so we can compare how unit changes in the predictors affect the Response. We can see that on its own Aeration is hardly having any effect on the Response as the line is almost flat. Oz_Conc has a moderate positive effect but Oz_Press is having the strongest positive effect.

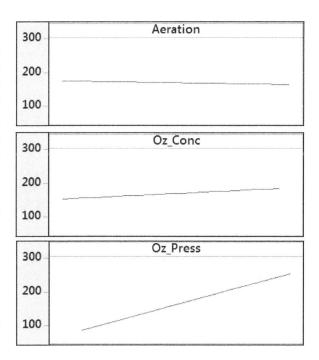

On the Diagnostic Report, not shown here, we are shown the Residuals Vs Fitted values plot and told that we have 2 points with large residuals. These two points are not too far away from the rest of the data and we would expect around this number of points to have large residuals so I am not going to take any action based on this finding.

On the Model Building Report we get to the heart of the Multiple Regression procedure. At the top centre we get the Final Model Equation. As stated in the Summary Report it contains the 3 predictors and the interaction term. It does not contain M_Speed as this was not significant to the Response.

On the Left we have the Model Building Sequence as generated by the Stepwise Procedure. Initially Oz_Press was added to the model as this was having the most effect on the Response. Then Oz_conc was added, it still had a P-Value of 0.000 but did not have as much impact on the Response. Then Aeration was added and as you can see that it had a P-Value of 0.381 which is above the Significance level of 0.10. However, this had to be added as the interaction term Aeration*Oz_Press was significant. This is one of the rules of model building. You can't include higher order or interaction terms without including the parent predictors.

On the top right we have a bar graph showing the Incremental Impact of the predictors on the response. M_Speed is greyed out as it is not included in the model.
Below that we have a bar graph showing the impact of each term regressed on all other terms.

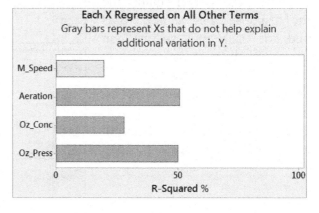

The Report Card, not shown here, gives us a warning about the unusual data points and tells us that our sample size was sufficient for a precise estimate of the strength of the relationship and large enough so we don't have to worry about the normality of the residuals.

We have completed the Multiple Regression Study in the Assistant and formed our Regression Equation. Now if we were worried about multi-colinearity, due to the correlated predictors, and were worried that the coefficients within the regression equation were poorly estimated we could check the VIFs using the Regression Procedure in the classic menu's. In the last section we have a simpliefied method showing you how to check the VIFs just for the regression equation you previously formed knowing the significant terms in the model.

14. Click **Stat<< Regression<<Regression <<Fit Regression Model**

15. In the menu that opens enter COD as the response and Aeration, Oz_Conc and Oz_Press as the 3 significant predictors.

16. Click on the **Model** button to get to the Model sub menu. Here you will see the predictors used to form the model at the top of the menu and the terms in the model at the bottom.

17. In order to add the Aeration*Oz_Press term into the model do the following in the top section for Predictors. Click on Aeration, Hold the Control key and then click on Oz_Press, release the Control key.

18. With both terms highlighted click on the top **Add** button which is in-line with the text 'Interactions through order:'. This will add the single interaction into the model.
19. Click on OK and OK again to execute the procedure.

Navigate to the Session Window and find the Coefficients table. We see that the VIFs are high, above 10 indicating strong multi-colinearity. This is due to the interaction term being correlated to its parent predictors. However, the Assistant uses Standardised Predictors so let's do the same.
20. Click on the Edit Last icon or press Ctrl+E to return to the Regression Menu.
21. Click on the **Coding** button.
22. On the drop-down menu next to 'Standardize continuous predictors' select 'Subtract the mean, then divide by the StDev'.
23. Click OK & OK again.
Navigate to the Session Window and find the new Coefficients table. The new VIFs are now okay and you can see that the P-values used in the Coefficients table are the same as that generated by the Assistant. Additionally the regression equation is exactly the same.

```
Coefficients

Term                    P-Value      VIF
Constant                  0.000
Aeration                  0.029    20.63
Oz_Conc                   0.000     1.11
Oz_Press                  0.000    64.28
Aeration*Oz_Press         0.014   123.29
```

Standardize continuous predictors:

Subtract the mean, then divide by the standard deviation ▼

```
Coded Coefficients

Term                    P-Value      VIF
Constant                  0.000
Aeration                  0.381     1.70
Oz_Conc                   0.000     1.11
Oz_Press                  0.000     1.56
Aeration*Oz_Press         0.014     1.03
```

In Summary, we found moderately to strongly correlated predictors. This made us cautious as we wanted accurate coefficients in the regression equation. We then formed the regression equation in the Assistant and we entered those terms into the traditional regression menu to confirm that the VIFs with standardised coefficients were satisfactory.

Maybe we were overly cautious but now at least you know how to confirm if your coefficients have suffered from multi-colinearity if you had correlated predictors when using the Assistant.

```
Regression Equation in Uncoded Units

COD = -439 + 4.11 Aeration + 0.919 Oz_Conc
      + 5.11 Oz_Press - 0.0521 Aeration*Oz_Press
```

```
X1: M_Speed  X2: Aeration  X3: Oz_Conc  X4: Oz_Press

              Final Model Equation
COD = -439 + 4.11 X2 + 0.919 X3 + 5.11 X4 - 0.0521 X2*X4
```

Example 12.6.2 Optimisation of Solar Cells

Woody is leading a Six Sigma DMAIC project for a solar cell manufacturer. The team want to assess the technologies available for solar cells and reach a target of >54% energy conversion to electricity. After initial studies the team have narrowed down the inputs to two continuous predictors which are glass purity (Purity) and array conductivity (Conductivity). There is also a categorical predictor with three levels, this is the actual photo voltaic material (PVM). The team have used the following designations for the categories A=Mono crystalline silicon, B=Gallium Arsenide & C= Cadmium Telluride. Help Woody form the Regression equation and then find the optimum settings to achieve >54% energy conversion. Display the settings on a contour plot. All data for this chapter is in '12 Regression.xlsx' and the data for this example is in the worksheet called 'Solar'.

To start off we are going to check if any of the predictors are correlated.
1.   Transfer the data in to Minitab. There are 4 columns of data.
2.   Click **Stat**<< **Basic Stats**<< **Correlation.**
3.   Enter the 2 numeric predictors so we can check if they are correlated. These are Conductivity and Purity. Click OK.
4.   Go to the Session Window to check the results.

The Pearson Correlation Coefficient indicates only a very weak correlation and it is not deemed significant. This should mean that we can conduct the analysis without any worries of poorly estimated coefficients.

```
Variables:

Conductivity Purity
```

Correlation: Conductivity, Purity

```
Pearson correlation of
Conductivity and Purity = -0.240
P-Value = 0.064
```

5. Click *Assistant<<Regression.* Click on the *Optimize Response* box.

6. Enter Efficiency as the response. We can choose a target for the Optimisation but I know that 54% will be at the maximum. Therefore select 'Maximise the response' from the drop-down menu.

7. Enter Conductivity and Purity as our two continuous predictors.

8. Enter PVM as the Categorical X Variable.

9. Click OK to run the procedure and produce the 5 page report.

In the top left corner of the Summary Report we have two decision bars. The first confirms that there is a relationship between the Response and at least one of the Predictors.

The second tells us that 60.94% of the changes in the response can be explained by changes in the predictors. This indicates a reasonable model.

At the bottom of the Summary Report we are given 3 scatter plots. We have two for the continuous predictors against the Response. It looks as though Purity has a stronger linear correlation with the response than Conductivity. We also have a scatter plot of the categorical predictor against the response. It can be clearly seen that the middle level, B, gives the highest values of the response.

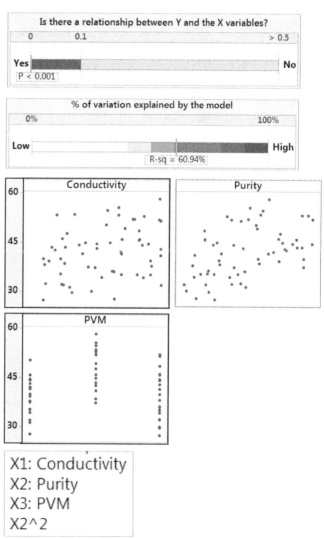

In the Comments section in the top right of the Summary Report we are told that there are four terms in the model. The three predictors and a quadratic term for purity.

On the Diagnostic Report, not shown here, we are shown that we have one point with a large residual. It's not too far from the rest of the data so I am not going to take any action.

Previously, on the Model Building Report we had the final model equation at the top centre of this report but as our model contains categorical variables we have to wait until the next plot before we see the equations.

On the Left we have the Model Building Sequence as generated by the Stepwise Procedure. Going from top to bottom you can see the order that the terms were added to the model with the quadratic term being the last added to the model.

On the top right we have the bar graph showing the Incremental Impact of the predictors on the response. We see that in terms of R-Sq% the terms had almost the same incremental impact on the model.

On the Models Equations Report we finally get the model equations. We get three equations one for each of the levels of the categorical variable.

Next we are going to move onto the Prediction and Optimization Report which is added if you select the Optimization option.

Initially, we wanted to maximise the response so right at the top of the report we are given the highest predicted level of efficiency that we can achieve, which is 55.06%. Next to that we have the settings we need to get 55%. Keep in mind that the first panel you make could actually have an efficiency anywhere between 44.34% and 65.78%. Eventually, after enough panels are tested the average should settle down to 55% using those settings.

PVM		Final Equations
A	Efficiency =	$22.90 + 0.1442\,X1 + 0.1673\,X2 - 0.000523\,X2^2$
B	Efficiency =	$30.20 + 0.1442\,X1 + 0.1673\,X2 - 0.000523\,X2^2$
C	Efficiency =	$23.52 + 0.1442\,X1 + 0.1673\,X2 - 0.000523\,X2^2$
		X1: Conductivity X2: Purity X3: PVM

Goal: Maximize Efficiency

Predicted Y	55.0615
95% PI	(44.346, 65.777)

Solution: Optimal Settings

X1: Conductivity	79.536
X2: Purity	159.876
X3: PVM	B

Below that we have 3 optimisation plots showing the optimal setting in the form of a dashed line. I have to say that the Response Optimizer in the classic menus is much better as it is dynamic. You can move the predictor settings around and see the effect on the response.

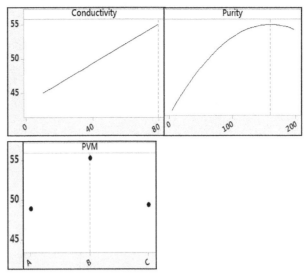

On the bottom left we are given the top five alternate solutions. Note that all of them involve panel type B.

The Report Card, not shown here, gives us a warning about the unusual data points and tells us that our sample size was sufficient for a precise estimate of the strength of the relationship and large enough so we don't have to worry about the normality of the residuals. It also says that once we have settled on the optimal values we should conduct 20-30 test runs in order to validate the results. This is good practical advice.

X1	X2	X3	Predicted Y
78.318	131.962	B	54.4736
62.233	197.058	B	51.8503
77.974	76.029	B	51.1470
54.239	190.437	B	50.9307
57.64	114.666	B	50.8274

The final part of the task was to form the Contour Plot. This must be done in the classic menus. There are two ways of navigating to the contour plot. The route shown below is better as it will automatically pick up some parameters from the regression model.

10. Click *Stat<< Regression<< Regression << Contour Plot*
11. You should find that the Response and the Variables have the relevant data columns auto-filled. If not enter the data as shown.

12. Click on the **Contours** button. We are going to change the contours on the plot to focus on the region we are interested in and not be spread evenly over the map. Select the radio button for 'Values' and then enter '51 52 53 54 55'. Placing a space between each number.
13. Click OK and return to the root menu.

14. Click on the **Settings** button. We need to lock in a value for PVM of material B. Select 'B' from the drop-down menu. Then click OK and OK again to form the contour plot.

I have added a flag to show you where an efficiency of 55% can be achieved.

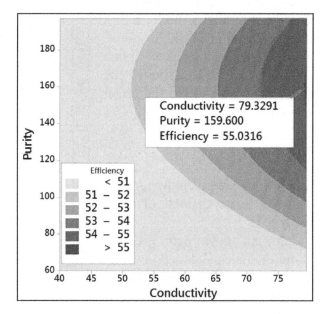

12.7 Regression Exercises

Exercise 12.7.1 Simple Regression Study
Data has been collected on a process where a single predictor affects a continuous Response variable. The data has not been collected in time order. Conduct the appropriate Regression analysis and answer the questions below.
The data in File 12 Regression.xlsx worksheet Exercise1.

1) What order of equation best fits the data and is significant?
2) How much of the variation in the Response can be explained by changes in the Predictor?
3) Are there any unusual data points in the study and are they an issue?
4) Using this process could we reasonably expect a data point to appear at 60 for the predictor and 200 for the response?

Exercise 12.7.2 Multiple Regression Study
Data has been collected on a process where four predictors are thought to affect a single continuous Response variable. The data has not been collected in time order. Conduct the appropriate Regression analysis and answer the questions below.
The data in File 12 Regression.xlsx worksheet Exercise2.

1) Are any of the predictors correlated?
2) Are all the predictors significant?
3) How much of the variation in the Response can be explained by changes in the Predictors?
4) What terms are present in the model?
5) Are there any unusual data points in the study and are they an issue?
6) What are the top solutions to obtain a value of 200 in the Response?

13 Design of Experiments

13.1   What is Design of Experiments

Design of Experiment (DOE) is a lot like Regression where we have a response variable and we want to link it mathematically to two or more predictors. Except we now call the predictors factors. We can still include interaction terms and higher order terms in our model as well. The difference is that with DOE we plan the series of experiments that we are going to conduct and we pre-plan the levels of the factors we are going to use. Whereas in Regression, it's usually the case of grabbing pre-existing data and throwing it all into the Regression Calculation. As DOE is meticulous in the planning stage it is usually more efficient in terms of the number of experimental runs that are required to obtain the same information. Therefore, where runs are difficult or expensive to conduct DOE is the preferred choice.

There are many different types of experimental design each with its own specialty. There are screening DOE's used to reduce a large number of possible factors to the ones that are really affecting the response. Modelling designs that allow you to optimise the factors to give your required output. There are designs used to look for curvature, reduce the effects of noise variables and deal with mixtures. DOE could be a three book trilogy becoming a four film quad ology in itself. The classic menu's allow you to run all these types of DOE. The Assistant on the other hand takes the most commonly and easily used elements and guides you through screening to modelling to looking for curvature. However, if you don't want to do a screening experiment you can go straight to modelling. It provides a really useful tool that you as a Green Belt will find useful and easy to use.

13.2 DOE Terminology

Let's say we are doing an experiment to see if a gas conforms to the ideal gas law. We have a seal chamber with a set mass of gas. We can change the pressure and the temperature and we are going to be measuring the volume as the response. Pressure and Temperature are our factors. In this particular DOE we are going to be testing each of the factors at two levels, a high level and a low level. It's actually called a 2 Level Factorial Design.

Compared to the predictor versus predictor scatterplots generated in regression the scatterplot produced by plotting the predictors in a DOE study is much neater. Additionally, with this type of

Pressure	Temperature	Volume
20	15	
40	15	
20	40	
40	40	

DOE Factor Scatterplot

experiment there is no correlation between the predictors and therefore no multi-colinearity. We say that we have an orthogonal design. Bear in mind that not all DOE studies are orthogonal.

For now we have only looked at the set-up of the gas experiment. I will conduct the experiment and write the results into the table.

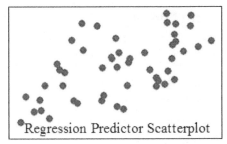

Regression Predictor Scatterplot

Pressure	Temperature	Volume
20	15	108
40	15	81
20	40	125
40	40	90

Having conducted the experiment I can produce the Main Effects (ME) plot. We have produced these before and we know that the ME plot isolates the effect of each factor. The Y-axis on the ME plot is the response and the scale is common to both factors. What is not common is the units for the X-axis. Minitab uses the same horizontal distance to represent the change between the high and low levels for each factors not the units of the factors or their values.

The change from the low level to the high level for Pressure produces a longer steeper line than temperature. For this reason we say that Pressure is having more of an Effect than temperature. Also, when Pressure increases the response decreases so we say that it is having a negative effect.

We need to understand the term 'Effect' as the Assistant uses it when reporting the power of the experiment. Let's have a look at how we actually calculate the effect of a factor

Effect of Factor = Average of responses at high levels - average of responses at low levels.

$$Pressure\ Effect = \frac{90+81}{2} - \frac{108+125}{2} = -31$$

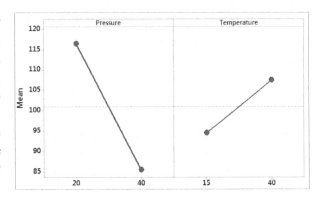

Term	Effect
Constant	
Pressure	-31.00
Temperature	13.000

If the line were horizontal then the factor would not be having an effect on the response. We still need P-values to tell us if the effect of the factor is significant.

Finally, with a 2 Level Factorial experiment we have to assume a linear response between the high and low levels of the Factors. We can look for curvature, in the form of quadratic terms, but when we do this we need to add more points to the study.

13.3 The DOE Flowchart in the Assistant

We will work through the complete flowchart when we go through detailed examples. The DOE procedure in the Assistant has to start with the creation of a worksheet. The created worksheet tells the experimenter at what levels to conduct the experiment and in what order. The created worksheet tells the assistant that it is dealing with a DOE study. If you want to reduce a large number of factors to a significant few you should start with a screening DOE. If you find between 2 & 5 significant factors when you analyse your screening DOE Minitab can then create a Modelling worksheet for you. Once the Modelling DOE has been analysed you can look at the settings required to optimise the response to your requirements or if curvature is detected add additional points to fit a quadratic model. On occasion you may have enough data to go straight to the quadratic model without further experimentation.

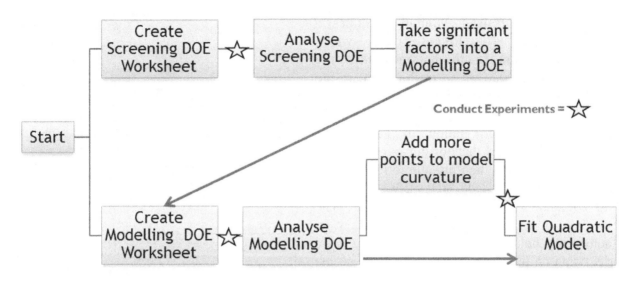

13.4 DOE Considerations

Whenever we have used the Assistant before we have used it to conduct distinct studies. For DOE the Assistant offers a sequential process. This means that the intention is that the user conducts a series of smaller experiments to reach an overall conclusion. The advantage is that a series of smaller studies will be more efficient in terms of the number of experimental runs that we need to do. The reason for this is that a lot of the insignificant factors will be removed in the screening design and won't be carried through the entire study.

Before you go into the DOE you will have identified your single response variable and a number of factors that you feel could be affecting the response variable. If you have between 6 and 15 suitable factors you should use a screening DOE to reduce the number of possible factors to between 2 & 5 significant factors. 'Suitable' means that the factors are controllable and that the high and low levels identified for the experiment can be set independently of each other. You will have confirmed the measurement system for the response already, if you were following DMAIC, you may want to check your measurement systems for the factors prior to starting the experiment. The high and low levels for the factors should not be extreme but set to the levels that experience tells you will change the response. When you have finalised the factors and their levels you can then choose the number of runs within the experiment. Increasing the number of runs used in the screening design will improve the detection ability. Once you have selected the number of runs you can then create the screening design.

This will generate a worksheet with four of what I call DOE 'Admin Columns' and then the columns showing you the levels that the factors need to be set in order to get data on the response. Each row on the worksheet represents one experimental run. The worksheet can be printed and used as a record sheet. To save yourself some typing it is worth saving the worksheet, even though there is no response data, at this stage. The reason for this is that the worksheet is automatically randomised to minimise noise factors effecting the experiment. The first two of the 'Admin Columns' are StdOrder and RunOrder. StdOrder is the non-randomised order for the experiment and RunOrder is the random order for conducting the experiment. To get round the randomisation issues for the examples I sort the columns on StdOrder so we all get the same worksheet.

On creating the worksheet Minitab generates a Summary Report and Report Card which summarises the design. On the bottom right of the Summary Report we are given information on the detection ability of the experiment. This is very different to the power bars we have seen previously and takes a bit of interpretation. In the example shown we are being told that for our experiment to achieve a power of 80% the minimum effect that we will be able to detect is 1.06 StDevs. We looked at how to calculate the effect in section 13.2. The StDev being referred to here is of the response when the factors are held. Therefore, only if you have historical data on the response can you establish the minimum effect that you can detect whilst achieving an 80% power. However, there is some advice below the power bar on the relative size of the effect that can be detected. With our 1.06 StDevs at 80% we should be able to detect a small effect.

At this point you conduct all the experiments and enter the results into your saved Worksheet. The screening DOE will look for main effects only. This means that at this point it is not looking for interactions. The Assistant also uses a significance level of 0.1 and not the usual 0.05. Personally, I think it is a shame that the Assistant does not allow you to select a user defined significance level. If you remember, going from a significance level of 0.1 to 0.05 will select more terms as being significant but it also increases the chance of a Type 1 error from 5% to 10%.

The point of a screening design is to reduce your initially selected 6 to 15 factors to between 2 and 5 factors to allow modelling and optimisation of the factors. It is unlikely that you will get more than 5 significant factors but if you do consider holding the levels of what you perceive are the least significant factors so that you can go into the next phase. If you get less than 2 significant factors repeat the brainstorming exercise to establish if you have missed any significant factors. If you have one significant factor and a good fit it may be the case that the relationship is only dependent upon a single factor. You can then use Simple Regression to model the relationship.

Once 2 to 5 significant factors have been identified you can go into the modelling design. When you select Assistant<<DOE<<Analyse & Interpret and then click on the Create Modelling Design button Minitab will give you the option to change the factor levels that you are using. But as far as possible Minitab will auto-complete the menu for you, which is nice as there is less typing to do. You also get the option of stating the purpose of the study, is it

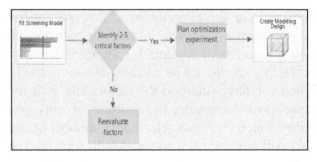

optimisation to a max, min or for stated response level. You also specify how many replicates you want to run. Replicates are repeat runs of the experiment which will improve accuracy and will on occasion allow you to look for curvature straight away.

Once you have selected the number of replicates to be used in the study you can print the worksheet. Again, always save the worksheet.

Once you have the results for the modelling experiment you fit the linear model. This looks for significant main effects and interactions at a 0.1 significance level. If curvature is detected you will be given the option to add additional runs to the modelling design or you will be able to look for curvature straight away.

We will now go to the examples and see how the sequential process works. We will go through screening to looking for curvature in the examples. As the DOE procedure in the Assistant does not display the regression equations we will even form the regression equations using the regression routine learned in chapter 12.

13.5 DOE Examples

Example 13.5.1 Bacterial Growth Screening DOE

Dr Foster has identified a number of factors that could be significant to the growth rate of a bacteria he is attempting to culture. Some of the factors relate to the agar jelly which the bacteria feeds upon and others are concerned with environmental conditions. Create a worksheet for the screening DOE and hand this over to Dr Foster so his team can conduct the recommended experiments.

When Dr Foster has run the experiments for the Screening DOE analyse the results and establish which of the factors are significant to the response, GrowthRate. Then wait for further instructions.

The screening DOE factors are listed below using the following format 'Factor Full name (Column Heading, Lo setting, Hi Setting)'.

Lipids concentration in feed (Lipids, 1, 10)
pH (pH, 2, 8)
Sugar concentration in feed (Sugars 5, 100)
Temperature (Temperature 6,25)
Micro Enzymes in Feed(Micro_Enzms 1,100)
Light Levels (Light 1, 100)
Mutagen concentration in feed (Mutagens 1, 100)
Humidity (Humidity 10, 1000)
Percentage of Nitrogen in atmosphere (%Nitrogen 1, 100)

We can't start this sequential DOE process without creating a worksheet so the first thing we need to do is create the Screening DOE Worksheet. We are starting off with screening as we want to reduce the 9 possibly significant factors to between 2 and 5. Actually, even 1 significant factor is acceptable as long as the model error is low.

In order to create the worksheet we don't need to import any data into Minitab.

1.   Start with a new project and then click ***Assistant<<DOE<<Plan and Create.***

2.   Click on the ***Create Screening Design*** box.

3.   We need to set-up the worksheet in the menu that opens. Enter 'GrowthRate' as the response variable.

4.   Dr Foster has given us 9 factors so we will enter '9' as the Number of factors.

5.   We then need to enter all the factor details. We need to enter the short factor name, the data type and then the high and low levels to be used for the factors in the experiment. Note, we can use categorical factors with two levels as well. However, for this experiment we only have continuous factors. Note, only 8 factors are visible at a time. You will need to use the slider or tab button to make space to enter the 9th factor.

Enter the name of your response variable: GrowthRate

Number of factors: 9

Enter your factor names and settings:

Name	Type	Low	High
Lipids	Continuous	1	10
pH	Continuous	2	8
Sugars	Continuous	5	100
Temperature	Continuous	6	25
Micro_Enzms	Continuous	1	100
Light	Continuous	1	100
Mutagens	Continuous	1	100
Rel_Hum	Continuous	10	1000
%Nitrogen	Continuous	1	100

6.   The minimum number of runs required for the screening DOE is 12. However, Dr Foster has decided that it would be beneficial to be able to detect a smaller effect and has decided to increase the number of runs by folding the design. Select '24 (fold design)' as the number of runs.

Adding runs allows you to detect smaller effect sizes.

Total number of runs in your design: 24 (fold design)

7.   Click OK to produce the worksheet, Summary Report and Report Card.

8.   A menu opens asking if we would like to print the data collection forms. Click No but in the real world this would be worth doing.

Print data collection forms?

You can print data collection forms, one for each block.

If you do not print the data collection forms now, you can print the worksheet at any time and use it as a form.

Do you want to print the forms now?

Yes   No

We have created a worksheet that tells us how to conduct 24 experimental runs in 24 rows. It has 13 columns, the 4 DOE admin columns and then 9 columns showing the factor settings. The 14th column, with heading GrowthRate, is where we will enter the response data when the experiments have been completed.

Experimental Goal

Reduce the number of factors down to the critical few that have the greatest influence on the response.

Let's have a look at the Summary Report that was created for the screening experiment. In the top left we are reminded of the goal of screening designs. And below that we are given a summary of the design. We are reminded that the base design was 12 runs but the 24 run option was used.

On the right hand side of the Summary Report we get information on Effect Estimation and Detection Ability. We are told that this design will estimate the linear effect of factors but won't do interactions. As we don't know if all our factors are significant yet we are quite willing not to get any information on interactions at this point.

Design Information

Response	GrowthRate
Base design	9 factors, 12 runs
Total runs	24

Effect Estimation

This design will estimate the linear main effects for all factors. Interactions will not be estimated with this design.

Y | | Main effect: Describes how the response (Y) changes if you change the setting of one factor (X).
X

On the bottom right of the Summary Report we are given information on the detection ability of the experiment. The power bar shows us that to achieve a power of 80% the minimum effect that we will be able to detect is 1.07 StDevs. In the guidance given below we are told that we will be able to detect down to small to moderate effects of the factors. I can tell you that had Dr Foster not added the extra runs we would only have been able to measure effects down to 2.3*StDev.

Dr Foster and his researchers work hard and complete all the experimental runs and the data is recorded in 13 DOE.xlsx worksheet 'Bacteria Screen'. As the auto-randomisation will create worksheets where everyone's StdOrder is different the Excel worksheet has been sorted on the StdOrder column. This means we can't just copy the response column into Minitab. We need to copy the entire Excel worksheet and transfer it into Minitab.

9. In Minitab highlight column C1 to C13 from row1 to row24. Do not delete the title row.

10. Right click and then left click on 'Delete Cells'. This will clear the Minitab worksheet leaving only the column headings.

11. Go to the Excel worksheet 'Bacteria Screen' and copy cells A2 to N25.

12. Paste those cell into Columns C1 to C14 directly under the title bar. That brings the complete screening DOE including the response data into Minitab. We can now analyse the screening DOE.

13. Click *Assistant<<DOE<<Analyze and Interpret*.
14. Click on the *Fit Screening Model* box.

15. Even though you have just indicated you wish to fit a screening model you get a pop-up menu that asks the same thing again. Clicking on 'Yes' will produce a 4 page analysis report on the screening model.

The top left of the Summary Report has the Pareto Chart of Effects. This shows which of the Main Effects or Factors were found to be significant. These are the effects that extend past the dashed line which indicates significance at the 0.1 level. We see that Sugars, Temperature, pH & Light were significant factors.

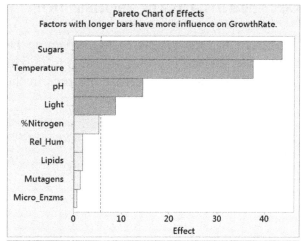

We are told that changes in these four factors explain 94.68% of changes in the response. Which is a very good fit.

On the Effects Report we have the Main Effects plots for all the factors. The non-significant factors have been greyed out. Light is the only factor that has a negative effect on the response. We can also see that Sugar has the largest effect followed closely by temperature.

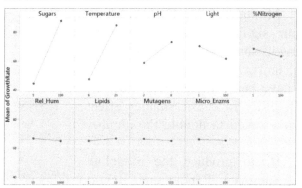

At the top of the Diagnostic Report we have the Residual Vs Fitted values plot. We have one point with a large residual. It is not that isolated from the other data. Therefore no action will be taken.
The plot below that is the Residual Vs Observation Plot, not shown here. This loses its impact as the results of the experiments were sorted and are no longer in time order.
The Report Card, not shown here, only warns us of the point with the large residual.

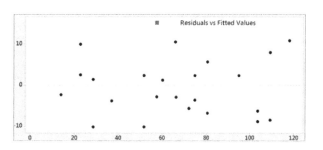

Example 13.5.2 Bacterial Growth Modelling DOE

Now that Dr Foster has the results of the screening DOE he wants you to create a worksheet for a Modelling DOE. He advises you that he wants to maximise GrowthRate, leave the factor levels where they are and that he is happy to increase the runs in the experiment to improve the effect that can be observed.

16. Click *Assistant<<DOE<<Analyze and Interpret.*

17. Click on the *Create Modeling Design* box.

18. A menu box will appear and ask you if you wish to enter new factor levels. Click on No and you are taken to the Modeling Worksheet Creation Menu.

Set new factor levels?

You set low and high levels for your factors when you created a screening design. For a modeling design, the factors are often set closer together.

Do you want to set new factor levels?

Yes   No

19. Type in 'GrowthRate' as the response.
20. From the selector for 'What is your response goal?' Select 'Maximise the response'. Minitab will have already selected our significant factor and their levels saving us some typing.

21. For 'Number of Replicates' select 2. We could have had a design with only 19 runs but in order to detect smaller effect sizes we have opted to double the number of runs.
22. Click OK to produce the modeling worksheet, Summary Report and Report Card.
23. A menu opens asking if we would like to print the data collection forms. Click No. But in real life you would give a copy of the file to Dr Foster so his team could complete the experiments.
On the bottom right of the Summary Report we are given information on the detection ability of the experiment. The power bar shows us that to achieve a power of 80% the minimum effect that we will be able to detect is 0.9 StDevs which is equivalent to small effects.

Dr Foster and his team complete the experiments for the Modeling DOE. They return the results in Excel worksheet 'Bacteria Model'.

24. Go to the Minitab worksheet where our modeling DOE worksheet was created. Delete everything but the title bar and then transfer the data from the Excel worksheet into Minitab. It's the same as we did for the screening model but the cell references are different.

25. Click *Assistant<<DOE<<Analyze and Interpret.*

26. Click on the *Fit Linear Model* box.

27. A menu for the Response Goal opens. If the goal is not listed as 'Maximize the response' change it to that. Click OK. This will produce a five page report.

Starting at the top left of the Summary Report, which has the Pareto Chart of Effects. We see that Sugars, Temperature, pH & the interaction between pH and temperature were significant factors at the 0.1 level. Light is no longer a significant factor.

Sugars and Temperature are still having the greatest effect on the response.

Again the model is a very good fit and we can explain 94.25% of the changes in the Response through changes of the main effects and interaction term.

On the top right of the Summary Report we are given the Design Information for our experiment, not shown here. Below that we have the factor settings that we should use to get the highest response value possible, which as a single value is 114.354.

On the Effects Report we are shown all the interaction plots and main effects for the factors. Only the significant factors and single significant interaction are highlighted and all the others are greyed out.

At the top of the Diagnostic Report we have the Residual Vs Fitted values plot. We don't have any unusual data points so I have not shown the chart here.

Below that we have the Residuals Vs Observation order chart. It's worth noting that Minitab will automatically split this experiment into two halves, as each is a repeat of the other, and it will compare the two halves to check if there was a significant difference between the two halves or Blocks. Minitab is checking to see if anything changed when you did the experiment. You can manually change the split between the Blocks if you feel like investigating a noise variable in your experiments.

Next we have the Prediction and Optimization Report. This is added to reports to tell us what settings we should use to achieve our aim with the response.

Dr Foster wants to maximise GrowthRate so right at the top of the report we are given the highest predicted level of GrowthRate that can be achieved, which is 114.345. The prediction interval for single experiments is 95.98 to 132.73. Just on the right of that we are given the settings that should be used to achieve the maximum GrowthRate.

Goal: Maximize GrowthRate	
Predicted Y	114.354
95% PI	(95.977, 132.73)

Solution: Optimal Settings	
A: pH	8
B: Sugars	100
C: Temperature	25

Dr Foster notes that the maximum response is achieved at the upper limits of the three factors and that in future projects it would be worth using even higher levels of the factors to check if GrowthRate could be further increased.

Below that we have 3 optimisation plots showing the optimal setting in the form of a dashed line.

On the bottom left we are given the top five alternate solutions.

Top Five Alternative Solutions			
A	B	C	Predicted Y
2	100	25	108.979
8	100	6	79.4485
5	52.5	15.5	64.1513
8	5	25	61.7292
2	100	6	59.0735

The Report Card, not shown here, does tell us that Blocks were not significant. This means there were not any unexpected changes which affected the results between the first repeat of the experiment and the second. The Report Card also tells us that there was no sign of curvature detected. This is a really useful insight and tells us if more experimental runs might be useful in improving the model.

Dr Foster is excited with the results so far. As curvature was not detected in the linear model it would not be advisable for Dr Foster to conduct more experimental runs trying to find curvature. Dr Foster and his team will now look at conducting experiments with the significant factors at higher levels in the future.

Example 13.6.1 Fuel Efficiency Screening DOE

Zaf is not someone who is in denial regarding mankind's impact on the environment and feels that he can conduct an experiment to improve the fuel efficiency of his 5.0 ltr EM 5 car. He brainstorms 7 factors that he thinks will have a significant effect on fuel efficiency. These factors are listed below. TEL, Ferrocence & MMT are all fuel additives. Fuel Magnets are powerful magnets used to align the molecules in the fuel lines before combustion. The type of tyre is Eco or Normal, where Eco indicates a fuel saver tyre which is ecologically friendly.

The efficiency tests are conducted on a rolling road in order to reduce noise variables.

Help Zaf and his team save the environment by generating a Screening DOE design. Pass the design to Zaf and then analyse the data that he gives you. Continue this process through to the Modelling DOE up to a quadratic model. Zaf will advise you on the number of runs he is willing to support.

The screening DOE factors are listed below using the following format 'Factor Full name (Column Heading, Lo setting, Hi Setting)'.

Air pressure in the tyres (Tyre_Press, 25, 35)
TEL (TEL, 1, 3)
Ferrocence (Ferrocence, 1, 3)
MMT (MMT, 2,5)
Generic Type of Tyre (Tyre, Eco,Normal)
Fuel Magnets (Fuel_Mag, Off, On)
Air Conditioning (Air_Con, Off, On)

We start the sequential DOE process by creating a Screening DOE Worksheet. We want to reduce the 7 possibly significant factors to between 2 and 5.

In order to create the worksheet we don't need to import any data into Minitab.

1.   Start with a new project and then click
Assistant<<DOE<<Plan and Create.
2.   Click on the ***Create Screening Design*** box.
3.   We need to set-up the worksheet in the menu that opens. Enter 'Efficiency' as the response variable.

4. Zaf has generated 7 usable factors for an experiment so we will enter '7' as the number of factors.

5. We then need to enter all the factor details. We need to enter the short factor name, the data type and then the high and low levels to be used for the factors in the experiment. Note that Tyre, Fuel_Mag and Air_Con are categorical factors. The high and low levels must be typed in exactly as shown for the procedure to run without an error.

6. The minimum number of runs required for the screening DOE is 12. However, Zaf has decided that it would be beneficial to invest in the extra runs and be able to detect a smaller effect. He has decided to increase the number of runs by folding the design.

7. Click OK to produce the worksheet, Summary Report and Report Card.

8. A menu opens asking if we would like to print the data collection forms. Click No but in the real world this would be worth doing.

We have created a worksheet that tells Zaf how to conduct 24 experimental runs in 24 rows. It has 11 columns, the 12th column, with heading Efficiency, is where Zaf will enter the response data when the experiments have been completed.

In the previous example we covered a lot of the information on the Summary Report that was created for the screening experiment so that won't be repeated here.

The really important piece of information on the bottom right of the Summary Report is the detection ability of the experiment. The power bar shows us that to achieve a power of 80% the minimum effect that we will be able to detect is 1.06 StDevs. In the guidance given below we are told that we will be able to detect down to small to moderate effects of the factors. This is a similar level to the last example.

Response and factors

Enter the name of your response variable: Efficiency

Number of factors: 7

Enter your factor names and settings:

Name	Type		Low	High
Tyre	Categorical	▼	Eco	Normal
Fuel_Mag	Categorical	▼	Off	On
Tyre_Press	Continuous	▼	25	35
Air_Con	Categorical	▼	Off	On
TEL	Continuous	▼	1	3
Ferrocence	Continuous	▼	1	3
MMT	Continuous	▼	2	5

Adding runs allows you to detect smaller effect sizes.

Total number of runs in your design: 24 (fold design) ▼

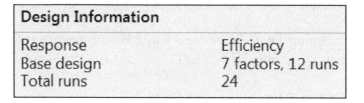

Design Information

Response	Efficiency
Base design	7 factors, 12 runs
Total runs	24

Detection Ability
What effect sizes can you detect with this 24-run design?

< 40%   60%   Power   80%   100%

0.81   Effect   1.06

Effect Size (Shift in the Mean)

Small — < 1 std dev shift
Moderate — 1-2 std dev shift
Large — 2+ std dev shift

Zaf and his team of modders have a great time collecting the data and complete all 24 experimental runs. The data is recorded in 13 DOE.xlsx worksheet 'Efficiency Screen'.

As the auto-randomisation will create worksheets where everyone's StdOrder is different the Excel worksheet has been sorted on the StdOrder column. This means we can't just copy the response column into Minitab. We need to copy the entire worksheet in.

9. In Minitab highlight column C1 to C11 from row1 to row24. Do not delete the title row.

10. Right click and then left click on 'Delete Cells'. This will clear the worksheet leaving only the column headings.

11. Go to the Excel worksheet 'Efficiency Screen' and copy cells A2 to L25.

12. Paste those cells in Columns C1 to C12 directly under the title bar. That brings the complete Screening DOE including Response into Minitab. We can now analyse the screening DOE.

13. Click *Assistant<<DOE<<Analyze and Interpret.*

14. Click on the *Fit Screening Model* box.

15. Even though you have just indicated you wish to fit a screening model you get a pop-up menu that asks the same thing again. Clicking on 'Yes' will produce a 4 page analysis report on the screening model.

Fit Screening Model

The top left of the Summary Report has the Pareto Chart of Effects. This shows which of the Main Effects or Factors were found to be significant. These are the effects that extend past the dashed line which indicates significance at the 0.1 level. We see that we have only two significant factors and these are Ferrocence and Tyre. There are a number of factors that are almost significant but they just miss the 0.1 level.

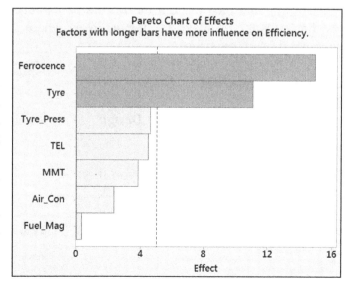

We are told that changes in these two factors explain 65.72% of changes in the response. This is an okay fit, it does warrant a conversation with Zaf to ask him to review if there could be a missing factor that was not in the experiment.

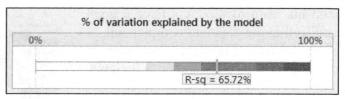

On the Effects Report we have the Main Effects plots for all the factors. The non-significant factors have been greyed out. We see that increasing the Ferrocence additive increases the efficiency and the Eco tire also increases the efficiency.

At the top of the Diagnostic Report is the Residual Vs Fitted values plot. We don't have any unusual points .
As we have sorted the data the Residual Vs Observation Plot, not shown here, is not relevant.

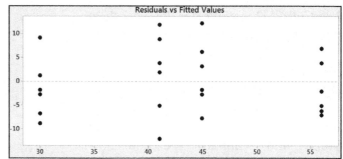

The Report Card does not give us any warnings that we need to be concerned over. The Report Card does tell us that for our 'Next Steps' we can create a modeling experiment using the two significant factors. Strangely enough that's exactly what we are going to do.

Example 13.6.2 Fuel Efficiency Modelling DOE

With these results Zaf is keen to get started with the Modeling DOE. Create the worksheet for a Modelling DOE. Zaf advises you that he wants a fuel efficiency of above 50 mpg. This means you need to target 50 mpg and then tell Zaf the factors he can change if he wants to go above 50 mpg. Zaf also advises that he wants to leave the factor levels where they are and that he is willing to go up to 25 experimental runs at this stage.

16. Click *Assistant<<DOE<<Analyze and Interpret.*
17. Click on the *Create Modeling Design* box.

18. A menu box will appear and ask you if you wish to enter new factor levels. Click on No and you are taken to the Modeling Worksheet Creation Menu.

19. Type in 'Efficiency' as the response.

20. From the selector for 'What is your response goal?' Select 'Achieve a target value' from the drop-down menu. As per Zaf's requirements enter a target of '50'.

21. For 'Number of Replicates' select '4'. This will create an experiment of 24 runs. If we select 6 replicates then that would give us 36 runs which is more than Zaf is willing to accept at this stage.

22. Click OK to produce the modeling worksheet, Summary Report and Report Card.

23. A menu opens asking if we would like to print the data collection forms. Click No. In reality we would probably give a copy of the worksheet to the experimenters for them to complete.

On the top left of the Summary Report for Model creation we are given the experimental goal. Strangely we are told that the goal is 'Construct a quadratic model..'. This is strange as we were expecting a linear model. Also in the bottom left we are told that this design will model curvature. As the curvature can only be associated with the numerical factor and not the categorical factor it does not take a great many runs to investigate the single factor for curvature. We get that investigation as a bonus within our specified runs.

Zaf and his crew complete the experiments for the Modeling DOE. They return the results in Excel worksheet 'Efficiency Model'.

24. Go to the Minitab worksheet where our modeling DOE worksheet was created. Delete everything but the title bar and then transfer the data from the Excel worksheet into Minitab. It's the same as we did for the screening model but the cell references are different.

25. Click *Assistant<<DOE<<Analyze and Interpret.*

26. Click on the *Fit Quadratic Model* box.

Response

Enter the name of your response variable: | Efficiency

What is your response goal? | Achieve a target value

Enter your target: | 50

Replicates

Adding replicates allows you to detect smaller effect sizes.

Number of replicates: | 4

Experimental Goal

Construct a quadratic model that describes the relationship between the response and critical factors. If the model is adequate, use it to find optimal settings for the factors.

Modeling Curvature

This design will model curvature in the data.
Your goal is to target Efficiency at 50.00. When you plot the quadratic effect, you typically get a curved line. Your design can help you find the point on the curved line where Y equals the target, if that point exists in the current experimental region.

Fit Quadratic Model

27. A menu for the Response Goal opens. If the goal is not listed as 'Achieve a target value' change it to that and then enter the target as '50'.

28. Click OK to produce the five page report.

Starting at the top left of the Summary Report, which has the Pareto Chart of Effects. The terms that extend past the red dashed line are significant. We see that Ferrocence and Tyre are both significant but the Ferrocence quadratic term is also significant. The interaction term between Ferrocence and Tyre is not significant.

The model fit has improved by a few percent and is now up to 69.16%.

On the top right of the Summary Report we are given the Design Information for our experiment, not shown here. Below that we have the factor setting that we should use to obtain the target response value of 50. To get Efficiencies higher than 50 we would have to increase the level of Ferrocence. There will be more on that later.

On the Effects Report we are shown the interaction plot for Ferrocence*Tyre. This is greyed out as it is not significant and it is not shown here.
The ME plot for Ferrocence shows a curve which is typical of a quadratic term. The ME plot for Tyre shows that the Eco tyre was more fuel efficient than a normal tyre.
At the top of the Diagnostic Report we have the Residual Vs Fitted values plot. We don't have any unusual data points and there are no patterns that we need to worry about so I have not shown the chart here.

Below that we have the Residuals Vs Observation order chart which shows how the experiment was split into two blocks. Again, as we had to interfere with the run order these are not worth examining.

Let's have a look at the Prediction and Optimization Report. In the top centre we are given the 95% prediction interval we can expect to achieve when conducting runs at the settings given to achieve an average mpg of 50.

Goal: Target Efficiency at 50	
Predicted Y	50.0000
95% PI	(39.219, 60.781)

We are then shown the settings that we need to set in order to achieve our target response using main effects plots. We can tell Zaf that a Ferrocence level of 2.635 will achieve his minimum target value. Increasing the Ferrocence level up to 3 will further improve fuel efficiency. We don't predict what happens above 3 as that would be extrapolation and as good Six Sigma practitioners we don't do that.

Solution: Optimal Settings	
A: Ferrocence	2.63503
B: Tyre	Eco

On the bottom left we are given the top five alternate solutions. Some of these solutions even attempt to use the Normal tyre. However, as can be seen from this data even using the hi level of Ferrocence of 3 a response level of 50 would not be achieved with the Normal tyre.

The Report Card, not shown here, does tell us that Blocks are not significant.

Top Five Alternative Solutions		
A	B	Predicted Y
3	Normal	47.0612
3	Eco	54.7081
2	Eco	44.3816
1	Eco	42.1606
2	Normal	36.7347

Example 13.6.3 Fuel Efficiency Regression Equation

We thought that the results of the DOE would keep Zaf happy but we were wrong. Zaf has realised that ECO tyres are more expensive than normal tyres by £9.55 per tyre and that Ferrocence cost £0.5/ltr. Zaf is willing to do the maths but he wants us to give him the regression equations for this DOE so that he can understand the costs associated with his fuel economy.

29. Click *Assistant<<Regression.*

30. Click on the **Optimize Response** box. We could have selected the Multiple Regression option but the selection that we used gives us additional verification that the model used in DOE and Regression within the Assistant is the same.

31. The Optimize Response menu opens. Enter Efficiency as the response. Set up the menu to tell Minitab we want to achieve a target of 50.

32. Enter Ferrocence as the continuous predictor variable and Tyre as the categorical predictor. Note, the tick box to investigate higher order terms is engaged by default.

33. Click OK to run the procedure and produce the 6 page report.

We are going to go through this report very quickly as we only want two things. The first is that we want to confirm the regression model is the same as the DOE model and then we want the Regression Equations. Unfortunately, the regression equations do not appear in the DOE report.

Let's go to the Summary Report first and check the R-Sq value. It is 69.16% which is the same as the DOE report. Great!

Next we are going to jump to the Prediction and Optimization Report which is added if you select the Optimization option.

The settings to achieve a response of 50 and the 95% PI are the same as the DOE model. This means we can conclude that the models are the same.

Now let's go to the Model Equations Report. This is where we find the two regression equations that we need to give to Zaf. Zaf said he would do the maths but let's just think about what he needs to do. For the tyres he needs to work out the life of the tyre and the cost of petrol the tyres would consume in their life. Then work out if the extra cost of Eco tyres is less than the cost saving in fuel. The same type of arithmetic needs to be done for Ferrocence as well.

Response (Y) variable

Response variable: Efficiency

What is your response goal? Achieve a target value

Enter your target: 50

Continuous X variables:

Ferrocence

Categorical X variable: Tyre

% of variation explained by the model

0%		100%
Low		High

R-sq = 69.16%

Goal: Target Efficiency at 50

Predicted Y	50.0000
95% PI	(39.219, 60.781)

Solution: Optimal Settings

X1: Ferrocence	2.63503
X2: Tyre	Eco

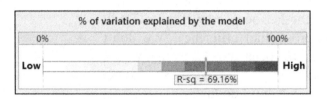

Tyre		Final Equations
Eco	Efficiency =	48.05 - 9.94 X1 + 4.05 X1^2
Normal	Efficiency =	40.40 - 9.94 X1 + 4.05 X1^2

X1: Ferrocence   X2: Tyre

Apart from the next exercise this brings the book to a close. I hope that you found it useful and that you learned a lot from it. Please leave a quick review as it helps authors reach a greater audience if users leave reviews. Please take a couple of minutes and complete the feedback form that can be downloaded within the Chapter 1 area. This will greatly help me improve the next book.

If you have any quick questions you can email me at admin@rmksixsigma.com, there is no charge for this.

Also, if you think your company would benefit from receiving this book in the form of a training course please drop me a line at admin@rmksixsigma.com or if you want more detailed help.

13.7 Sequential DOE Exercise

13.7.1 Starship Engine Power

You are helping Jock, the Chief Engineer, increase the engine power of the Starship Emoji. Jock has identified 8 factors and level that he wants investigated. Your mission is to boldly identify significant factors and maximise the response, Power, using a Screening DOE. Once significant factors have been identified run a Modeling DOE with the intention of maximising the response using existing levels. If curvature is detected conduct additional runs to characterise the curvature.

The screening DOE factors are listed below using the following format Factor Full name (Column Heading, Lo setting, Hi Setting).

Engine Temperature (Temp, 9k, 12k)
Magnetic Field Density (MFD, 180, 230)
Magnetic Field Flux (MFF 26, 49)
Scones, Cream or Jam (Scones 0,1) Categorical
Reaction Initiation, Crank or Fusion (Initiation 0,1) Categorical
Core Wavelength (Wave 13k, 21k)
Plasma Input Angle (PIA 14, 26)
Plasma Input Flux (PIF 80, 120)

Made in the USA
Middletown, DE
06 December 2018